Solo in the New Order

Solo in the New Order

LANGUAGE AND HIERARCHY IN AN INDONESIAN CITY

JAMES T. SIEGEL

Princeton University Press
Princeton, New Jersey

Copyright © 1986 by Princeton University Press
Published by Princeton University Press,
41 William Street, Princeton, New Jersey 08540
In the United Kingdom: Princeton University Press,
Guildford, Surrey

All Rights Reserved
Library of Congress Cataloging in Publication Data will be
found on the last printed page of this book

ISBN 0-691-09427-6

Publication of this book has been aided by a grant from the
Albridge C. Smith Fund of Princeton University Press
This book has been composed in Linotron Palatino

Clothbound editions of Princeton University Press books
are printed on acid-free paper, and binding materials are
chosen for strength and durability

Printed in the United States of America
by Princeton University Press
Princeton, New Jersey

For Ben Anderson

Table of Contents

Solo in the New Order

"It should be pointed out that certain . . . concepts retain their meaning, and possibly their foremost significance, if they are referred exclusively to man. One might, for example, speak of an unforgettable life or moment even if all men had forgotten it. If the nature of such a life or moment required that it be unforgotten, that predicate would not imply a falsehood but merely a claim not fulfilled by men, and probably also a reference to a realm in which it is fulfilled. . . ."

Walter Benjamin

"Keep the memory and keep the chance—is this possible? And, chance—can it be kept?"

Jacques Derrida

Introduction

To SPEAK JAVANESE, indeed, to be Javanese, one must translate. Children first speak Low Javanese. They are not considered fully adult, fully Javanese, however, until they also use High Javanese, a code or speech level they learn as a second language. This fact has often troubled scholars. The Dutch philologist J. Brandes, for instance, says, "However much traditional one finds in *Kromo* [High Javanese], *Kromo*, if we consider it carefully, is essentially a morbid phenomenon, an outgrowth on the real stem of the Javanese language, often highly deformed; *Kromo* lies superficially on Javanese, . . . it is in great measure mannered. . . ."[1] Brandes's strong moral tone is exceptional amongst scholars, yet his assumption of an underlying "stem" and a "superficial," "mannered," and even "morbid" and "deformed" outgrowth expresses a common notion of the authentic and the derivative. One's true intentions are formed in the first language; a second language masks those intentions.

The vehemence of Brandes's language indicates that something important is at stake for him. There is a "real" Java and an inauthentic one and, by a linguistic Gresham's law, bad drives out good. High Javanese is "largely the product of a pedantic schoolmasterishness under which all Javanese have been gradually weighted down so heavily that now the important and ordinary person finds *Kromo*, the polite form, more elegant and prefers it over healthy *Ngoko* [Low Javanese]."[2]

The distinction between the authentic and the inauthentic in language, one aligned with the original the other with the learned and artificial and, by extension, the written, repeats an old argument in Western thought, one exposed by Jacques Derrida.[3] The original here is not only what is first, it is also what is natural and what is associated with the voice. What comes through the voice comes spontaneously, as though the voice, comprising the physical means of producing language, were closer to our thoughts than writing, which takes place outside the body.

What is merely formal lacks substance or intent. It lies on the surface of Javanese. True Javanese, like all true language in this view, is language governed by intent; intent is interior: it lies within the speaker. When language seems governed by the inauthentic, it is as though whatever comes from the superficial reaches of language in the form of schoolteachers and their books dictates what people must say, obliging them to suppress their "natural" inclinations to speak spontaneously.

I do not believe that Brandes's characterization is entirely inaccurate. The Javanese in various ways indicate that in order to speak High Javanese they are obliged to suppress Low Javanese. Moreover, so far as the scanty evidence allows us to know, the capability and desire to speak High Javanese has increased, even during the period after the national revolution, when many expected equalitarian forms to replace the use of speech levels.

Brandes aligns the formal, superficial, and unnatural with what stifles spontaneous expression. For Western readers to see what was at stake for him when translation was introduced into the heart of Javanese society, they must imagine not being allowed to speak their first language on most occasions within their own society. It is as though one had to substitute German, for instance, for English each time one spoke to one's father. One imagines the stifling of speech. One speculates that a certain fear would invade each utterance. One might think that the life of the culture would end, there no longer being any interest in expression.

This would be exaggerated. But I believe it is true that there is a pervasive anxiety about language in Java as there may be in most places. Indeed, I have tried to map that anxiety as it affects the course of ordinary life. But alongside it there is also a strong interest in High Javanese that has to be accounted for. I give examples drawn directly from linguistic practice later. Here I want to give a different sort of example.

In January 1980, the Oriental Circus Indonesia came to Central Java. I found the acrobats to be the most daring I have seen. The high-wire acts were performed mainly by children and young teenagers. They balanced on one leg, lay down on the wire while others walked over them, formed pyramids by leaping on each others' shoulders with a naturalness more appropriate to movements on the ground. However, they scarcely stimulated the attention of the audience, which was enthralled by the clowns. The major clown act consisted of a row of men seated facing the audience. Behind them were other clowns dressed like ferocious animals, gorillas particularly. The costumes were elaborate but not realistic. It was obvious that these were merely men dressed as animals. Yet it is not too much to say that the audience found them thrilling. Animal-suited men would approach those seated from behind. The figures in front gave every sign of being unaware of their presence. The animals would come suddenly and unavoidably into view, and there would be a chase accompanied by shrieks from the audience. The scene was repeated later with other disguises. No one, I learned later, seemed to believe that the disguised clowns really were dangerous animals. Rather, they were interested in the costumes, which meant to them precisely that they were costumes, simulations of animals rather than the real thing. But, by a logic we will develop later, if these were merely the contrived forms of animals, it meant that the 'actual' animals were elsewhere. Seeing the obvious contrivances meant that one became aware of the 'real' thing somewhere else—somewhere else, but still brought near by means of the formal, the mannered.

My own interest remained with the acrobats. Watching them, their loops and arcs, the acrobats' suspension in the space between the swinging trapezes, I realized it was not the skill of the acrobats I appreciated; skill is merely something learned, an accomplishment open to human talent. I was, rather, thrilled by them to the degree to which I thought they were doing something beyond ordinary skill. It was as though physical laws were momentarily suspended and they were actually flying. I believe the Javanese audience was not particularly interested because many of them knew that people can fly. There are stories of people with such power who used it to fight against the Dutch, for instance. The audience may have thought they were seeing only a skillful performance. I, on the other hand, wishfully assumed I was seeing something impossible, something more than I could comprehend. While some children were forming a pyramid on the high wire, the strand broke. Several plunged to the wooden floor and were whisked backstage, to be replaced by the clowns. The acrobats' fall jolted me, not only out of concern for them, but also because it let me see the foundation of my wishfulness: death was the consequence of trying to exceed the "possible." I was obliged to believe that nature is serious in order to be fascinated with the possible breaking of her laws.

The audience, its wishfulness taking them in a different direction, did not markedly increase its interest. They remained concerned with the costumes and the suggestions they aroused. One could say their interest was governed by conventional representations. Formality here had the opposite effect from what Brandes might have expected. Theirs was an interest in the "inauthentic," in the merely representational. Mine, governed as it was by assumptions about nature and death, was an interest in the real or authentic—the opposite of theirs, but still not entirely different. My thrill rested on the "almost," on the closeness to making a mistake that could be fatal. The audience's interest also involved the "almost." In their case, seeing the costumes and thinking that dangerous animals were elsewhere was a way of thinking they existed. It brought to mind what they could not see.

The audience's interest in the clowns brought them, too, into a connection with death, since "death" in Java is linked with the invisible. Death, moreover, in its Javanese sense, is closely connected with the operations of translation between speech levels. It furnishes one of many examples of how the movements between languages take Javanese speakers where they do not necessarily wish to go, and at the same time reassure them.

The audience's delight in the artificial is comparable to delight in translation. It indicates that translation can sustain a culture as well as stifle it. I will show that the pleasure that speakers of High Javanese take in their speech is connected with its preservation, indeed its establishment, as a language, rather than an attempt to suffocate speech. Pleasure nonetheless comes associated with fear, because what is at stake is the preservation of language, of linguistic ability itself. This fear I will show to be a fear of an intrusive element that makes discourse impossible; the pleasure is the reassurance that comes with having courted this danger and evaded it. The issue is not the authentic versus the inauthentic as the means to sustain any particular culture, but the drawing of a line that defines one language in relation to another and, I will show, thereby distinguishes language from nonlanguage.

It may seem that this is a question that belongs to philosophy and linguistics rather than to anthropology. This is not necessarily the case. I am concerned with showing how the issue permeates social discourse. My aim is to say something about Java, or at least part of it, at a certain moment, and on that basis to speak about the general issue. The book is organized around the description of social situations that I observed in Surakarta, Central Java, a city of about a half million inhabitants. The city was founded when the kingdom of Mataram moved its capital to Solo between 1743 and 1746. Along with Jogjakarta, it was one of the two centers of Javanese court culture, known for the refinement of its arts and language. It was and is a center of the batik cloth industry, batik being also one of the arts practiced inside the palace. But Solo was a stronghold of nationalist sentiment as well, one of the important sources of support for President Sukarno.

Indonesia is a country with hundreds of local languages. As such, the question of local languages in a national setting is pervasive, no less so because the national language, Indonesian, is one of the great accomplishments of the nationalist movement. There is no question that Indonesia has a national language and that only in remote corners is it not accepted as such. And yet it is accepted as a second language. Here again we see the institutionalizing of translation.

Javanese, however, is unique in the national setting because its speakers comprise about two-thirds of the nation's population. They are strongly represented in governmental administration, to the point where they are sometimes accused of dominating it. And Indonesia's national culture and language have been heavily shaped by the Javanese. This does not mean that Solonese always see themselves reflected in the products of Jakarta, the national capital. Like those in other regions, they too feel threatened. As Sukarno supporters, they are sometimes unsure of the man who replaced him, President Suharto. Suharto is the founder of the New Order, a term used to distinguish the present regime from that of Sukarno, a term said to have been chosen with knowledge of its political resonance. The Javanism produced by the New Order sometimes appears unassimilable to Javanese in Solo.

In politics there is uneasiness about the stability of the New Order, particularly about the capacity of Suharto to remain in control. This anxiety comes not only from the political situation as such, but also from an apprehension that is built into translation. I have attempted to isolate it first by describing the operation of speech levels within Javanese, showing how the process involves the assumption of a threat to language, a threat I speculate was formulated during the colonial period.

Translation and hierarchy are intimately intertwined in Java. One is left out of discourse, remaining "not yet Javanese," unless one can translate into High Javanese and thereby show respect. The formation of social hierarchy and translation thus appear inseparable. In the description of social scenes that constitute the bulk of this book, I show how social order is constituted through movements between Javanese languages, how during the New Order what is heterogeneous to this interplay is accounted for, and how, in a moment of social disruption, it was not. If hierarchy is constituted by language, language can also work against it. I conclude with three cases where undomesticated language became apparent.

The interest of the circus audience was not in the animals' costumes themselves, but in what they caused spectators to bring to mind. My interest in the acrobats likewise was not in them as such, but in what I imagined about them. Both of us saw something that was not there and for that reason became interested. I had another interest besides the acrobats, since I was also concerned with the reactions of the audience. Their reactions were different from mine, but this difference was not important; even if our interests had been identical, whatever captured their attention would have been important to me. The existence of their interest itself was what mattered. It is at this point that I tried to describe their activities.

This description is already a translation in the sense that it substitutes my words for their activities. Even had I written my notes in Javanese, there would have been the substitution of one code, written ethnographic description, for another, the enactment of conventions governing spectacles. It is at the point of interest that different idioms or codes arise, that translation takes place and, for that reason, that differences between peoples are consolidated.

The alternative might be some form of transcription, though obviously one still has to choose what to transcribe. The result of sheer transcription is to transfer without assimilation. Had I attempted this the result might look like lumps of Javanese in the midst of English. But in fact the foreign elements would be "Javanese" only to those who knew about it before hand. Otherwise they would remain only indecipherable elements, without provenance. Mechanical comparison of differences that only notes that "they" do this and "we" do that approaches such comparison. An interest in interest, which usually produces a description of differences, seems to govern most anthropological fieldwork; it is the reason few ethnologists accomplish the project they had planned before they left home.

The procedure suffers from the major difficulty of recognizing the interests of someone else without conflating them with what one already knows and already is interested in oneself. Its advantage is the exposure of concerns and information not otherwise accessible. The procedure rests on the opening of cross-cultural communication, a process that comes through misunderstanding and even confusion. I address this matter in the final chapter. Here I want only to note that the analogous procedure in psychoanalysis has been treated with particular incisiveness by Samuel Weber.[4] I have tried to answer him in my final endnote.

The cultural geography of interests of course varies from place to place. This study maps those differences in Java and, in exploring the formation of absence that triggers interest, looks at its stabilization in social relationships, its breakdown, and its reformulation. I have subsumed all of this under the rubric "translation." I do so because of the prominent place translation occupies in Java and in ethnography. In doing so I want to acknowledge my debt to Jacques Derrida, particularly but not exclusively for his essay, "Des Tours de Babel," as well as to the piece by Walter Benjamin on which it is based, entitled "The Task of the Translator: An Introduction to the Translation of Baudelaire's *Tableaux Parisiens*."[5]

I want to stress how various Java is. Whatever claims I make about it should be understood to refer to Solo alone, relieving me of the tiresome duty to qualify my statements in every instance.

Since the book is based primarily on my fieldwork, and since Solo is a larger city than a person working alone can be sure of comprehending, I want to relate a little about the conditions of my study. I went to Solo first in 1978 to study Javanese and to develop a project. I was struck at that time by the profusion of imagery there and resolved to make that the focus of my study. The results are included. I discovered, however, as I continued to learn Javanese, that the fact of translation and its connection to the setting of boundaries around Javanese had to be included to understand imagery. This shifted the focus of the study.

I spent the summers of 1978 and 1979 in Solo. I lived during that time with the family of an entrepreneur in the area near the palace reserved for those with connections to the court. I had the advantage of knowing the students in the house, there being six of them, two studying in universities, the others in high school and grade school. I returned in September 1980 to stay another 16 months, making 22 months in all. I lived at first in the house of a widow from the court of Solo's junior royal line. I ate my meals during this time in the nearby house of the head of the Mangkunegaran library, R. T. Moehamad Hoesodo Pringgokusumo. I am more than grateful to him and to his wife for the help they offered me in learning Javanese and much else. During the final year in Solo I lived in the neighborhood described later. I am nostalgic when I think of my neighbors there; I thank them for their generosity to me. Half of my time in Java was given over to studying Javanese, half to fieldwork.

I want to thank Ben Anderson, who offered me full advantage of his unparalleled knowledge of Indonesia, especially of Java, and of his considerable critical abilities. I thank Timothy Bahti also for his discussion of theoretical questions. I want to thank Ellen Burt, Cynthia Chase, J. A. Day, Richard Klein, Pietro Pucci, Vincente Rafael, Shiraishi Takashi, Tsuchira Kenji, Samuel Weber, and John Wolff, who helped me understand many of the issues raised in the following pages. And I want to acknowledge the many kindnesses of Helen and Jeremy Evans in Solo.

The Cornell Southeast Asia Program enabled me to study Javanese in Surakarta and continued to support the project in a number of ways. Funding came from fellowships from the John Simon Guggenheim Foundation, Fulbright-Hays, and the Social Science Research Council. Though the labor involved was only my own, excluding my Javanese teacher and my typists, such research is costly. I appreciate receiving the support, and I appreciate also the cooperation I received from the Indonesian Council of Scientific Research (LIPI) and the Fakultas Sastra of Universitas Gadjah Mada.

Chapter Ten first appeared in the journal *Indonesia* (no. 36, October 1983) in a somewhat different form and with illustrations; it appears here with the kind permission of the editors.

Personal names have been changed in Chapters Two and Three, though I have not been able to disguise the name of the place.

PART ONE

Language and Hierarchy:
The Establishment of Translation

CHAPTER ONE

The Javanese Language and Related Matters

JAVANESE IS two languages,[1] High Javanese, or *Kromo*, and Low Javanese, or *Ngoko*. Though High Javanese has only a few hundred vocabulary items, these include most of the items used in ordinary speech.[2] Javanese is one of those languages whose speakers frequently complain that they cannot speak it. What they mean is that they cannot speak High Javanese; occasionally a Low Javanese equivalent will slip out where it does not belong. (The opposite does not seem to happen.) Their complaints, however, are exaggerated. One knows this by the way they deprecate themselves when hearing a foreigner speak High Javanese; nearly always they say, with apparent conviction, that the foreigner's Javanese is better than their own, though this is never the case. It is nonetheless conceivable to them that it is so, since no one has High Javanese as a first language. It is always learned after one can speak Low Javanese.

One should speak Low Javanese to children and to those with whom one is *intim*, a term that comes from the Dutch equivalent of "intimate" but that is not properly translated as such. To all others one speaks High Javanese or a mixture of the two languages.[3] One thus cannot speak Javanese without making a statement about one's hierarchical position vis-à-vis the second person. The Solonese warn foreigners about learning Javanese. It is not merely that it is difficult, but that the consequences of making mistakes are not only linguistic but also social: one might address the second person as though he were of low rank.

To speak inappropriately could thus wound one's listener or even anger him. Since, however, the Solonese consider it unmannerly to show their anger, and since manners are important, one might never know if one has offended someone. As it would be a solecism for someone to notice a mistake in usage, one can worry for a long while, not merely that one has been offensive, but that one has made an error of speech. The concerns are identical; thus foreigners find themselves reviewing their words, trying to remember not what they said, but what words they used.

High Javanese is often conflated with other forms of Javanese: the literary language, still used in shadow-puppet performances, which is little known to most Javanese; court language, whose existence is known but which is unavailable to most; Old Javanese; and even Javanese script. Ability to read and write the latter is vastly admired; most people seem to have the ability to decipher letter for letter, but few ever use the script. When Javanese complain about the difficulty of High Javanese, they sometimes have in mind all of these, the languages of high culture.

When such authority does infiltrate one's language, it is not possible to behave improperly. A man told me that as a boy he used to quarrel with his brother. His mother forbade the brothers to speak Low Javanese to each other. Not until they realized they could use Indonesian did they begin to fight again. By the same reasoning, to make a linguistic mistake in High Javanese itself would be to betray authority.

Nervousness about language is also nervousness about behavior. As in other Indonesian languages, it is also true that speaking properly is equated with behaving properly. Speaking *Kromo* properly is the most essential ingredient of being *alus*, the desirable standard of Javanese behavior that is usually translated as "refined."[4] To be *alus* in speech is to speak appropriately, that is, to use the language appropriate to one's listener and to please, or at least not to upset, him or her. In most circumstances this means not merely using the vocabulary suitable to one's listener's social status, but also speaking in a tone that is cajoling, pleasing, and without sharp edges. If one is speaking High Javanese, it means phrasing one's sentences so that they are long and, if possible, full of archaisms. Given the right opportunity and a skilled speaker, the result can be a pleasing vacuity, one that stills whatever tumultuous feelings one's listener might have while one says as little as possible. For example, an orator at a funeral was greatly admired, the person next to me saying with a certain awe that "he has spoken for a long while now and said nothing." Given that his topic was the biography of the deceased, this was, indeed, an accomplishment. In ordinary conversation nothing quite so extended would occur. Nonetheless the tone of High Javanese is chosen in the first place not to suit the content of one's remarks, but to please one's listener. The aim is not to match one's feelings to one's words, but to one's listener's sensibility.

High Javanese can be thought of as a second language in the sense that it is not the speaker's "own" language. Identification between the "self" or speaker and his speech is avoided. One sees this in the way in which *Kromo* is taught. Javanese children learn Low Javanese in a way that seems not to differ from the way children acquire languages anywhere. In the case of High Javanese, however, the child, when he speaks to an adult, will have his words rephrased by the adult in High Javanese.[5] Thus the child does not appropriate the language of his parents for himself, taking over their authority with their words. Rather, he imitates adults speaking the way children ought to speak, in this way picking up an imitation of a language, one that is divorced from the person of the speaker and that indicates social inferiority. By speaking it, however, he at once indicates his own adherence to social norms and is allowed, indeed encouraged, to say nothing of substance. One understands how speaking High Javanese successfully, demonstrating social obedience, can alleviate fear.

That *Kromo* remains a second language to its speakers is due in part to it being taught in the context of the child's mistakes. When he speaks *Ngoko* to adults, his words are pushed aside and replaced with *Kromo*. Control of language means not the ability to say what one wants to say, but the ability to replace one's "own" words, the words one would ordinarily use, with others. But these strange words honor others and, at the same time, give the child who speaks them a certain standing. He is on the way to becoming someone who can behave like an adult—in Javanese parlance, on the way to becoming "Javanese," the opposite of which is not another ethnic label but "animalish."

Just as one only speaks proper High Javanese when one speaks slowly, softly, and uses many words, Low Javanese is quick, abbreviated, abrupt, and usually harsh. Many conversations with three people thus involve constant switching of tones. For instance, the following incident occurred between myself and an upper-class couple: I asked them about sending a package through the post, a topic appropriate in its triviality for *Kromo* conversation. It led, however, to technical details about string, knots, paper, and glue and their acceptability by the post office, then to a difference of opinion about these matters between husband and wife. They, quite correctly, spoke to each other in *Ngoko*, but both addressed me in *Kromo*, and I answered them in *Kromo*. Thus I would ask if the post office would accept staples. The woman said yes, but the man said to her "No," in a tone that can only be said to convey that the wife was an idiot, that only a fool could have such an opinion, etc. The wife replied, saying something about string, using the same tone. Without understanding the conversation—listening, that is, only to the harshness, loudness, and abruptness of the exchange— one would assume that the couple was not merely disagreeing but actually having a quarrel. This is unlikely. It is merely that Low Javanese often sounds as if the speakers are quarreling. To speak Low Javanese means that one need not attend to the position of one's hearer, to his social standing. Stripped of the tones that designate consideration for others, Javanese sounds quite harsh. Often one hears indirect discourse. The speaker will repeat something that has been said to him and his own reply. It is not unusual for the speaker to reproach himself in the gruff tones of Low Javanese while the voice of the person who spoke to him is given the wholly distinct tones and vocabulary of High Javanese. Such examples could be multiplied.[6]

To speak High Javanese is to choose one's words to suit the hearer. In this sense it is not a second language at all; it does not seem to the speaker as if he has a choice of languages, as though one's hearer understands both French and English and one will speak whichever is most comfortable for both parties. The Javanese speaker has to choose his words not according to his listener's capability to understand, but as though languages are not arbitrary matters. He or she has to find out where the hearer fits in society, and then speak as though the words were attached to the status, part of the nature of the world. The ability to speak High Javanese is assumed to be the ability to read signs inscribed in the world itself. To speak High Javanese, then, is constantly to uncover the unchanging nature of the social world. The result is a picture of the world as absolutely steady, provided only that its hierarchical quality is realized in Javanese speech. Furthermore, to speak High Javanese is to demonstrate that one has the ability to read such signs and therefore has a place in society. Merely to speak Low Javanese will not do; that is not considered an acquired ability, but rather something that anyone at all is capable of doing. It does not reflect the structure of the social world, and thus gives its speaker no place in it. Nervousness about speaking High Javanese therefore comes from the fear not merely of offending someone, but of losing one's place in a world that appears immutable.

The history of High Javanese is still unstudied. It seems, however, to have developed as a court language. What is remarkable about its development is that, though designed to mark differences of status within the Javanese feudal world, it has lost no ground in a period of nationalism and independence. It has done this by encompassing all new statuses. Not just court officials but anyone with a recognized position of any sort is ordinarily entitled to be spoken to in *Kromo*. Thus government officials, army officers, and schoolteachers, for instance, all persons considered to be, we might have once said, "respectable," will usually receive this form of deference.[7] In addition, the old are always deferred to. Every adult, in fact, is ordinarily given some degree of linguistically expressed deference. In the marketplace this might take the form of a very low form of Middle Javanese (*Madyo*); but Middle Javanese is still considered part of High Javanese, not of *Ngoko*. It can happen that someone will speak such a low form of *Madyo* that there is little way of telling whether or not it is, in fact, *Ngoko*. But ordinarily a high form will be inserted every once in a while, in order to indicate that one is, after all, not speaking Low Javanese.

Gradations of status can be quite fine. To an old person of low status, for instance, one might speak Low Javanese in keeping with his general status; but one would also use High Javanese pronouns and certain other High Javanese words out of respect for his age. Such speech would be considered by the Solonese to be a form of deference. That one can actually defer to someone lower than oneself is possible because of the line that the Solonese draw between *Ngoko* and all other forms of Javanese. Reciprocal speakers of *Ngoko* do not recognize each other as equals; rather, the question of each other's status is not reflected in their speech. (Equals, those of the same rank, might well address each other in *Kromo*.) To speak some form of Javanese that is not *Ngoko*, even though it is not pure High Javanese (*Kromo Inggil*) but is linguistically almost undistinguishable from *Ngoko*, is still thought to confer recognition of the listener's social worthiness. One thus defers to the social order itself.[8]

Indonesian, the national language, has been given a place in this hierarchy.[9] It is the language used for public meetings, for instance, when people speak as citizens. It replaces High Javanese in certain settings such as classrooms; there, students speak to each other in Low Javanese and to their teachers in Indonesian because the schools are national. It is also used to avoid hierarchy. When, for instance, a prince, head of the junior line of the Surakarta nobility, spoke to a cabinet minister, himself from Surakarta, during a celebration in honor of the former's ancestors, they spoke Indonesian to avoid the difficult problem of different hierarchies. When Javanese hierarchy is bypassed through the speaking of Indonesian, it does not mean that such hierarchy is degraded by speakers. It is precisely to avoid doing anything that might diminish the status of the prince that the minister spoke Indonesian; for the prince, it was the sort of subtle gesture of concern for the other that a highborn Javanese should show, as well, of course, as being the act of a citizen. In such ways Javanese retains its public nature, including its sense of encompassing, even defining, public hierarchy.

One can compare this to the relation of another regional language, Acehnese, to Indonesian. In the 1960s, when I last was in Aceh, a province of Sumatra, Acehnese was the usual language of villagers on all occasions, including meetings with government officials. Acehnese was also spoken in the city. There, however, it had changed character. In the city, Acehnese was used in the home and between people who knew each other. Otherwise, particularly in government and university circles, people spoke Indonesian. (In government offices in Solo, though Indonesian is used on formal occasions, office workers generally speak to each other in Javanese.) Acehnese was thus on its way to becoming a language associated with household and privacy and being stripped of its public functions. Javanese, by contrast has retained all of its public nature, including its sense of defining the public hierarchically.[10]

The undiminished hierarchical quality of Javanese poses a problem. The burden of High Javanese is put on those who speak up, who show deference through speaking High Javanese. Given the opportunity to avoid the implication of social inferiority by substituting Indonesian for Javanese (and in Solo as a rule people speak fluent Indonesian), why should Javanese have kept its vitality? In certain respects, this repeats the problem of the origin of High Javanese. Though originally a court language, it developed, to the best of our knowledge at least, under the pressure of colonialism.[11] At the time that the Dutch were eating away at the independence of the courts, High Javanese developed as a language and then was adopted by all Javanese. One can understand the eagerness of the court to bolster itself through the exaggeration of forms of deference. What needs explanation is why those low in the social scale took on the burden of showing it. In the largest sense, such an explanation is beyond the scope of this book, needing as it does historical and linguistic treatment. What is open to us here, however, is to show the advantage to the speaker of High Javanese.

To do this, we must first return to Low Javanese, or *Ngoko*. If High Javanese is the language of social location and self-consciousness, what then is Low Javanese? And who is the speaker of Low Javanese? Javanese claim that they think *Ngoko*; it is the language they speak when they are excited or when they lose control or when they talk in their sleep. Asked if they talk to themselves in *Kromo*, they often laugh. To speak to oneself in *Kromo* is absurd to them, a bizarre proposition since it raises the question of who is being honored. To talk to oneself in Javanese of any kind is embarrassing if one is caught at it, for reasons similar to those that hold for a speaker of English. For an English speaker, the listener knows what the speaker is going to say before he finishes; he is therefore incapable of interpreting the speaker's words and so being a distinctly different identity. Insofar as the listener's registration is found to be a moment separate from that of the speaker's utterance, there is duplication of the self that contradicts the notion of an ideally unified person in control of his speech.

The problem for the Javanese speaker is different only in certain respects. In attending to himself while he speaks, the listener brings the speaker into view. The embarrassment is equivalent to the embarrassment when a bit of *Ngoko* slips out in place of *Kromo*. It is not strictly the duplication that is embarrassing but the revelation of the speaker. The speaker should have remained hidden but did not.

As in English, there is no embarrassment in speaking to oneself in Javanese unless one is discovered, by oneself or by another. After asking Javanese off and on for two years what language they used when talking to themselves, I did find one person who said he spoke to himself in *Kromo*. When he was angry with himself, he would say, *"Piye, Mas?"* He considered this to be High Javanese, even though the word *piye*, meaning "what about it?" is Low Javanese, since the word *Mas* ("older brother," a frequent term of address) he considered to be High Javanese. This reverses the ordinary situation. For a Javanese person to become angry with someone often means that he drops down the language hierarchy, not only because he thereby insults the hearer, but also because in excitement his first thoughts turn to what he wants to say rather than to the status of the hearer, the latter entailing the right degree of *Kromo*. The person in our example spoke to himself as one would where there is a conflict of hierarchies, a solution like that used in addressing someone older but of lower status. Here the Low Javanese, as is always the case, indicates the lack of a need to take regard of the listener. It is just for this reason that the speaker also used a deferential form for himself, the hearer; otherwise the "person" with whom he was angry could disappear. The speaker of *Ngoko* is apparently undiscoverable even by himself in ordinary circumstances.

Merely to speak to oneself in *Ngoko* assumes, until one is found out, that instead of there being a division, albeit unproductive, between speaker and listener, the two are collapsed into one, and the object of one's anger disappears. This follows from the nature of *Ngoko*, which simply by being *Ngoko* announces that it takes no cognizance of the hearer. His or her status is not noted; one thus does not allow for any difference between speaker and listener. It is as if the latter is not there at all. Lower status is, in fact, better recognized by a lower degree of High Javanese than by pure *Ngoko*. *Ngoko* is reserved for those people—children and spouses primarily—who are, in the first case, not fully human, or in the second, completely identified with oneself. It is not a question of relative status in the social hierarchy but of a certain lack of recognition altogether. The person angry with himself, then, had to behave ridiculously, had to pay himself respect, because only by doing so could he make himself the recipient of his anger.

Just as the person speaking *Ngoko* to himself cannot bring himself into view, he cannot do so in speaking to others. Because the persons to whom one speaks *Ngoko* are those one need take no notice of, the ability to speak to them in Low Javanese brings no recognition of oneself in return. When children answer one's Low Javanese with High Javanese, it is worth little since, from the start, they do not count as social beings. When one's spouse answers one's Low Javanese in the same language, Javanese say that it is because they are *intim*. This "intimacy" is, however, formal. It is what spouses should speak to one another, regardless of whether they are feeling intimate or feeling angry or, as is often the case, just not taking much notice of each other's presence. The usual meaning of *Ngoko* is that one's speech forms do not have to reflect the difference of oneself and one's hearer. The result can be conversations where talking to one's spouse and talking to oneself are practically indistinguishable; there is no recognition of otherness in either case. Thus neither the reactions of others nor the reactions of oneself can make the *Ngoko* speaker self-aware—the reverse, of course, of the situation with *Kromo* where the language one speaks appears as a function of one's hearer and the speaker becomes known as one capable of making that evident.

The *Ngoko* speaker seems, then, to disappear from view. This can have striking results in the eyes of an outsider—for instance, in triangular conversations where two speakers use *Ngoko* reciprocally and the third addresses them in *Kromo* and is replied to in kind. In the example earlier of such a conversation between myself and a married couple, the tone of the *Ngoko* used between the couples was harsh and abrupt. But all the tones indicating consideration were restored in addressing me. Soothing tones of deference followed harsh tones with no embarrassment at all. The outsider in such conversations is not excluded from the interchange. Everyone can understand all levels. It is rather that, so long as speech levels are in accord with the recipient's status, there is no attempt to integrate the various usages in terms of a single speaker. The speaker who switches tones along with levels does not betray himself as "really" uncaring, uncouth, or perhaps emotionally disintegrated; he merely makes no claims for himself and gets no recognition for using *Ngoko*, providing that it does not supplant *Kromo*. It is as though he is not there when he speaks *Ngoko*.

The *Ngoko* speaker comes back onto the scene as the perpetrator of errors or, more frequently by far, as the potential perpetrator of errors. This happens mainly in contrast with *Kromo*, but not exclusively so. There are in fact conversations when the sense of being honored comes not from *Kromo* at all, but from Indonesian. In such conversations, one knows that something else is being given up in order that *Kromo* or Indonesian may be spoken. We have mentioned the case of public schools; students in the presence of their teachers speak *Ngoko* to each other but Indonesian to their teacher. In doing so, they recognize the school as a national institution in which Indonesian is the appropriate language and the teacher is the representative of the school. It is evident in this situation that the sense of respect comes because students give up their ordinary speech in order to speak Indonesian. Similarly, when Solonese worry about being able to speak *Kromo*, they imply that speaking *Kromo* means suppressing their ordinary speech.

When two persons speak *Kromo* to each other, particularly pure *Kromo* (*Kromo Inggil*), *Kromo* unmixed with lower forms, one sometimes feels one can detect this suppression. One might expect that in a language that unavoidably designates status, people would compete to have the highest possible forms addressed to themselves while giving the lowest possible forms to others. This, indeed, does happen. For instance, there are notorious eccentrics who are reported to speak only *Ngoko* to anyone and who are consequently labeled "arrogant" (*angkuh*). In the face of such people, most speakers merely ignore their bad manners and speak to them in return in High Javanese. There is not much of this, however, nor are there many of the less extreme cases whereby each tries to give the lowest possible forms of High Javanese to the other. Rather, it seems to be the other way around. On most occasions people seem to delight in speaking High Javanese. Partly they delight in the ability to show that they are in control of that language, that they can, in fact, manage the highest forms of deference.[12]

Such conversations are likely to take place when people meet accidentally; they might be seated next to one another at a ceremony, or they might meet on the street or run into each other while visiting a mutual friend. The substance of such conversations is ordinarily meager. There is a standard conversation for foreigners—do they eat rice in America, can you eat rice, is it cold there—that runs almost always into a discussion of Javanese: Javanese has two levels, one has to be careful not to insult anyone, Solo is the center of the most refined Javanese, etc.

Between Solonese themselves topics are less standardized but are treated with equal vacuity. However, the tone is scarcely one of boredom. Rather, there is a certain delight that is supposed to show through in one's voice and that is part of being *alus* or refined. In part this indicates one's eagerness to please the other. The vacuity of the conversation comes in part as a way of avoiding offense. It is a means of showing that one has the other fully in mind and is eager to please.

This deference, however, lacks all sense of subservience for several reasons. In part it is in the nature of Javanese that its speakers can practice the emotional detachment (*iklas*) they so much value by speaking of things in order to avoid being possessed by them.[13] Thus Javanese dislike being surprised, and consequently they frequently exclaim, "*lho*," indicating that they are surprised, in order to avoid feeling it. To indicate deference, by the same reasoning, is to free oneself from having to experience a feeling of inferiority. In this sense the conventional nature of *Kromo* is used for self-protection. That, however, would by itself mean only a neutrality of tone, whereas what is involved here is a feeling of pleasure.

It is hard to explain the length of such conversations when they could often be shorter, or their frequency when they could often be avoided altogether, without attributing some gain to the speakers. The delight people take in showing that they can manage the language is part of this;

it points to the way each person is secretly congratulating himself. One has to add that these congratulations would not be so frequent or so pleasurable unless people were congratulating themselves not only on speaking High Javanese, but also on performing the substantial feat of not speaking their "own" language, Low Javanese.

This explains another feature of these conversations: not only are they pleasurable, but they often have an air of complicity, as if the speakers were sharing something no one else knew about. Since the speakers are rarely saying anything of substance, one has to assume that what delights them and what furnishes an air of intimacy (as if to say, "we will continue this later") that *Ngoko* itself often lacks is what is not being said, what is kept out of the conversation. The thing between speakers that brings them into a feeling of closeness despite the formality of *Kromo* is that they share a secret; they both know without saying that they are not speaking *Ngoko*. What makes *Ngoko* thought of as a "natural" language—one untaught, easy to pick up, simple, appropriate for talking to oneself, in short, one's "own" language—is that it is brought to mind when one is not speaking it. It is that which is reserved for oneself. When it is actually used it loses that character. But when it is kept out of Indonesian or High Javanese, its very absence makes the language felt.

Of course, the lone fact of the suppression of *Ngoko* tells us nothing of the gain for the speaker of *Kromo* that makes him or her want to speak *Kromo* whenever possible. A further clue comes in the phenomenon known as *latah*.[14] *Latah* is the term used when someone is obliged to repeat another's words or gestures, or when, in response to a certain stimulus, someone utters obscenities or crude words. For instance, one Javanese woman in Jakarta is obliged to respond "in, out, in, out, in, out" whenever anyone says to her "penis."[15] In her article on the subject, Hildred Geertz has described *latah* in this way:

The symptoms of *latah* are an involuntary blurting of obscene words or phrases, compulsive imitation of the words or actions of others, and compulsive unquestioning obedience when ordered to perform actions which may be ridiculous, improper, or even dangerous. The stimulus to such behavior is any sudden loud sound, a tickling prod in the ribs, or an abrupt gesture. While an inanimate stimulus such as the sound of a door slamming, can bring on a *latah* attack, more usually the stimulus is interpersonal, and in fact, most often, in the form of deliberate, malicious teasing. The blurted obscenities, in Java at any rate, are always sexually obscene; there were no anal references noted, and no blasphemous or otherwise offensive words were used. In many of the cases that I observed, the obscene words were mixed in ordinary sentences, often replacing an ordinary word which was closely similar in sound to the obscenity.[16]

Geertz points out that those who suffer from *latah* are mainly lower-class persons, frequently servants. She notes a large number who are former employees of the Dutch. Contrary to her report, however, not all those who are noted as suffering from *latah* are women, though most seem to be. *Latah* is not considered a disease by the Javanese but rather a breach of manners.

Geertz sees *latah* as a psychological disorder in which "the symptoms [are] determined primarily by a cultural tradition" since, involving "the value for elegant and polite speech, the concern over status, sexual prudery and the dread of being startled," *latah* furnishes an image of quite a lot of what is most disvalued in Javanese behavior.[17] *Latah* is, thus, "comprehensible at an unconscious level to any Javanese." It is nonetheless not considered a disease because the actions are thought to be involuntary, making them "not offensive but entertaining."[18] The Javanese thus recognize the element of compulsion in the inability of some to practice correct linguistic behavior.

It is interesting to note in Geertz's examples just how *latah* is triggered. The Javanese, as Geertz says, intensely dislike being startled. One reason for this is seen in *latah*; fear of surprise for *latah* sufferers is fear of not being sufficiently on guard to prevent oneself from linguistic slips. The turn that these slips take is often association of sounds. Thus Geertz reports that a *latah* sufferer offered a cup of tea to someone, with the words "Please have some vagina;" the word for tea is similar in sound to the word for vagina.[19] Geertz also gives this incident:

> In one mild case, the *latah* was startled in the midst of a conversation about baskets. The Javanese word for basket resembles the word horse, and the *latah*, meaning to say, "Hand me that basket there," cried out "Go have intercourse with a horse," a sentence which the Javanese find deeply shocking.[20]

It is in this context that one understands Javanese concern for proper pronunciation, which seems to be a way of suppressing associations with other words. In teaching English, for instance, I frequently noticed how much more concern Solonese students showed about getting sounds right than do Western students learning foreign languages. Their embarrassment at making mistakes in pronunciation was noticeably greater and more frequent than in the case of making other sorts of mistakes.

The role of *Kromo* in producing such suppression is seen again in this context. It is a remarkable fact that though the Javanese suffer from *latah*, they do not seem to do so in Solo or Jogjakarta, the two places always mentioned as the centers of refined language.[21] When, for instance, I asked why Javanese in places such as Kebumen, west of Jogjakarta, suffer *latah*, I was told several times that it was likely to be because of the sounds of Javanese there. Javanese in Kebumen, I was told, sounds harsher and is

spoken too quickly. Rapid speech is not considered refined, perhaps because its rapidity alone sets one's mind
working to simply follow it, whereas the desired effect of
Kromo is to produce a certain tranquility. People from East
Java also are said not to speak very refined Javanese, to
be deficient in the capacity to speak *Kromo*, and to suffer
from *latah*. (Indeed, Geertz's examples all come from East
Java.) One could then argue that where the ability to speak
Kromo is better established and where High Javanese is
spoken more as a matter of course, a speaker is protected
from *latah*. We have not said much more here than we
have already reported: *Kromo* takes the place of forbidden
speech. In doing so, it offers a certain protection to its
speakers.

As I have mentioned, *latah* is said not to exist in Solo
and Jogjakarta; many people, in fact, do not even know
the term. When *latah* symptoms are described to them they
report never having seen such incidents. There is, however, one sort of behavior in Solo that looks very much
like *latah*, involving mimicry as it does. Small children,
hearing foreign languages spoken, are inclined to repeat
what they take to be the sounds of that language. This
has an element of mockery to it. When I heard myself
imitated not by children, but by some young women, I
felt I was being mocked. I am now inclined to think that
this was not the case. The women were neighbors of mine
and were among the people with whom I felt on the closest terms. On no other occasion did they show any behavior that I interpreted as hostile. Moreover, they did
not mimic my English, but my Javanese. On one occasion, for instance, as I returned home, they told me that
someone had been looking for me. I thanked them and
said, as is customary, *"Ora apa-apa,"* "it doesn't matter."
It was this phrase that they repeated.[22] That it was not a
case of mockery but of a certain compulsion on their part
to imitate is, I believe, shown by the fact that, not only in
this incident but in each case where they mimicked me,

my pronunciation when I said the phrase "*ora apa-apa*" was distorted. I had thus reproduced the situation that occurs in *latah*, where indistinct pronunciation leads to associations that ought to be suppressed. The mimicry of my pronunciation can be interpreted as taking the place of the trains of association that such pronunciation might have aroused. Mimicry here would then be a way of preventing something worse.

The behavior of these young women was by Javanese standards quite rude. Given that they displayed no other instances of rudeness toward me, I take it that their behavior, as in the case of those afflicted with *latah*, was compelled. It is this compulsion that gives us the clue to the advantage for the speaker of *Kromo*. The associations released by bad pronunciation or triggered by being startled are, of course, the speaker's "own," not those of the person who triggered the *latah*. However, the teasing of *latah* sufferers shows us how such people are at the mercy of others. The words in one sense may be their own, but they did not choose them. Their own words thus were put entirely at the disposal of others. Geertz, indeed, says that "the compulsive imitation of the words and gestures of another person, and compulsive obedience to commands, are acts which are at base unconscious parodies of the social relationship between inferior and superior."[23] The point, however, is that this parody is what would be the case if the inferior, the speaker of the higher forms of Javanese, did not have control over his or her own actions. It is the speaking of *Kromo*, the giving of deference, that restores control to the inferior. If the speaking of *Kromo* is the giving of deference, it also preserves the speaker's "own" language from the possession of the other.

Speaking *Kromo*, then, results in the trading of deference for relief from compulsion or subservience. It gives the speaker control over his own words, over his own *Ngoko*, at those moments when he is not speaking it. He is most in control of his "own" speech at those times when he suppresses it. It is no wonder that people are eager to defer to one another, that forms of deference developed and spread at the time when Javanese political strength was ebbing in favor of foreign domination. In this sense, the frequently repeated claim that Javanese is the language of the defeated seems to me to be true. But it is also a language of a profound national self-assertion. At the moment of defeat, it created a space immune from control by others, or at least the feeling that there was such a space. And it did so not by creating a private sphere, but by marking out the very center of the act of deference for the speaker. Acknowledging defeat, it at the same time shored up Javanese social life.[24]

CHAPTER TWO

A Neighborhood in the New Order: Hierarchy and Social Order

AT ONE TIME, one could hear adults in Surakarta speaking in the roughest possible Low Javanese and being answered in *Kromo*. The Low Javanese speakers were nobility with close associations to the palace. The existence of such people in the hierarchy is important; it assures the rightness and potency that are assumed to inhere in forms of deference. This has been definitively explained by B. R.O'G. Anderson in his seminal exposition of the idea of power in Java.[1] Power in Javanese thought is a substance that can move from person to person. It can be cultivated by mystical practices. The possessor of power becomes the apex of the hierarchical pyramid, the king and even the center of the universe; people are drawn to him, and in this process society assumes its hierarchical shape. When the ruler loses power, the realm itself declines and loses its distinctness.

The absolute authority of those at the top of the pyramid combines mystical and political power. People near the top who can speak in the lowest possible language to other adults embody a force that compels deference. Such compulsion guarantees that the reserve we spoke of in the last chapter remains in place. And for this reason, the world is thought to be a safe place, since the forces that might ordinarily disrupt it, embodied as thieves, for example, are kept under control by the power of the ruler.

Surakarta today is governed as a municipality with the same status as other Indonesian cities. The holder of the title of the Surakartan dynasty is not involved in city government and is also thought to be without power in the Javanese sense, the last "powerful" ruler of Solo being his grandfather, who died shortly before the Japanese occupation. The dynastic heirlooms, however, are still considered by many to contain magical potency. On the night of the first day of the Javanese month of Sura these heirlooms, mainly magical spears and daggers, are paraded through the city, borne by palace retainers and accompanied by the nobility. In 1981, however, this holiday became the occasion for further realization of the ruler's current "powerlessness."

Part of the elementary abilities of any person with magical "power," ruler or not, is the capacity to control the weather. In 1981, the Sunan, holder of the Solonese title of ruler, had announced the procession for 11:00 P.M. As usual, the streets were lined with those who hoped to profit from contiguity with the magical implements, many if not most of whom had walked in from the countryside, often for miles. On this occasion, however, the ceremonial procession was delayed for over three hours by a downpour. This was taken as a further indication of the titular ruler's inability to provide safety for his subjects, and as an indication that spirits had convened in neighboring Mt. Lawu. During the next week there were alarming reports of robberies from every part of the city. In the neighborhood I am about to describe, for the only time during my 11 months of residence there, spirits known as *tuyul* who specialize in robbery were said to be at work. For seven consecutive days there were reports of yet someone else who had been robbed by these spirits. Many people took special measures: some set out charms, while several others went without sleep, in one case reportedly for four nights, one way Javanese believe they will gain the spiritual strength to stave off unwanted events.

These anecdotes illustrate the current lack of strength at the top of the hierarchical pyramid. When the ruler is "powerless," the nation loses its stability; robbers enter when they should be kept out. Solonese, however, do not rely on the old nobility alone to be the pyramidal apex. During the Sukarno period, Solo was a stronghold of nationalism and of Sukarno supporters. Solonese generally regret Sukarno's downfall. They do not, however, blame the person responsible, Indonesia's current president. They rather see President Suharto as having failed to replace Sukarno sufficiently, as lacking the special "power," in the Javanese sense, that Sukarno, at least in retrospect, is thought to have enjoyed.[2]

As Anderson has pointed out, the cyclical view of history that the Javanese inherited from India is not, in practice, cyclical at all.[3] It is rather a question of whether a ruler has been blessed with power or has, perhaps with equal suddenness, been deprived of it. In the latter case, the assumption is that power may have devolved on someone else. Part of current Javanese efforts concern looking for that someone else. The extraordinary popularity of a new type of magical curer that, unlike most previous Javanese curers, works cures in front of vast audiences, illustrates Javanese hopes. Such healers are widely rumored to have the *wahyu*, divine power. Within a day or so of their appearance, thousands of visitors come, some to be cured, some merely to watch and perhaps share in the "power" by their proximity. The political potential of these curers is indicated by the fear they inspire in the authorities. They are frequently forbidden to practice in certain localities and forced to move on by government officials. The reasons given are various, but one can see in them the officials' fear that behind the existent hierarchy, another is taking shape.[4]

Within Solo itself, however, the dominant reaction to the sensed absence of power is different. It is marked by a lack of interest in *Kromo*. There is, for instance, the decline of interest in Javanese literature and the current lack of popularity of Javanese theater that depends on refined language (*wayang, ketoprak,* and by comparison, *ludruk*). These theatrical forms either use refined language as their medium or show a world that depends on that usage. The lack of interest in refined language by no means indicates skepticism about the value of deference. Quite the opposite. Rather, the sort of deference that the New Order commands is too often built on force, an indication to the Javanese that true power is lacking; the ruler blessed with power should be able to govern effortlessly. The problem for Surakartans is that the current government does not command the sort of respect that would allow for the extreme forms of deference that I described in the beginning of this chapter. It as is as though *Kromo* today marks the shell of a structure that will at some point be filled with more powerful figures. In the meantime, deference to the national hierarchy is important; but it is as though that hierarchy exists independent of the present government.

The alternative is not a movement to family or privacy, however. We have seen how, within the family, those who speak *Ngoko* to each other achieve no social identity by doing so. For that reason the family cannot furnish an alternate social identity apart from hierarchy and cannot function as a refuge from hierarchy. "Intimacy" itself, in its Javanese understanding, is dependent on hierarchy, thus again making it impossible to think of privacy as a retreat from hierarchy. Indeed, because intimacy and hierarchy are linked, it is necessary for Javanese to find a community of some sort, rather than retreating into a private area.

The problem is illustrated through the *tuyul* stories. On the one hand, since the thieves are not human, they are not named or nameable. The circulation of the stories indicates the extent of the fear felt by those who told and retold them. The implication was that anyone could be next: anyone could be the victim of a loss whose agent could be at best only vaguely located. On the other hand, although vague, the stories also did give a location to the fears aroused by the display of failure of supernatural devices of protection. There were things one could do to protect oneself against *tuyul*.

The assuaging of fear may be of less consequence than the effect of locating it in the spirit world. The latter allowed Solonese to give their sensation a name; one was *wedi*, "afraid."[5] This particular sentiment is the proper one to have for spirits. But *wedi* also means "respect." In Javanese thinking, it is good to be *wedi*; it is even necessary in order to behave properly. The display of the ruler's powerlessness aroused anxiety that had no locus. The panic aroused by bad weather could not yet be called *wedi*. It began to take on that name when people repeated that spirits had gathered on the mountainside outside Solo. Once stories of thievery circulated, the relation of any listener to a source of danger was clear. He or she could take on the attitude proper to such an occasion. And in so doing, he or she also generated the sentiment underlying the payment of deference and set the way for the re-establishment of the social hierarchy.

The question that this incident raises, however, is where this deference was to be paid. The *tuyul* stories implicitly acknowledge the inability of the existent hierarchy to protect those who pay deference, and at the same time generate the sentiments necessary for deference to be paid. It is as though there is a proto-hierarchy underlying the actual one. I see the lack of interest in *Kromo* in present-day Solo as an indication that the present hierarchy is thought insufficient to generate or absorb the energy of deference. Instead, sentiments of respect or fear are generated outside the *Kromo-Ngoko* hierarchy and become attached to local structures. In the remainder of this chapter, I want to show how fear is localized and made into hierarchy on the same principles as the operation of *Kromo* and *Ngoko*, but without the use of *Kromo*.

The community I am about to describe is a neighborhood in the center of Solo. It was originally the residence of court musicians. Amongst the older residents there are still today some musicians. The former court connection is maintained as well in land ownership. The family of one former court official still holds title to about 25 percent of the land of the community I surveyed. As in a great many Surakartan neighborhoods there is a mixture of social types—for instance, a few well-to-do merchants, the principal of a high school, as well as some schoolteachers and some "agents" (that is, persons who live by dealing in whatever they can, often living quite marginally). Kemlayan, the name of the administrative subdivision (*kelurahan*), is also a center for merchants who buy old shoes, renovate them, and then resell them on the sidewalks surrounding the neighborhood. The bulk of the population is poor though there are many exceptions. Most households have been in the neighborhood for two generations. There is no head of household whose great-grandparents lived in Kemlayan. But most people have lived there for at least a decade. People speak with pride of the neighborhood, as if everyone had been there for generations.[6]

There are a few neighbors who cooperate in their economic ventures. For instance, one man hunts out used shoes, which he sells to neighbors who repair them for resale. But Kemlayan is not a community linked by common economic interests; disparities of wealth and the fact that people earn their livings in various places outside the neighborhood account for this. That it is a "community," that the people who live there feel they have common interests and an important stake in each other's well-being and good behavior, is nonetheless the case. What people feel is important in the community is security. Kemlayan is known as a safe neighborhood, one that thieves are afraid to enter.[7] Its residents think of it as a place where the sorts of occurrences that are said to have happened after the celebration of the month of Sura do not happen.

The primary reason Kemlayan is thought to be safe is

the nightwatch, or *ronḍa*. This is a voluntary organization of youths that patrols the neighborhood after dark. The *ronḍa* is widely known to have killed thieves in the past. It is seldom specified just when this happened or what the circumstances were. It does seem, however, that at least one thief, sometime in the early sixties, was beaten to death when he was caught stealing a towel someone had left out. It is, indeed, the custom in Solo for thieves to be beaten and sometimes killed.

The nightwatch formed from the bulk of the youths who took credit for keeping troops out of the neighborhood in the period after the presumed coup of 1965. At that time troops hunted out communists. In Kemlayan there were only a few, the great majority of residents then being nationalists, PNI (Nationalist Party of Indonesia) supporters. The youths blocked off the entranceways to the neighborhood, making sure that neither soldiers nor gangs from other parts of the city entered. In return, they promised to see that whoever was actually a member of the PKI (Communist Party of Indonesia) would be dealt with appropriately. Apparently they were able to manage this by convincing army authorities that there weren't many PKI members in the neighborhood and that those that were members were only nominally so. Two persons I knew of were members of PKI-affiliated organizations and were neither imprisoned nor killed. In the section of Kemlayan that borders on the neighborhood, one person was killed by an intruding gang. One resident, himself a leftist, claims that the nightwatch stories are a hoax, that, in fact, gangs wearing black masks roamed the neighborhoods at night, and that one person was killed, not by gang members at all, but by neighborhood youth, the body later being dumped outside the city.[8]

In the riots of November 1980, however, the *ronḍa* indisputably did protect neighborhood residents. At that time, Chinese were the targets. Chinese families living in the neighborhood, whose shops, only yards away on the main streets, were badly damaged, were unmolested in their homes. Again the *ronḍa* set up barricades to make sure that none of the rioting youths could enter. At the same time, however, many Kemlayan youths were themselves out on the streets and successfully entering other neighborhoods. What is important is not sentiment about Chinese, which varies from hatred to mild dislike, but the feeling of neighborhood solidarity, which is all the better demonstrated when it extends to those one dislikes; in particular, the reputation of the *ronḍa* and its ability to defend the neighborhood are at stake.

The *ronḍa* sees itself as responsible for keeping order. It does this basically in cooperation with the police, but partly on its own terms. Of course, for the *ronḍa* to kill anyone is contrary to Indonesian law. But as the youths repeat, when questioned by the police each will step forward and claim that he did the killing himself, stymieing the police. The police in any case are not too particular, being happy to have the help of the neighborhood in carrying out their duties. A police officer tours the various neighborhoods nightly, checking in on the *ronḍa*; relations are quite friendly.

The *ronḍa*, however, often takes matters into its own hands. In one case a house newly rented by a Chinese family was seen to have male visitors late at night. The members of the *ronḍa* suspected that the daughter of the family was a prostitute. They informed the head of the neighborhood organization (the Kepala Rukun Tetangga) and then the chairman of the overarching organization that links several neighborhoods (Kepala Rukun Keluarga), but neither official acted. One of the *ronḍa* members then wrote an anonymous letter to the brother-in-law of the man who resided in the house, threatening to "take steps" because they were "dirtying the name of our neighborhood." The family moved out. In another incident, the *ronḍa* informed the family that they could not have visitors after 11:00 P.M. and would have to keep the curtains open in the evenings. They did so, and the matter was closed. The latter case, one member of the *ronḍa* told me, was particularly satisfying since it resulted in the reform of the girl.

What is involved, again, is not morality in an absolute sense, but the reputation of the neighborhood and the responsibility of the *ronḍa* to maintain it. The *ronḍa* members make no secret of their own visits to prostitutes; these, however, take place outside Kemlayan. *Ronḍa* organizations operate in most, but not all, Solo neighborhoods, taking on the maintenance of security. In another neighborhood on the outskirts of the city, in which residents are exclusively batik workers, boys who are out of school and unemployed are trained to be batik stampers (*tukang cap*) and helped to find work. Those who refuse such training are driven out on the grounds that idleness leads to trouble.[9]

The ability of the *ronḍa* to take such action is based on the belief that it controls violence and that in so doing it maintains, if not creates, the moral order. Indeed, the line between coercion and a sense that what the *ronḍa* enforces is naturally right is sometimes difficult to see. The *ronḍa*, for instance, is supported by voluntary monthly contributions. Chinese, however, pay several times the amount Javanese pay. It is not that they are asked to give that much; each household is only expected to pay what it can afford. That Javanese families with comparable incomes pay less is due to the nervousness Chinese feel.[10] It is not only Chinese who feel the pressure of the *ronḍa*, however. When levies were made for paving the lane that ran through the neighborhood, there were a couple of families who paid only nominal sums. The people sent around to see that they gave a bit more were all *ronḍa* members.

The myth of the *ronḍa*—that Kemlayan is a community because of it, that there is safety and order in the neighborhood because of *ronḍa* efforts—overrides any other sense of community. Thus the community's historical connection with the palace does not figure much in people's thinking about the neighborhood. What recurs in conversations, rather, are the stories of thieves. The importance of these stories is shown by the primacy they are given over the history of the events of 1965 or 1980. What is repeated is that the *ronda* kills thieves and therefore thieves are afraid to enter the neighborhood. Questioning will reveal that the last thief was killed in Kemlayan before 1965 at a time when in a certain sense there were no *ronda* at all. At that period the nightwatch was organized by the Pemuda Rakyat, a communist organization, with the help of the lurah's office. (The lurah is the lowest district administrator in the mayor's office, corresponding to the village head in the countryside.) Thus the *ronda* has taken deeds not strictly their own for themselves, joining their reputation to that of an outlawed group. This does not reveal a secret political sympathy, but rather represents consideration that the youth were all local and shows the need for the myths of stymied theft.

Thieves are not merely apprehended in these stories; it is stressed that the thief was beaten or stoned.[11] It is the violence, therefore, to which we are obliged to turn our attention.

When I spoke with *ronda* members, they insisted that the thief had to be *kapok*, had to have "learned his lesson"; that was why it was necessary to beat him. None thought that jail, for instance, would do this. It was necessary for the thief to "suffer"(*lara*), and for some mark to be left on him. Indeed, when I told a friend of mine who had earlier described how he stoned a thief that I had just watched a thief being beaten, what he wanted to know was not the circumstances of the theft—what was stolen, how the thief was caught, who caught him, who he was and so on—but what the thief looked like, meaning was he bruised, and if so where.

I want to put such violence, the violence that involves

beating, in the context of language levels and gestures, since blows have a certain place in Javanese speech. They occur, actually, in two places. First, when there is contradiction in status, there are sometimes playful blows. Thus the senior administrator of Solo's junior dynasty was talking with the guardian of one of the dynasty's graveyards one day in November 1980. The caretaker was an old man, but of considerably lower rank than the rather senior official. At one point the administrator made a joke; the caretaker gave him a playful kick in the pants. On another occasion I asked for directions from an old palace retainer of low status; hearing me speak Javanese, frequently a joke to Solonese, he kicked me in the pants. What happens on these encounters is that a certain irregularity of behavior—especially an irregularity that is unexpected and that could possibly arouse uncalled-for behavior—is resolved through a mock blow. An old person could get away with such a gesture, as it asserts the privilege of age. What is important to us here is that it is only a mock blow, a self-conscious miming of childish behavior. It is this self-conscious quality that gives it a place in speech levels.

A more common sort of blow occurs between children. Brothers and sisters in particular, as part of the teasing that is common amongst them, resort to blows. It is the younger who hits or slaps the older; the older merely takes it. One finds this gesture repeated between lovers and friends in later life in mock form, where it becomes a means of touching. Brothers and sisters speak *Ngoko* to each other, as do lovers. Judging by context, then, jabs and blows become part of intimate speech, of *Ngoko* discourse.

Close inspection of "intimate" gestures shows that they are not to be identified with Western notions of intimate gestures, of touching in particular. Touching, in the Western conception, is intimate because it seems to bypass speech, conveying intentions as they are most fully felt without the loss that is assumed to be involved in putting them into words. The energy of one person is thought to be transferred to another as directly as possible. For contrast one might consider this touching between two market women, one in her early twenties, the other in her early thirties, that took place at a coffee stand inside a Kemlayan market. It is like touching that occurs in the neighborhood. What follows is an edited transcription from the notes I made as I watched them:

> The younger's right hand lies on the older woman's left arm. As she speaks she slides the pads of her fingers up and down the arm. Emphasizing something, she jabs lightly into the arm, but pulls back with a scooping motion.
>
> The whole gives the impression of fluttering, the gestures rapid and, aside from the emphatic gesture, unrelated to the woman's speech.

As I continued to watch, I realized that the jabs did not actually come at moments of emphasis in speech, that I had merely assumed that. Also, the second woman made no response to the gestures. It was as though they had gone on in the air, perhaps even somewhere else, rather than on her body. Not only is there the light rubbing of the skin, but also after the jab (really a tap) the fingers are withdrawn, as I have noted, and in the process, they skim the skin's surface rather than pushing into the body.

When a younger brother or sister beats his or her older sibling, slapping or pounding him with fists, the older sibling at most scrunches up, but accepts the blows, never hitting back. All that can ordinarily be expected by way of return is, sometime later, for the older sibling to say how he adores his sister or brother, proving it with a pinch that can produce screams. The passivity of the older sibling at first looks like a role reversal—the subordinate party is supposed to restrain himself—but this is not so. The older sibling is merely acting the part of older sibling, one who takes care of his younger sibling, and beyond that, by not responding, acting the part of an adult; one is in general capable of social action because one can restrain oneself. Later, the relationship of older and younger becomes the model for lovers and for spouses, who call themselves "younger sister" (*dhik* or *jeng*) and "older brother" (*mas*). The blows of childhood have been drained not only of their hostility, but also of their expressive function. Rather than the energy of the toucher being passed on to the person touched (or the energy of the person touched being sensed through bodily contact), the scooping motion, pulling back toward the toucher's own body, mimes the holding of energy within the body of the toucher. This quality of restraint makes the blows into a version of those of siblings, but drained of their intent.

Such touching by no means occurs in all *Ngoko-Ngoko* exchanges; it is found only where there is great informality, where consequently there is a partial lifting of the restraints in most other speech forms. The gestures signify as little as possible. At best they are indications of escaped energy that never reaches a destination. It is as though they make visible what in more refined speech would be held back altogether.

These gestures belong to the *Ngoko* that pertains between adults: spouses or lovers for instance. Though drained of their signifying function, these gestures, unlike *Kromo*, do not restrain or replace another code. Rather than suppressing anything, they manifest energy that is merely excessive. They can be seen as repetitions of an earlier form, the blows of childhood, made acceptable by being drained of content. They occur only in the freest relationships, and then only with an increase in the level of excitement. They are a form revived in the more permissible context of *Ngoko* speech, but still divorced from it in that they contribute nothing to the communication of sense. They are, rather, signifiers that seem to escape despite anyone's intention.

With this in mind, we can return to the beating of thieves. Here I apologize for the unpleasant graphic details required for our explanation. One evening at about 7:15, some members of the *ronḍa* caught a youth who had tried to snatch a purse from a young woman. They beat him before they were discovered by a police patrol, and all were brought to the police station, where the beating continued. When I arrived a few minutes later, the beating was still going on, visible through the open doors and windows of the one-room police post in the market. A crowd of about 150 had gathered. The boy was bound to a chair, having been stripped to his shorts. He was being hit with the palm of the hand across his face. As he was struck, his head would swing with the blow. His mouth was open with his cheek muscles taut. He did not wince as he was hit. His eyes stayed wide open. It was not that he was focusing on anything. Rather it was as though by keeping his eyes open, he was refusing to shut out whatever was before him—refusing, that is, to even brace himself for the beating. He did not cry out as he was hit, even though judging by the look of his face he must have been hurt.

A *ronḍa* member told me the thief was *kapok*, had learned his lesson. His silence was taken as the indication of this. He was not being beaten in order to confess; there was no question in anyone's mind of what had happened or of the need for proof. In that sense there was no attempt to get him to speak. It also would not have been acceptable for him to have cried out when the blows landed. To do so would have been to express his own state: not simply to show that he felt the blows, but to answer, as it were, with his own reaction. To say that he was *kapok*, on the other hand, meant something quite different. It meant that he accepted what he had received and kept to himself what would have been his "own" reaction. As I have said repeatedly, this is the state of one who is capable of Javanese social action, and, identically, of proper Javanese speech. The need for bruises arises just because of the thief's desired silence. Bruises are a way of knowing that

it really did hurt, that, therefore, there was a reaction that
the thief, in his terror, held back.[12]

The thief's silence, his self-restraint, is thus like the self-
restraint of an older sibling beaten by a younger. The difference in the situations comes in the nature of the blows.
The blows of a younger sibling are often heartfelt; there
is no mistaking the sincerity of his anger. The attitude
toward thieves is somewhat more complicated. Thieves
are disliked: I sometimes had the impression from the en-
thusiasm with which *ronḍa* members spoke that they would
just as soon have thieves enter the neighborhood so that
they could catch them. This, however, does not mean that
the beating they administered was angry, or even felt violent. The blows came slowly and evenly with a certain
regularity that is contrary to the furious slaps of children.
The deliberateness of the slaps delivered to the thief plus
their intent—to make him *kapok*—allows these gestures to
have a place in the nexus of Javanese. Like the caresses
of *Ngoko* touching, they are not spontaneous transfers of
energy. However, whereas *Ngoko* touching is drained of
significance altogether and works independent of speech,
the beating of a thief retains an intent. It is distinguished
from its possible origin in the violence of children, though,
by having this intent made deliberate rather than spontaneous.

These blows thus also have a place in *Ngoko*. Given the
silence of those doing the beating, one might see blows
as standing in the place of speech. They are an even more
kasar or crude form of language than *Ngoko* itself. They
nonetheless have a precise linguistic locus; they are the
way in which one talks to thieves. As it is proper to speak
Kromo to one's superiors, it is proper to beat a thief. Both
are linguistic actions with their own places in the Javanese
hierarchy.

The thief thus has a certain place; he is the figure who
does not belong. He is not an unknown quantity, but a
type with a defined locus. I would like to be able to report

that thieves discovered living in the neighborhood are driven out, but I do not know this for a fact. What is true, however, is that theft can become the focus for proto-witchcraft beliefs. In the case of the *tuyul* discussed earlier, at the end of the week one *ronda* member said he discovered that someone had been making offerings to the *tuyul* in order to get their loot. He named a person with whom he had been having a long dispute and for whom he had displayed (privately) feelings of enormous hostility. In his mind at least, to make his enemy into a thief was to get rid of him.

It is significant that in most stories of theft the thief has no name and his origin is not a given. He figures not as a person in his own right, but as that which does not belong. The boundaries of the community are defined as the area from which he is excluded, the area protected by the *ronda*. (In the same way, the *ronda* is thought to consist of all the youth of the neighborhood; everyone has an obligation to support it, and all youth, it is said, would identify themselves as the killer of a thief if it were necessary to do so to stymie a police investigation. But only certain youths are active in the night patrols.)

A thief thus needs no name of his own, nor any origin other than "outside." He is the figure of one who does not respond to language, but who can be made *kapok*, made to learn in the act of expelling him. In that sense, he is a figure of the limitation of Javanese, as Anderson has pointed out in his interpretation of a story of Pramoedya Ananta Toer.[13] To make him *kapok* is to teach him how to respond linguistically; it proves he did not know how to do so before. The thief is thus shown to not know language and to belong outside the community in the same gesture. The community then becomes those protected from him, all of whom can speak properly.

The neighborhood is thus founded on violence. Yet this violence is not primordial; it is not what came first, out of which Javanese arose. It rather implies the prior existence of language levels. The deliberate character of the beatings, the distinction between them and childhood beatings alone would indicate this. In that sense too, the awareness of violence in the foundation of the community does not lead to a sense of the arbitrariness of its institutions but rather the opposite. No one says that certain people risked death in order that this community might exist, that out of the possibility of their own annihilation came what we have today; death is not used as a way of showing how things might have been different—how at a certain moment there was nothing, and then a certain order emerged, as though another order might well come about if someone else were to take the same risk. In the story of the thief, there is no special heroism accorded the *ronḍa*. The risk of death is all on the side of the thief. One never hears of *ronḍa* members killed trying to apprehend a thief; only the thief seems ever to be killed. Indeed, the thief is usually solitary, whereas the *ronḍa* members are always multiple. The beating of the thief implies a whole linguistic order that already existed and that is only preserved by the thief's expulsion. Beating the thief is predicated on the assumption of the prior existence of speech levels. It gives that assumption a local manifestation.

The neighborhood as a community is marked by the fact that neighbors, with some exceptions, speak *Ngoko* to each other. The assumption made in doing so is not that all are equal, but that all are, ideally, mutually dependent. One woman, the wife of a retired captain, who had once lived in an Army camp, put it in a statement reminiscent of Toqueville:

> I did not like it in the barracks. There everyone was the same rank and there was intense competition. So if there was an *arisan* [a revolving lottery; members put in a determined amount regularly and the winner moves from one to the next] there was competition to dress up

and serve fancy food. If you didn't have a special dress you were ashamed to attend. But in Kemlayan there are all sorts—rich, poor, bureaucrats, merchants, laborers. And there is mutual help. If anyone needs something someone helps him.

For her, and she expressed the general attitude, the neighborhood does not represent an equality that underlies differing statuses, but a sense of shared security. This limited sense of commonality is the basis for the mutual speaking of *Ngoko*. The assumption here is not that status is momentarily forgotten; to say that all types live in the neighborhood and still to speak *Ngoko* is to keep in mind that status based on *Kromo-Ngoko* for the moment is merely not being considered. In this sense the community takes hierarchy as a given that is not in any way challenged by the fact that individual statuses outside the neighborhood are not reflected in speech levels within the neighborhood.

The myth of *ronḍa* control of violence we have seen to be one that simultaneously implies speech levels and community order. The assumption of order as founded on suppression is evident in the *Ngoko* spoken between neighbors, just as the suppression of *Ngoko* is evidenced in *Kromo* speech. It is the *Ngoko* of adults as distinguished from that of children. *Kromo* is spoken at the expense of *Ngoko*; in that context *Ngoko* remains the language of unself-consciousness. But in the community, the myth of violence underwrites *Ngoko* as itself a language of self-consciousness or status within the confines of the community. It does so by placing something under *Ngoko*, a language that is even lower than it—namely blows. By contrast alone *Ngoko* appears as restraint.

It is important, again, to compare these blows with those of children, the latter being spontaneous, contrasted with the deliberateness of blows brought into the hierarchy by the preciseness of their intent—to make the thief *kapok*—

and the limitation of their target. It is not merely that people speak *Ngoko* rather than being violent, but that a certain sort of violence is already within the linguistic order.
Adult *Ngoko-Ngoko* discourse does not replace the possibility of simply acting in an uncontrolled way with the
use of "language," but rather replaces the possibility of
using one code by the application of another. The significance of the myth of the *ronda* is to have given the language of the community, *Ngoko*, the possibility of doing
what *Kromo* does, of establishing who a person is, his
possession of a social location. The myth of the thief shows
that those who speak *Ngoko* also are capable of social intercourse, that they too recognize the worth of the other
since they too could speak an even more "natural" language—blows—but do not do so. How close this suppressed language can come to the surface is evident in
their gestures.

It is not *Ngoko* in relation to *Kromo* that gives the community a feeling of security and orderliness, but *Ngoko* in
relation to something it suppresses. Once this process is
begun it takes many forms. One can see this realization
of *Ngoko* as a language comparable to *Kromo* in those activities where people come together as neighbors. One such
occasion was the circumcision of a twelve-year-old boy,
the son of well-to-do batik traders. Boys are usually cir-
cumcised just before puberty. If they do not exactly look
forward to it, they still want it done because they are otherwise the target of other boys' teasing. The ceremony can
be large or small, depending on the means of the parents.
In this case there was an early breakfast for about 20 men,
all of them neighbors (relatives from outside the neighborhood came for a *selamatan* after the operation). The boy
knelt at the knees of his grandmother and his mother in
turn and received their blessings. Then, in two hired
minibuses, guests were taken a few blocks to the *bong supit*,
the performer of the operation, who welcomed them in

High Javanese. Dressed in a white doctor's smock, he ushered them into a room that had been partitioned by a white curtain. On one side were some chairs, on the other, a cot and a cabinet of instruments. A short prayer was recited, and a cassette of Indonesian popular music was put on, which was later changed for one of Javanese music. The guests settled down to wait. Or at least some of them did. Others went outside to an open window just above the operating cot to peer in; some leaned around the end of the curtain and watched from there. Most, however, stayed in the guest room and chatted. The subject was circumcision: who the best circumcisers were, how much they charged, how long the operation takes, what it was like when they were young. One would have thought they were not at all bothered by what was going on, that the possible consequences of the operation were not brought to mind. That this was not entirely the case, however, was shown by the father. Rather than stay with the guests, he went out into the lane by himself. He said later that he couldn't bear it, and that he could scarcely contain himself until the operation was over. It was not a lack of kindness that prevented any of his friends from keeping him company but the opposite. Realizing his inability to control himself, they left him to himself, out of sight.

Those who remained seemed to be having an especially pleasant time talking about circumcision, apparently not only unaffected by the thought of dreaded consequences, but actually enjoying themselves. The tone, in fact, was just that of those *Kromo* conversations where there seemed to be a feeling of delightful complicity between speakers. That certain associations were being suppressed became evident, however, through my own crude behavior. Being made nervous by the occasion, I resorted to pointed and sometimes explicit jokes, all of which were ignored, just as though I had said nothing whatsoever. However, when the operation was over, one of the guests, someone my own age, pointed to me and, actually leaping off the ground, said, "Pak Jim is next," a joke that he repeated several times not only then but also later during the *selamatan* that afternoon. Clearly it had taken an effort on the guests' part to shut out the sort of worries that had bothered the boy's father.

All of this was done in *Ngoko*, but the suppression involved took the same form and the same tone it does in *Kromo* and, moreover, had the same consequences. The father, like me, identified with the boy. His worries, which he could not contain, made him feel as though he were in the boy's place. The people talking in the guest room and the men peering at the operation itself, however, did so on the assumption that not only was there no danger but there was no connection between themselves and the boy. None of those whose heads, poking through the open window, were only a few feet from the boy, felt that they should reassure him. In keeping their own thoughts to themselves, a difference between self and other, comparable to that which pertains in speaking High Javanese, was established.

The connection between this incident and the notion of "community" in the Javanese sense became clear through another incident that occurred in the preparation of this ceremony. As in all cases where someone is going to give a *selamatan*, a committee is formed of neighbors to take charge of the various tasks. The committee is the *wong tua* of the neighborhood, a term that means literally "old people" but that, as in the Malay equivalent, refers to those who are thought for nearly any reason to be established persons of some importance. This committee meets to decide who will do what. Beyond the statement of the giver of the *selamatan* that he will hold it on such and such a date, a fact that is made known when the meeting is called, there is no business discussed at this meeting. There does not have to be, since the same people do the same thing each time: there is Wiro,[14] in charge of seeing that chairs are put out; the head of the neighborhood organization; and a few others who always are in charge of greeting guests and so on. The committee, when it meets, discusses anything at all, topics of vacuity equal to any *Kromo* conversation. At a certain moment, however, someone says *"Wis,"* meaning, in this case, "Okay?" and people nod and make an exit. It is as though it takes such a meeting to make the committee official. But what makes something official is not an agreement between people who might have different notions of how things should be done—a possibility that seems not to be brought up—but simply the emergence of *adat*, custom, as though it becomes apparent by itself.

It is not exactly by itself, however, that *adat* emerges. The conversation, though it was not about the *selamatan*, was necessary to make the occasion "official," since it demonstrated, through its very vacuity, the capacity for social action that results in "custom." Form or custom is not thought to be a product of human invention; whatever its source, however, it emerges when humans put themselves in a state of readiness for social action, a state that depends on suppression of one's "own" thoughts.

One sees this operation at work in the most common of neighborhood rituals, *soré*. *Soré* is the late part of the day when it begins to get cool. It is a time when people have returned home from work and, often, napped. Either before or after bathing, it is the custom for neighbors to lounge about in front of their houses or in the main lane that, in any case, is quite close to everyone's house. When as an ethnographer I discovered that people in Kemlayan spoke *Ngoko* to each other and spent the late afternoon in such activities I had many expectations. It is difficult for a Westerner to find anyone willing to speak *Ngoko* with him. Here, I thought, was my chance to use the language of intimacy and find out the real workings of Javanese life. This did not happen. It is not, however, only with me that little is said. I believe I can verify that this is the case between neighborhood residents as well. On the whole there is not much conversation at all. Most time is spent simply watching. One has to picture standing in the same spot each afternoon and looking at the same thing for anywhere from ten minutes to an hour to feel the atmosphere that prevails during *soré*.

Although people congregate on the lane during the day as well, at *soré* the atmosphere is affected by the fact that it is after work. This is a time of relaxation; it is a matter of taking one's mind off of one's work through some other activity. (We will leave aside the conception of work in Solo for later.) Not merely Javanese but also Indonesian has a difficult time with "relaxation," the words for it frequently being changed. Nonetheless, the idea of taking one's mind off of something after work, and after sleep as well, prevails in Solo as it does in America. This involves a drifting, as if the mind wandered to subjects without conscious choice of those topics. Such vagueness of mind is considered dangerous in Java. In such a state, for instance, one can become possessed by spirits. *Soré* is an attempt to rectify this state.

Just how it does so was made clear when I recalled an event that took place before I moved into Kemlayan. One afternoon, *soré*, I had been riding my bicycle down various lanes when I realized I was lost. As it happened, I found myself in the neighborhood into which I was later to move, though at that time I did not yet have any idea that I might do so. I stopped, got off my bike, turned around and mounted again. As I rode off, one of my future neighbors turned to someone standing next to her and said, "Ah, he's turning around." To understand what was going on in her mind one must think of all the things she did not say. Although it is true that an occasional European does pass down that lane, it is not a frequent occurrence. Yet instead of asking who this middle-aged European on a bicycle was, where he was going, where he was coming from and so on, she focused on the one indisputable fact: I was, indeed, turning around. That she commented at all indicates that my presence was not a matter of total indifference to her; what I recall as her initial "ah" ("he's turning around") indicates that she thought she had solved something: the riddle of my appearance. What she did was to reduce all questions to one unshakable fact, as if all the wandering, diverse thoughts in her mind at that time of day, thoughts she could only be partly aware of, had materialized into something she knew indisputably.

To say "ah, he is turning around" is to say that one has seen such things before. The presence of a European bicyclist, instead of being a new event in neighborhood history, becomes something that is already known and, in a sense, has already been seen. By pushing everything strange outside of awareness in favor of the one aspect that is familiar, the whole event becomes familiar. There is thus a process of instantaneous archaizing, as though the event did not happen for the first time on the first Wednesday of December 1980, but had happened the Wednesday before that as well, and so on as long ago as anyone can remember.

This is the working of *soré*. The same thing seen at the same time every day becomes an object fastened on to be recognized. In searching out things that one already knows, one finds in them as well those new thoughts that are set loose by the rhythm of the day. It is to say "ah, that is what it is," and to have that answer for every stray thought in one's mind.

This archaizing tendency creates the sense of custom (*adat*) in the neighborhood. It is not that every circumcision has always meant a *selamatan* and that every *selamatan* has required a committee and that the person in charge of chairs has always been Wiro that gives local activities a sense of antiquity. The actual age of such practices is immaterial. What matters is that the sense of it always having been so, of having already known it, comes not from the activity itself but from the suppressed thoughts. Without there first having been forty-five minutes of desultory conversation on any topic but the proposed *selamatan*, it would not have been possible to reach agreement on the arrangements for it, not because there is a difference of opinion about the arrangements, but because there needed to be a time in which to generate thoughts left unsaid, which could then be absorbed by that which is called *adat*.

On another occasion I was looking at a bank that had been built, apparently, on the model of A & P grocery stores; it was of red brick with painted white columns, actually not columns at all but boards slightly raised from the facade to look like columns, with white-trimmed leaded windows—"neocolonial" in several senses. Wiro, when I asked him what he thought of it, said "authentically Javanese" (*asli Jawa*), though to find anything beyond the suggestion of columns that would justify this statement would, on historical grounds, be difficult. In saying the building was "authentically Javanese," Wiro insisted on the familiarity of the building to him. And he insisted also that whatever he recognized had to be Javanese. In making his statement, whatever aspects of the building retained a foreign quality for him were nonetheless subsumed under the rubric, "Javanese." It is in this way that what is said becomes a sign of all that goes unsaid. When done in concert in the neighborhood, the result is institutions that feel antique.[15]

CHAPTER THREE

Neighborhood Politics

THE PERCEIVED weakness of the national hierarchy affects local politics. There is an attempt locally to reestablish hierarchy. The divisions that emerge can be seen as correlates of the attempts at suppression associated with the issues of language that we have raised. I want to show how the correlation occurs by examining a series of incidents that took place in connection with the celebration of the Indonesian independence day in 1981.

The residents of Kemlayan take special pride in their nationalism. The local holiday they talk most about is Independence Day, August 17. In 1980 they raised Rp 90,000 (approximately $150.00) through local contributions, a sizable amount considering local incomes, for the celebration. A committee was formed for the purpose, but most of the members were also *ronḍa* members, the *ronḍa* identifying itself closely with the celebration. People talked about the celebration and made plans for the coming year (1981) months ahead of time. They thought they would put up a gateway where the main alleyway debouched onto the street and hold a nightmarket as they had in the past.

When August 17, 1981, approached, however, there was not much activity. Talk about the celebration seemed, in fact, to have decreased. I went to a close acquaintance, a member of the *ronḍa* who had told me enthusiastically about its plans, and asked what was happening, were there any plans? He thought not. Why? Well, in the past there was always an announcement from the head of the neighborhood association that there would be a celebration; then the neighborhood youth went out and did the work. He told me again what they had done last year. "The atmosphere is different now," he said, and he told me I should ask the head of the neighborhood organization (the Kepala Rukun Keluarga).

I found the head of the neighborhood organization, the Pak R. K. as he is referred to, in the alleyway setting out flags for the seventeenth, which was the next day. He was doing this without help from anyone else, unusual since for public occasions in particular preparations are made cooperatively. I ask him if there were any plans. He told me, "Ask the youth [*pemuda*], the *wong tua* [senior people] are a bit tired." He went on to say that there would be a badminton contest later that afternoon, a chess tournament the next morning, a ceremony at the Heroes' Cemetery at midnight the next night, and a ceremony on the palace square the following day. But all of this was outside the neighborhood.

The problem was that the Pak R. K., like most of the other neighborhood officers, was a pious Muslim. Such people were not numerous in Kemlayan; only 14 of 69 households in a survey I made could be so counted, and 4 of these were not Javanese at all. Muslims (I use the term as an abbreviation for pious Muslims; most of the remainder of the families were called *Islam simpatis*, or "sympathetic to Islam," meaning that they counted themselves as Muslims for purpose of burial at least, but in general followed syncretic Javanese religious practices) held most of the leading offices, however; the heads of the administrative district (Rukun Keluarga) and two of its subdivisions as well as the secretary of the district were Muslims.

Bad feeling had broken out between these Muslims and their Javanese neighbors. This animosity arose along with the perceptible nervousness about forthcoming national elections to be held the following May (1982). The one important office that the Muslims did not hold locally was the office of *ronḍa* chairman. The *ronḍa* chairman was not elected, but rather was appointed by the chairman of yet another local body, the LKMD, an organization that was supposed to look after questions of sanitation, safety, and cultural activities. The incumbent was *kejawen*, that is, he was nominally Muslim, but he followed Javanese practices. He was a lieutenant in the police who, at the time of revolution, had been a recruit in the palace guard. He left that position to join the police. Nominally retired, he still worked, holding an administrative post that brought him more in special office perquisites than his salary, which, since his retirement, was less than a dollar a day. He was moderately well-off, owning not only his own house but a larger, two-story one that he rented out to some Chinese who had a nearby shop. He was an example of most of what Muslims disapproved of: he raised pigs in a village nearby, he made graveyard vigils, he drank (but, in fact, only a little beer), and he gambled. In most of this he was identical to his neighbors, differing from them mainly in the pride by which he obliquely let it be known that he did all of these things. Both his character and tension over the upcoming elections prompted the incident I am about to relate.

Bulet, the *ronḍa* chairman, was attacked in a public meeting in March 1981. At that time elections were held for the head of the administrative district (Rukun Keluarga). Heads of local households were present and decided, under the guidance of a representative of the lurah's office, that it would be done through a committee: the household heads would select certain people to represent them; the old head would also have a representative, as would the lurah. It was then announced that the heads of the 11 subgroups had been polled, and all but one supported the incumbent. The committee was left to report at some future date, when they would make the choice.

With this out of the way, the report of the present Pak

R. K. was distributed in mimeographed form as written by the secretary of the organization, also a pious Muslim.[1] This report was unexceptional aside from the section on the *ronḍa*. That section of the report, which was read aloud by the secretary, said that no account could be given of *ronḍa* finances since the head of the *ronḍa* had failed to submit the required information. When the reading was finished, the chairman of the *ronḍa*, Bulet, arose and said he was "insulted" (*tersinggung*).[2] He had only gotten notice of the meeting that morning. The treasurer of the *ronḍa* was out of town, in Jakarta in fact, and so there had been no chance to submit the information. Someone then suggested that the official report be delayed until Bulet could gather the necessary information. The Pak R. K. thanked the man for his suggestion and, without saying whether it would be accepted or not, called on the next speaker, the official from the lurah's office. Whether or not the suggestion was ever put into practice I never discovered; in any case the insult had been delivered. The official from the lurah's office went on for ten minutes about the need to make up "shortcomings" without once mentioning what these might be. When he was finished, Bulet, who had interrupted the proceedings to make his statement, rose again and slowly tore his copy of the report to shreds, letting the pieces fall on the living room floor of the house, which happened to be that of another pious Muslim. Bulet then made an exit, and the meeting continued.

General sentiment was in favor of Bulet and directed against the Muslim secretary. Interestingly enough, the Pak R. K. was not blamed.[3] The dispute went on for a couple of months, but sentiment obviously ran rather deep, as the events of August 17 indicated. When people came to talk about the events later, they said that Mahmud, the secretary of the neighborhood organization and one of the two Muslims most blamed for the events, had wanted to combine the celebration of independence with that of the end of the fasting month, the occasions occurring within two weeks of each other. There would then be a neighborhood *halil-bil-halil*, a celebration where people gather and are given the chance to mutually ask pardon. They wanted to do this, it was said, because they had so few supporters themselves, and this would make it seem as though they had the majority on their side. They were more than once accused of having no interest in national matters, putting religious concerns first. They of course denied this.

The celebration of the end of the fasting month illustrates the way in which religious celebrations, like national celebrations, are bent to local conditions. There was no neighborhood *halil-bil-halil*. There was, however, a torchlight parade in which Kemlayan children participated. A large number of *kejawen*, or nonpious Muslim children, joined in. Their parents, however, stayed indoors as the children were being lined up in the neighborhood lane. On the morning of the day after the fasting month, however, there was an early morning rush to ask forgiveness between neighbors. This was given a decidedly Javanese twist. In the Islamic conception, asking pardon is a way of showing that one has controlled one's desires by fasting during the previous month, thus putting oneself in a state where one can act as a proper Muslim by observing the fast. To ask pardon without fasting is, in this perspective, senseless. Solonese neighborhood practice goes further. In most places in Indonesia, the asking of pardon on Lebaran, the day after the fasting month, begins by going to those who have the most prestige.

In Kemlayan, the day starts with visits not to those who are most influential or wealthiest, but to the oldest residents. People who are not seen on the street because of their debilities and do not have the rank to be consulted on ordinary occasions become prominent on Lebaran. The reason that the aged are visited is not because they are repositories of experience; most of them are ignored on

occasions when decisions have to be made. It is not se-
niority that is honored on Lebaran, only age and, only
very old age at that. The nearness to death of such people
makes the blessings that they give in exchange for the
asking of pardon valuable in the minds of the Solonese.
In this way, an Islamic holiday is made into a Javanese
occasion.[4] The co-opting of holidays thus is something that
goes on from the Javanese side whether or not it is also
an activity of the Muslims.

On August 17 there were no celebrations within the
neighborhood. However, there was a meeting of neighborhood youth, including *ronḍa* members and the *ronḍa*
chairman. It was decided that in two weeks time they
would hold a celebration in any case, and that they would
ask the Pak R. K. to attend and give a speech. This plan
was carried out; there was a celebration with speeches by
the Pak R. K. and heads of the suborganizations and various kinds of entertainment.[5] This was not, however, a
happy solution. Stories that differed only in their details
circulated about how the Pak R. K. had had to be pressured to attend by the lurah, how some Muslims did not
come at all. During the celebration itself a complaint was
forwarded to the lurah, no one seemed sure by whom,
saying that the organizers did not have the necessary per-
mits and that the celebration should therefore be stopped.
This was the cause of many sarcastic comments on the
topic of what kind of people would oppose the celebration of Independence Day and what kind of nationalists
such people were; they obviously cared more for their religion than for patriotic causes. One person who came to
see the events was the brother of a woman who lived in
the neighborhood. He had been a member of the PKI, a
Communist. His presence was also reported to the lurah,
and on this basis it was said that people wanted to make
it seem that the celebration was really a leftist plot. This
led to a meeting in the lurah's office that I was not able
to attend, but that was said to be noisy, in which the lu-

rah tried to make peace between the two sides. This was the last incident in the series. The youths had planned to have a meeting to which they would invite the lurah and other officials and demand to know who had called the celebration a communist plot. The meeting never materialized however.

In Javanese eyes, this was a contest for the neighborhood. To say that, however, requires us to reconsider some other matters. We have to ask what, exactly, is involved. The Muslims in question might be called members of the lower middle class—they were minor bureaucrats and soldiers. The *ronḍa* head was a retired lieutenant of police, later replaced by a retired army lieutenant. The treasurer of the *ronḍa* was a wealthy batik manufacturer. The active *ronḍa* members themselves were drawn from the unemployed youth of the neighborhood and from those with menial jobs. They were supported in the neighborhood by many whose class status was comparable to the Muslims—bureaucrats and soldiers amongst them. Moreover there were no immediate economic interests at stake at all. The neighborhood, as I have pointed out, is not an economic unit; it required nothing in the way of cooperation for most of its members to make their living.

In my judgment the dispute would never have occurred if, under the pressure of the upcoming elections, differences that would have otherwise gone unnoticed had not come to everyone's attention. In the minds of the neighborhood residents, the elections meant not a possible change in government, but a time when they might have to declare themselves. Though balloting was to be secret, they felt that they would have to vote, and they would be on view. In an election for local neighborhood office, the necessity for such declaration was avoided in one case by having a committee make the decision. In other neighborhood elections that I witnessed, the choice was usually known in advance, and the election proceeded more like the committee meetings I have described, the topic being avoided until it seemed somehow to appear by itself, and then pass by. In the one case where there was an open discussion, it was prompted by a man known for his lack of manners and resulted in embarrassment.

These local elections are perhaps the best indication of what made people nervous about the national elections. In effect they were held on the assumption that elections should not evoke politics. Decisions should emerge by themselves in the way "decisions" about the division of labor in a feast did, as we have seen. Nervousness about elections is nervousness that one might, indeed, declare oneself, not by being anything that in itself was disapproved of—ex-Communists were barred from voting and thus had this possibility removed—but simply by asserting any position. To do so would expose one as the cause of disruption. In this climate, Bulet's character was not only distasteful to Muslims, it offered, in its flamboyance and assertiveness, a chance to blame him for any possible breakdown of order. Bulet could be blamed if security were broken; his lack of cooperation in official matters would make his culpability evident.

This probably was not quite the plot that the *kejawen* saw it to be; it was more likely the nervousness of Muslims about themselves and an attempt to blame others before they were themselves blamed; a way of saying that the person in charge of keeping things secure was the one at fault for any disruption. However much or little the Muslim faction intended to set off by their attack on Bulet, enough bad feelings were generated that it was forced to maintain an oppositionist stance when the time came to plan the August 17 celebration even though by that time Bulet had been replaced as head of the *ronḍa* and its oppositionism undoubtedly damaged the faction's own cause.

In part oppositionism was forced on the Muslims by Bulet's subsequent measures. The lurah was new and wanted to replace Bulet and the person to whom he was directly responsible, the head of the LKMD (the organization that is supposed to look after "social affairs," meaning trash collection, security, and so on). This was part of his effort to place new people in most neighborhood offices, for which reason he had called elections of the Rukun Keluarga and Rukun Tetangga as well as the LKMDs. His motive, then, did not have to do with this dispute; the lurah himself was in any case a Catholic. Two months after the attack on Bulet, Bulet was replaced, not with a pious Muslim, but with someone who was a friend of Bulet and who had served in a similar position in the Military Police. He was also acceptable to the Muslims. The reaction of Bulet and his friends to this was first to call the replacement illegal, claiming that there had not been the requisite meeting to replace the head of the LKMD, though in fact such a meeting had been held.

This led to a problem of valid signatures on the receipts given for the monthly *ronda* collections. These receipts were mimeographed and bore the facsimile signatures of Bulet and the head of the LKMD. Bulet complained to the Pak R. K. that if he and the head of the LKMD no longer held office, the receipts were invalid. But if his name was still on the receipts, he must be head of the *ronda* still. The Pak R. K. was stymied. He did not know what to do; "I am confused [*bingung*]," he said. In the course of this, the *ronda* member who made the monthly collection wanted to resign; how could he hand out invalid receipts when he made his collections? Bulet, however, convinced him not to resign, thereby showing that he had the security of the neighborhood at heart, and thereby also keeping alive the issue of the receipts and thus his claim to office. The Pak R. K., seeing this conflict, was thus forced into an oppositionist stand even after Bulet had left office. He felt, then, obliged to dissociate himself from the *ronda* when the time came later for the August 17 celebrations, a feeling that was afterwards only confirmed when Bulet was blamed for the insistence that the Pak R. K. be invited to speak at the belated celebrations.

The counters in this dispute are writings: the receipts and the report. It is through writing that matters become "official." Thus if, for instance, there is a death, there is a mimeographed announcement delivered stating the time of the funeral; so too for weddings and for other *selamatan*. These invitations are preferred to oral ones. They replace a custom prevalent still in villages whereby the persons giving the *selamatan* have a village youth circulate between households making the requisite announcement. When he comes to the door, the boy is greeted in whatever speech level is appropriate to him, and he replies accordingly. The announcement, however, is made in sentences as full of formulae and archaisms as possible. Thus the person holding the *selamatan* is effaced—it is not his own voice, not his own sentiment, but that of the community that is expressed when someone else speaks for him in a language as far removed from the "natural" language of either of them as possible.[6]

Language that is divorced from its origin is language that is replicable; anyone who knows the code could say the same thing. Mimeographed announcements are the same for everyone; their official character derives from this. Village ceremonies are often rites of passage: what makes them effective is the replicability of the ceremonial events; that is what pertains, always, on such occasions. The wedding not only announces marriage, it establishes a couple as wed. The fit between fact and announcement is not that the announcement simply expresses the fact, but that the announcement makes the fact what it is. It is this logic of writing that Bulet relied on when he said that because the receipts bore his name he was still chairman of the *ronḍa*. What is officially so is then factually so; and what is officially so is what is contained in the replicable language of the receipts. The Pak R. K. was "confused";

he knew that Bulet had been replaced by the lurah, but he also gave some credence to Bulet's arguments. The matter was resolved only when new receipts were issued bearing the name of the new *ronḍa* chairman.

A related logic pertained to the report. That Bulet was accused of not supplying information about *ronḍa* finances implied to me that he was misusing the funds. This was not a possibility that I could get anyone to agree with or deny. Bulet's supporters, for instance, would not deny that he had misappropriated funds. Yet I am confident that Bulet had not in fact mishandled the funds. The money was given as intended almost entirely to *ronḍa* members themselves for "cigarettes." The amount came to only Rp 5,000 (about $8.25) per month per member. This jibed with the amount collected monthly by the *ronḍa* members themselves, and I heard no complaints from them. The writer of the report may not have been averse to making that impression, but I never heard it circulated. It is rather a pure case of what is "official." The accusation against Bulet was just as stated—he had failed to provide information necessary for the report. It was not that the incomplete report officially implied his possible delict, but that he had caused the report to be less complete than an official report ought to be.

In this context one must understand the Javanese assertion that they have nothing against Muslims. They actually welcome their participation in the neighborhood, as the fact that they had, indeed, chosen them to be their leaders so often indicates. This parallels their feelings about Chinese and foreigners. In other contexts Chinese are despised; in a certain way, foreigners, if not despised, are thought contemptible. Nonetheless they are welcome in the neighborhood, providing that they participate in neighborhood activities. Chinese who stand outside during *soré* and who attend neighborhood functions are free of the accusations made about other Chinese, namely that they are *angkuh*, arrogant, holding themselves back from their neighbors. Solonese pride themselves on *toleransi*, toleration. The cost of this, however, is an assumption about the nature of participation. It is not a division of private and public, wherein people can practice whatever religion or customs they want apart from others so long as they abide by public rules. Rather it is an extension of Javanese assumptions about themselves to others. Participation, whether at *soré* or at a *selamatan*, involves a certain suppression, as we have seen. The presence of Chinese, Muslims, and foreigners in a Javanese community is an actual advantage because it shows how widely that suppression extends, how Javanese rules thereby encompass everyone. By that same reasoning, to see Muslims acting as Javanese proves the strength of Javanism, a strength that could only be challenged if Muslims were thought of as violating those rules.

The place of writing here is clear. Writing seems to the Javanese to carry out the potential of speech levels, being placed in replicable form and standing opposed to unique or spontaneous thoughts. What the receipts actually said had no importance in their function as a sign of payment until Bulet raised the question. Likewise, the report was wholly vacuous: one could get no sense of what had actually gone on in the neighborhood or what the association had done from reading it; ideally it would sound just like the report from the previous year or just like the report of another neighborhood. This vacuity is only valuable in contrast to what might have been said; in the same way, the possibility of the Chinese acting in a way that could not be shared by others is cultivated so that, by contrast, their behavior in the community is seen as a suppression of that activity. Participation, as opposed to simply not bothering anyone else through keeping one's differences hidden, is important because it is in participation that suppression becomes evident, and the rules, or *adat*, along with it.

Writing takes on the role of an empty form whose function it is to be played off against possible content. It becomes a matter of dispute when that form is disrupted by having the matter of its content actually raised, as happened with the reports and the receipts. "Participation" here means figuring in the writing through one's absence from it. Bulet as a character is present in the Rukun Keluarga report; his failure, withholding information, is, in the Muslim view, what one can expect from him: he was what was wrong with the report. To the extent that he did what he was supposed to do, his "own" character would be effaced. The question of his signature that either made the receipts invalid or made him still head of the *ronḍa* is similar. He inconveniently called attention to what the receipts actually said; they would have remained valid if people had not read them but merely looked at them, the issue of whose signature was on the receipts thus not being raised at all.

The vacuity of writing, therefore, is itself a source of value. It is this question of value that makes the place of writing somewhat difficult to grasp. For example, though literacy in Latin script is the rule in the neighborhood, the ability to read Javanese script is rare amongst Solonese today. The best that most people can do is make out individual letters; it is not exaggeration to say that they are illiterate in this script. Furthermore, very little is published in this script today. Nonetheless, the ability to read it is highly prized, and people will display their meager ability with pride, tracing the letters out and showing how to distinguish one character from another. It is, of course, widely known that there is Javanese literature, and this is somehow confounded with Javanese script. Even a few letters of such script, however, are looked at with some respect, though they say nothing. To the extent that literacy in Javanese script was widespread, one would expect the awe in which it is held to be reduced. It would eventually be on a par with Latin script, valuable for indicating the replicability and formality of its content. What would be irreducible would be the sense that Javanese script conceals something, that some great significance adheres to the sense of absence—hence, in Javanese conception, presence elsewhere—that it conveys. The "official" role of writing is based on this value.

This irreducibility is cultural rather than based on the nature of writing. Speech also contains the replicable element of writing in the sense that we understand one another's speech only by reference to elements—such as words in it, for instance.[7] Indeed, the example of village oral invitations shows how speech is comparable to writing in its capacity to distance itself from its origin; the very attempt to make *Ngoko* function like *Kromo* within the neighborhood illustrates the capacity of speech to express a certain vacuity. The cultural element in writing is seen in the report; without Bulet's contribution, the report lacked one section. That I could get no definite response about the implication of possible misuses of *ronḍa* funds was not because such an implication was not possible given that blankness in the report. The response was always a refusal to confirm or to deny, as though both were possibilities. Not only that implication, but any number of others as well are possible in such a situation. Such thoughts arise in the space of the blankness of the report because without the presence of writing, the process of recognition by which such thoughts are assuaged can not go on. It is as though people came out at *soré* to see the familiar landmarks of the neighborhood and everything had vanished. The possibility of saying, "Ah, that's what it is," and thereby absorbing the pressure to recognize one's own thoughts had been taken away.

The same is true in the case of the receipts. Looking at a dollar bill, we are not likely to read it. If we nonetheless do so and notice that W. H. Blumenthal is no longer Secretary of the Treasury, we do not suddenly fear that our money is invalid. Were we to do so we would start a process of interpretation—Blumenthal is not Secretary of the

Treasury now, but he was when the bill was issued; it is the office of the Secretary that has the right to issue money, not the person; and so on. A similar process was set in motion for Bulet. If writing led to aspersions on his character, he implicated its other possibilities, those usually ignored. The special position of writing is not due to a graphic element that distinguishes it from speech. Rather, it derives from its alignment in Javanese thought with absence in the interest of a stabilization of significance, as *Kromo* itself does. The result of this stabilization is "validity."

When the celebration was actually held, the lurah gave a speech saying how pleased he was that it had come about; the Pak R. K. thanked the youths for their efforts, and the head of one of the neighborhood suborganizations did the same. Nothing was said about the historical achievement of independence. What was celebrated was not independence, but the holding of the celebration. Afterwards I was told by various youths that the Pak R. K. practically had to be coerced to come, that it took not just their own request but also an emissary from the lurah before he would agree to be present. A few of the Muslims, including the hated secretary, did not attend. The Pak R. K. had at first refused to come on the grounds that he had not been invited to the meeting at which the celebration was planned. But, I was told, no one was invited. It was an entirely "spontaneous" (*spontan*) meeting, and usually the youths went on to comment on how well attended the celebration was. Before the Pak R. K. agreed to come, one youth said, it had been "tense" (*tegang*).

It was only after these events that I heard the word *spontan*, a word derived from Dutch and not present in the standard dictionaries of Javanese. The Pak R. K. possibly would agree that the meeting was *spontan*, at least in the sense that it lacked that which made it official, invitations. To the youths, however, the spontaneous nature of the meeting did not make it unofficial, but all the more a valid occasion. It meant in the first place that whoever attended was moved to do so; they would not deny that word of the meeting was spread and that people then came. But something made them come, and it is this insistence that they came without previous thought or intention that makes it, in their minds, *spontan*. They also said it was "odd indeed" (*lucu banget*) that anyone would protest the holding of a meeting of people who wanted to celebrate Independence Day, that it was the "right of all citizens." In acting spontaneously, then, they were merely doing what they had a right to do; beyond that the implication was that they were acting as citizens should act, as patriots. In this view it was the Pak R. K. who was less than perfectly nationalistic when he resisted the invitation to speak. To act "spontaneously," then, meant to do one's duty.

This spontaneous meeting had the feeling of the other meetings that I have described. That is, the talk was desultory and the tone relaxed. Decisions were not reached through discussion at the meeting itself, which went on for some hours with various people drifting in and out. The "spontaneity" of the meeting meant not the direct expression of intentions, but the recognition of something that emerged at the end as though without the intention of the participants. In acting "spontaneously," the youths of Kemlayan did something that they had never done before—planned to hold a celebration without the prior agreement of the Pak R. K. Their spontaneity in doing so was apparent to them later, not in thinking of an outpouring of their wishes or the novelty of their actions, but in recognizing that they had acted as patriots. What *spontan* meant was that they had acted in spite of themselves, in ways that they would not have expected from their daily behavior. Indeed, their "spontaneity" became apparent to them only later, when their actions were challenged and when it had become a defense of patriotism, no different than everyone's duty. They then saw themselves as having acted in old, recognized ways.

Spontan in this context is an answer to invitations, preferably written invitations. In the context of duty, of the general tone of the meeting as it went on, *spontan* means that the youths spoke with a certain language and not with a possible alternative. They spoke as "citizens" (*warga negara*) and as "patriots" (*patriot*), whereas their natural inclination would be to speak in their everyday voices. That the characterization of their actions as *spontan* emerged only later is because it could not be known as *spontan* at that time. The replacement of their own voices by those of citizens and nationalists could be known only after the fact; what they said became "patriotic" not because of what they actually said, which was very little, or because they wanted to celebrate Independence Day, though that had something to do with it, but because of their sense later that they had had it in their power to have spoken differently.

Their own interpretation was not the only one, however. It is for this reason that the Pak R. K.'s participation became an issue. They insisted that the Pak R. K. come. He would have been "trashed" (*dibom*) had he not, one youth said. Had they had their "own" celebration, with their "own" speakers, speaking as it were for themselves, the difference in voices would not have been self-evident. The equivalent of *Kromo* replacing *Ngoko* here is the Muslim Pak R. K. speaking for them. It was in the replacement of their own voice by another that, finally, their actions became indisputably official. They did not claim to have controlled the Pak R. K., nor did they say that he became their spokesman. In their view, he merely acted as he should have when he celebrated Independence Day. Their actual role was to have pressured him to do so. But they needed to think of him as merely acting as Pak R. K., as an official ought to act. For this reason Mahmud, the secretary, or another of the Muslims, was always blamed for the Pak R. K.'s bad actions. In the view of the youths, their spontaneous action was like the division of duties in a *selamatan*—issued on the basis of a common suppression. "Spontaneity" in their minds referred to the process of recognizing something that seemed to have emerged without them. Instead they were blamed for their actions, accused of acting without proper license, as though they had acted without restraint. When the Pak R. K. said not what they would have him say but merely what officially ought to be said, and when the Pak R. K. spoke in their place, thus putting them offstage, they could see their actions emerging despite themselves, "spontaneously," and they could have others see it this way as well. The Pak R. K. would become a sign of their own suppression, therefore of their rightness.

When the Pak R. K. finally did act as the youths hoped he would, he thanked them for their efforts, relegating these efforts simply to what youths ought to do for Independence Day. His innocuous words of course took no recognition of the conflict between them. But once he spoke, the youth could assume that no one need worry about the possibility of any actions that were not mentioned. In retrospect everyone would agree that spontaneity and duty coincided. The Pak R. K.'s speech could then function like the report of the Rukun Keluarga: so long as something was said it did not matter what it was; all possibilities of what might have happened would be put to rest in favor of what was official.

But too much had been brought into the open. Nothing "official" could rule out individual interpretations; further charges were made. The conflict ended not as the youth hoped, but with the actions of the lurah who clamped down on everyone. That he could do so successfully is worth comment. The fear that was generated by the conflict was the same fear that the national elections themselves aroused. Posters erected by the government urged people to "make the elections a success" in "peace and order" (*tertib dan tenteram*). "Success" was not winning the election but holding it at all without the social order unraveling. The nightmare that, with prompting, Islam has come to symbolize in some Indonesian circles is not the victory of Islam, but rather anarchy emerging under pressure from "those who might disrupt"; everyone might then turn against everyone else. It is a fear that all possibilities might be considered, that the "official" might not hold things under cover. It is for this reason that the lurah could so easily restore matters. The display of force he was reputed to have made in the meeting of various elements was not a victory for anyone. But it was effective because everyone feared a violence that was coincident with having all possibilities come up for consideration, and all were grateful to be able to put things to rest—at least temporarily.

What distinguishes pious Muslims from other Javanese primarily is their attitude, not about "death," but about graves. Muslims in Kemlayan stressed that one could not communicate via the "dead" with God, that such attempts deny the nature of God. They nonetheless believed in the efficacy of "power" in the Javanese sense, believing, for instance, that President Sukarno had certain "powerful" charms. They considered themselves nationalists and, in particular, admirers of Sukarno and the Pantja Sila. The Pak R. K. had himself fought against the Darul Islam in West Java. They followed the same conventions of speech levels as other Solonese, giving the same stress to etiquette and questions of refinement. In that sense they were no different than other Solonese in their regard for hierarchy. The difference came in the definition of the top. They, like other Solonese, felt there to be a lack of "power" at the apex of the pyramid. But in their view, Islam could fill this void. In this, however, they were realistic about their chances for national power, having seen themselves progressively put further and further to the side since the beginning of the New Order. It was in this context that they too turned to the local scene. Their feelings about Bulet generated a train of events that made them seem, from a *kejawen* point of view, "Muslims" and not "Javanese." From their own point of view, however, they remained Javanese, interested in the potential security of the neighborhood just like everyone else, but they remained the right kind of Javanese, that is, true Muslims.

From the perspective of class, it is significant that the small band of Kemlayan Muslims are no different in background than many of those they oppose and, moreover, that as bureaucrats their lives are encompassed within Javanese hierarchical arrangements. From that point of view one can understand that their wish is for a reform, for the right kind of Javanism, and one sees that they share the brand of nationalism inherent in speech levels.[8]

When the national campaign began, the Pak R. K. and two other Muslims displayed the paper lantern of Golkar, the government party, rather than the emblem of the Islamic party in front of their houses. (Others had not yet put out any party emblem at all when I left five months before the elections.) If Islam was to make a difference, it would have to be in the neighborhood itself. Yet local control is meaningless; it controls no significant funds ("Why shouldn't the Muslims hold the offices?" one *ronḍa* member said. "There is no budget."), and it makes no decisions about any important issue. The only way in which the neighborhood does matter is in the question of "security." This, in turn, implies the issue of hierarchy that is tied to it.

From the Muslims' own point of view, there was no conflict between Islam and nationalism. They were both Muslims and nationalists at once. If our analysis is correct, their own struggle in the neighborhood was based on their hopes to define "nationalism" by local action. In Javanese eyes, they could have all they wanted in the way of public office; indeed, their Muslim identification made them appropriate spokesmen for the community, providing only that they said nothing that they actually wanted to say, that they acted in unimpeachably Javanese fashion.

I have called the pressure put on neighborhoods a retreat from the precariousness of the total hierarchy. Yet it is not a refuge if this means giving up on the wider society. This can best be seen by the reverence accorded Sukarno. Everyone in the neighborhood, Muslims and *kejawen*, seemed to hold him in awe. His picture could be found not only inside homes but, in one instance, in a large framed case on the outside wall of a house. Partly this reflects the feeling that no one has really replaced him; no one has "power" in the sense that he had it. He remains at the top of the pyramid. (It is not wholly illogical that a dead person should be there by Javanese thinking.) What is important is just this sense that, though the word is used, thinking about Sukarno is not entirely "nostalgic."[9] Sukarno's photograph is an acknowledgment of his Javanese "death"—that is, of his absence here and presence elsewhere. It thus emblematizes the suppression by which the neighborhood assures its safety. In this it also indicates why the neighborhood is worth fighting for.

Javanese hierarchy is most apparent in Kromo-Ngoko exchanges. But the creation of something "official" by trying to find something suppressed beneath *Ngoko* is not limited to the neighborhood in the expectation of those who reside there. The hopes for something more emerging is what the display of Sukarno's photograph in the community indicates. There is no difference between the establishment of a *Ngoko*-speaking neighborhood and a total hierarchy of Kromo-Ngoko. Both are based on suppression in favor of "official" form; any form of instituting the possibility of social action implies the whole of Javanese, *Kromo* in relation to *Ngoko* and *Ngoko* in relation to blows.

Here we can return to the Javanese assumption sometimes invoked that a cosmic law exists that ensures that everything works out in a determined way. The alternative is to see the world as having a specific reality and a number of other possibilities. The failure of *Kromo*, though failure is too strong a term, is its present inability to ensure not just that other possibilities do not work out but, by reference to itself, to rule out the very admissibility of there being "possibilities." Such an admission would jeopardize the inevitability of a certain order to the world. It is this issue of ruling out "possibilities," of keeping them to "oneself," that motivated both sides, Islamic and nationalist. Each side exists as the object of the other's blame for making everything possible. The perfect fit between language and the world, between language and hierarchy, continues to elude Javanese.

Report of the Rukun Keluarga in Translation

Board of RK I Kemlayan

Surakarta

Re: Report of the   To the honorable:

RK I Kemlayan   Mr. Head of the Kalurahan

                                         of Kemlayan

                                         Kecamatan Serengan

                                         Surakarta

As almu' alaikum wr. wb.

With full sense of responsibility and gratitude to the Lord Who is One, allow us to submit the Report of the Board of RK I Kemlayan for the period of service 1978–81.

Our Report of Responsibilities covers four areas, namely:

    I. The Area of Administration;

    II. The Area of Finances;

    III. The Area of Inventory;

    IV. The Area of Activities.

Based on the aforesaid areas we are able to report as follows:

I. *The Area of Administration*

By certificate of the Camat[10] of Serengan dated 20-6-1978; number 994/Pemb/5/200/VI/1978 the administration of RK

I Kemlayan for the period of service 1978/1981 was established as follows:

-Chairman I   :Toegiman Wiryosukarno
-Chairman II   :M. Yusuf
-Secretary I   :Moeh. Nawawi
-Secretary II   :Danuwinoto
-Treasurer I   :Soenardi
-Treasurer II   :Sri Wiyono
-Assistant   :Y. Widjono

II. *The Area of Finances*

In fulfillment of the certificate of Mr. Head of the Kalurahan Kemlayan dated 7-3-'81 number 148/89/III/81 the report of responsibility in the area of Finances follows:

A. *Finances of the Ronḍa Kampung:*[11]
We cannot report on the finances of the ronḍa[12] Kampung within the working area of RK I Kemlayan at this point for several reasons, amongst them:
a. Administration/Finance of Ronḍa Kampung RK I is managed by the official appointed by LSD/LKMD KI Kemlayan.[13]
b. Up until this moment the Administrator of RK I Kemlayan has not/not yet ever received his report.
B. *Finances of BUKK:*[14]
We can report the finances of BUKK Permukiman[15] RK I Kemlayan as follows:

No.	Explanation	Income	Expenditure
	Received from routine collections from inhabitants from the month of April 1980 through February 1981	Rp 203,055,	
1.	Expended for honoraria for functionaries 11 × 2 × Rp 5000, . . .		Rp 110,000,[16]
2.	Collection for drawers		Rp 20,300,[17]

No.	Explanation	Income	Expenditure
3.	Purchase of parts and service of garbage cart		Rp 29,495
	Total..............		Rp 159,795,—
	Cash balance		Rp 43,255,—
	Total	Rp 203,050,–	Rp 203,050,—[18]

III. The Area of Inventory

Inventory owned by us:

		Number of Objects	
No.	Name/Type of Object:	Unit	Number
1.	Rubber stamp RK I Kemlayan	Object	1 (one)
2.	Sign Board RK I Kemlayan	Object	1 (one)
3.	Pennants (colored cloth)	Piece	1 (one)
4.	Pull-cart	Object	1 (one)
5.	Drum/Trash can	Object	6 (six)

IV. Area of Activities

During the period of service 1978/81 the Administrator of RK I Kemlayan held amongst other activities:

1. Scraping of the drains of RT 13
2. Repair of the special privy of RT 12
3. Repair of the public privies
4. Drain repair from Coyudan Street [Bawah Sawo] to Slamet Riyadi Street [Losmen Kota]
5. Scraping of the drains of RT 14
6. Scraping of drains and construction of privy skah[19]
7. Various other social activities[20]

Note: Activities 1 through 7 above were carried out via the contributions of the RK I Kemlayan community.

Thus our report with the hope that it will be perused and used as necessary.

Thank you.[21]

Wassalamu'alaikum
Surakarta, 12 March 1981
Administrators of RK I Kemlayan

Chairman[22]   Finances   Secretary

Copies to:

1. Chairman of the LKMD K1 Kemlayan
2. Administrator of the BUKK Kemlayan
3. Administrators of RT within the area of RK I Kemlayan
4. Community figures in the area of RK I Kemlayan[23]

PART TWO

The *Anéh*, or Oddity In and Out of Place

CHAPTER FOUR

Surakartan Theater Under the New Order

IT APPEARS to be impossible to write about Java without mentioning the shadow puppet theater, the *wayang*. The figures of the *wayang* permeate Javanese thinking to the point where the puppet theater is unquestionably the richest source of metaphor and imagery in Java. *Wayang* also has a close relation to *alus* or refined language, to High Javanese. Javanese rank theatrical forms by language: *wayang* is High Javanese; other theatrical forms are lower. It is not that the language of *wayang* is pure High Javanese. Much of it is literary language incomprehensible to viewers and either considered to be High Javanese or thought to be even higher. But it also includes the language of daily life, and enough of what is said is repeated in ordinary language to allow spectators to follow the action even when, as is usually the case, they cannot comprehend literary language. And even when they cannot follow the puppeteer's language, the puppets tell the story by their actions. When the Javanese see *wayang*, they thus see what Javanese means. The greater part of the puppeteer's rhetoric is inaccessible to viewers; nonetheless *wayang* figures appear on the puppeteer's screen, and with them language that otherwise would remain incomprehensible is embodied before the spectators.

In literary-historical terms, Javanese *wayang* plays come from Indian epics. But they are not thought of in that way. Nor do the figures emerge from a mythical or timeless past, outside history. Rather, they are what the world would look like if one could really understand Javanese thoroughly. Thus one occasionally reads in the newspaper that Semar, the clown-servant, for instance, has appeared in a photograph. Or Javanese search for *filsafat*, from the Dutch for "philosophy," the "real sense" of *wayang*. Such sense is never an understanding of the world that comes with asking certain questions; it is rather what the world actually does mean and what knowledge of the language itself reveals.

Wayang figures exist in the world, but only in the world open to Javanese. The difference between the two is a clue to understanding the interest in *wayang*. At the time of the national revolution and after, the potential of *wayang* to define the world was greatly exploited. *Wayang* was perhaps more than ever used as a source of metaphor. *Wayang* language was applied to national politics; non-Javanese people and situations were understood in *wayang* terminology. The international scene itself fell under the same set of rubrics. The language used was often not Javanese any longer, but Indonesian. This was possible because of the imagistic nature of *wayang*; the figures were detachable from their setting within the stories as told in Javanese. They could be used in everyday speech regardless of the language actually spoken. The hierarchy of figures within the *wayang* stories could thus be transplanted onto the national scene.[1] However, from a Javanese point of view, it is more acceptable to reverse the terms of the last sentence: via *wayang* imagery the world was recognized in Javanese terms even though the language actually spoken might be Indonesian.

Partly this means the Indonesian world was Javanized. There was a certain exhilaration in recognizing that a world that formerly had merely been excluded or ignored could be read in Javanese terms. What was involved was a process of recognition that might be termed "immemorial." It was not that persons were thought to leave traces of themselves, clues of speech or behavior that, when followed up, allowed one to see who they were. It was that regardless of whatever sociological, regional or national identity they might have, there was a mode of recognition that came into existence in a time beyond anyone's memory that could be used to find out who they actually were; one knew them not because one had ever seen them before in one's own experience, but because the world could be read in Javanese terms—perhaps best in Javanese terms.

Wayang thus became tied to a national hierarchy, one with President Sukarno at the apex, part of the success of the revolution. With the overthrow of Sukarno, the hierarchy lost its claim to guarantee security in the minds of the people of Solo, as we have mentioned before. The use of *wayang* as metaphor declined drastically. Over a period of three months, I made a list of the occasions on which I heard anyone use *wayang* imagery. There were only two occurrences. This remarkable decline, almost disappearance, of *wayang* imagery in ordinary speech reflects the uncertainty that the world can still be read in Javanese, an uncertainty that, as we saw in the last chapter, caused the Javanese to turn inward and look for the source of hierarchy in places such as the local community.

Hierarchy itself was never rejected, of course. For that reason, intrusions into the Javanese universe still had to be Javanized. But the principal way in which this is done in New Order Solo is through the Javanese language itself, by extending the use of *Kromo* to anyone who has a claim to status for whatever reason. We have seen, for instance, in the example of the neocolonial bank building, this mode of incorporation simply ignores all marks of a non-Javanese origin. Consequently, anything put into Javanese has a feeling of antiquity, of having always been "Javanese." By contrast, the use of *wayang* imagery never obliterated the foreignness of what it assimilated. A Sumatran, thought of in *wayang* terms, was always still Sumatran. The exhilaration in the use of *wayang* imagery came precisely from the feeling that the non-Javanese world was readable in Javanese terms; a space was thus created for the new and the foreign.

The process of recognition that prevails today, however, in which everything that doesn't fit is ignored, puts a burden on Javanese. What is to be done with everything that goes unrecognized? Anything recognized in terms of *wayang* was at least potentially part of a narrative schema given by the stores of the *wayang*. What was new, what was non-Javanese, could be talked about. But when recognition depends on ignoring the foreign character of whatever one has experienced, the question of where it fits in relation to everything else one knows arises. What happens to the memory of those things one has ignored? It is in response to this problem that a new form of theater has arisen in Surakarta, one that depends on laughter rather than narrative.

Comedy plays an important part in *wayang*, as well as in other forms of Javanese theater, such as *ketoprak*. But the comedy theater in the form we will discuss it dates from after 1965. It is thus a phenomenon of the New Order. The most prominent group is known as Sri Mulat, after its founder. The group today comprises three companies: one in Surabaya, one in Solo, and one in Jakarta. A few members of the troupe are sometimes rotated between locations, but there is a core of performers in each place. The head of the company, Teguh, tries to see that each company suits its local audience. The company is known nationally since it appears on television, though the Solo group had not done so as of the beginning of 1982.

Sri Mulat herself was born in 1905, the daughter of Raden Citrosoma of Surakarta. At the age of 22 she became an actress in *ketoprak*, a popular musical theater. In 1936 she formed her own *wayang orang* troupe. (*Wayang orang* is the theatrical form in which actors imitate puppets.) She was also a singer of *keroncong*, the form of popular music influenced by Portuguese sources. In 1946 she married Teguh, the present head of the company, though he was twenty years her junior. Teguh is Chinese, also born in Solo. He is a saxophone player, and he worked in Sri Mulat's troupe before they were married. Though he spends his time today managing Sri Mulat, he maintains his musical interests. He is particularly concerned that *keroncong* does not disappear in the face of contemporary popular music, and he features it alongside other popular forms of song in the performances of Sri Mulat. In doing so, he wants to counter "foreign cultural influences of a negative character."[2] He is also a supporter of *ketoprak*, wishing to "modernize" it, as he puts it. He has added realistic scenery of the sort to be found in *wayang orang* and has shortened performances to about three hours in the *ketoprak* theater that he maintains in the amusement park that he has leased from the city of Surakarta. One cannot claim, however, that these innovations have led to great success. *Ketoprak* audiences in Solo are limited to people from the countryside, and these audiences are small.

When Sri Mulat formed the company that bears her name in 1950, the comedians performed short routines that they repeated from place to place. Teguh felt that audiences lost interest. In 1966, after Sri Mulat's death, he took over the company and began writing longer stories. His innovation is thus to have created a new story for each performance and to have these each about an hour and a half in length. He retained the singers, who perform for about a half-hour before the comedy begins and again between acts. He is also responsible for introducing Sri Mulat's most popular character: each Thursday night, the night when the Javanese believe spirits are out, the plot centers around Draculla (*sic*), usually "Mrs. Draculla from abroad." Although there had already been *horor* ("horror") stories as part of skits before that, Draculla appeared first in 1969. Since that time, her success has been so phenomenal that one cannot be sure of getting a seat on Thursday nights. Her influence has spread to the point where she has been sighted in the neighboring islands of Madura and Bali.[3] There had been spirits in earlier comedy theaters, but they had all been Javanese. Draculla's popularity depends on her foreignness.

Titles of Sri Mulat performances are sometimes in English: "Killer of Play Papa," "Violent Papa"; sometimes in Indonesian: "Honeymoon with a Living Corpse" (*Bulan Madu dengan Mayat Hidup*), "The Undisciplined Who Rebel" (*Yang Binal yang Berontak*), "The Key to Dracula's Desire" (*Kunci Napsu Draculla*); sometimes in a mixture: "Metropolitan Girl" (*Gadis Metropolitan*), "Hot Love of Kuntilanak" (a *kuntilanak* being a type of spirit). The writer of the scripts makes up the titles a week or two in advance, in time for the posters to be painted (though he does not actually write the scripts until the afternoon of the performance). He is a high-school graduate with a little English vocabulary. The stories themselves, about a page or two of typescript, give little clue to the humor, which is the attraction Sri Mulat holds for its audiences.

"My Wife Was the Cruel Draculla" (*Isteriku Draculla Ganas*),[4] a typical example, begins like almost all performances with a monologue by a servant. He is visited by his parents who wish him to marry a village girl. He refuses because he hopes to marry his boss, an extremely pretty woman. Members of the nightwatch enter and announce that youths who come to the house all disappear, that the boss's mother is really Draculla. To test this they draw some blood from the servants. The servant is to mix it in her tea. If she drinks it, she is Draculla. Another youth enters; he has come to court the boss. The servant explains the situation to him. The mother herself comes in, drinks the tea, and proclaims it "refreshing." The woman goes offstage and Draculla herself (played not by the woman but by the actor who specializes in the role) enters. There is a chase ending the act. The next act (all performances are in two acts) begins in a graveyard. The nightwatch is there, including a very fat man, his obese wife, and two pretty girls who ask the fat man for protection against Dracula. In a typical scene, the wife is jealous and the women do battle. They all exit except the fat man. The village head man comes in with the boss of the previous act. They plan to kill Draculla by luring her into the graveyard and then stabbing her with a wooden staff. They lie down. Draculla enters. After another chase they are caught by her; just then the sun comes up and they are saved.

The plot is really an excuse for humor that has no connection with the story. For instance, in "The Undisciplined Who Revolt," two servants, a man and a woman, decided that the woman should marry the master for his money and that they should then split it. The plot turns into a never-resolved series of complications about who should marry whom. It opens with the two servants. The man tries to teach the woman to walk enticingly. The humor here is visual: he walks with an exaggerated swing of the hips, which she then tries, unsuccessfully, to imitate. She keeps trying to repeat his gestures but cannot. Finally he orders her to "sit down." Instead of doing so, out of the habit of imitating him, she repeats "sit down." At a certain point Pak Panggung, a 72-year-old actor and the star of the troupe, enters. He plays a merchant just returned from abroad. The servant asks him where he has been. He tries to say "Czechoslovakia" but cannot get it out. The servant says it for him, and he tries to imitate the servant, but can't. The servant says it, pausing between syllables; Pak Panggung repeats it, adding glottal stops for the pauses. The servant says it faster; Pak Panggung spits it out: "Czekkoslavakina." They go through it again, several times, the pace speeding up until the word becomes nearly unrecognizably garbled. This routine depends on the servant making the word sound like six even taps on a drum with each repetition of the six syllables increased in volume and tempo. As it goes on, Pak Pang-gung makes use of his lack of teeth to fold his face in on itself, seeming to thereby swallow his sounds. His face shrinks appreciably, his chin juts out, and his head tilts up as though the distorted sounds have hit him. At the climax his eyes, round to begin with, seem to enlarge, all comprehension having vanished. The words appear to strike him in the stomach, sending his behind out. The rhythm and sound of language have been made physical. "Czechoslovakia" is no longer a small, distant, unknown land; it is directionless energy tearing through Pak Pang-gung's body.

Pak Panggung's capacity to reduce language to embodied energy continued in the next scene, where the servant asked him what business he was in. After trying hard to answer without being able to say anything, he blurted out sheer nonsense (*"Wedang roti,"* hot bread drinks). Then he went on to try to say "import-export." He drew his lips into his toothless mouth for the "im," paused, and then popped out the "por" (*impor* in the Indonesian and Javanese version). Then he did the same for "ex," pausing, and finally saying "pect." Then in increasing tempo he exaggeratedly sucked his lips into his mouth and pushed them far out, saying *"impor, expor, impor, expor"* in increasing tempo, ending with *kaus spor*, meaning "sweat-socks," but possibly with the implication of "condom" as well. For no reason at all he later began to recite the months of the year, repeating them after the servant and garbling them: *"Januari, Februari"* (these in their correct Javanese and Indonesian versions), but for *Maret* (March), *"Na-brek,"* a word close to *nabrak* meaning "to collide." He then continued to elide the sounds of the next months into suggestive nonsense.

In thinking of the reasons why Pak Panggung's performance elicited such an enthusiastic response from the audience, one must attend to more than the linguistic humor. In the context of Javanese, language that tears unrestrained through one's body is practically an image of *Ngoko* speech at its worst. Furthermore, it is not only the servant who is unable to control his speech, but the rich man as well. In many cases the master is reduced to uncontrolled behavior. Nerimo, the actor whose specialty is the role of the master, is nearly always driven to fury by the antics of his servant. He demands *disiplin* and shouts, in a most crude fashion, to get it. One sees in these scenes (and they occurred in every performance I witnessed) the upper-class person driven to unacceptable behavior by his inferiors. And one thus has to ask whether one is seeing a certain wishfulness displayed by the audience; are they enjoying the sight of the social order turned upside down? We will turn to the nature of the audience later, but it is enough to note that the expensive seats are nearly always sold out, that amongst the persons enjoying this sight are not those who suffer under hierarchy but those who occupy its superior positions.

A similar condition pertains in the scenes where women dominate the stage. In Solo there are no female comedians. The local director explained that the role of women is to look desirable. When the action does center on women, however, it is almost always in a scene where they fight jealously over men. In the audience, women and men enjoy these scenes equally. Again the women occupying the expensive seats would be equatable with the jealous wife on the stage rather than the pretty girlfriend or servant.

To explain the nature of the identification that is involved, it is useful to turn to other spectacles. In August 1981, national television broadcast a prize fight between an Indonesian and an American. It was a chance for Indonesia to win the lightweight boxing title, and it attracted much attention. The papers were full of details about the fighters and the fight. Yet neither before nor during the fight was there comment on these matters. People kept track during the fight of who was ahead, relying on the announcer's comments. But they said nothing about the way the fight was proceeding, about what each fighter was doing. Nor did they comment, then, before, or later, on the fighters themselves. The facts that the Indonesian was from Timur Timor, the newly acquired and distant province of Indonesia, and that he was Catholic, were never mentioned. There was no talk about his family, nor about his past, nor about what he might do next. The points at which they could find similarities and differences with themselves, or see themselves in his bright future, did not materialize in speech. Their reactions during the fight, however, were intense, and they came always at the same point. Whenever he landed a blow, many of the 20 or so people watching the fight with me in my neighbor's house would make the onomatopoeic sound of blows. There were no sounds of sympathy for him when he was himself hit, however; only silence. They in effect identified themselves with what he did, but without ever identifying themselves with him. It was as though they could imagine themselves delivering those blows without ever thinking what it must be like to be him or to be in his place in the ring. When he was himself hit, their interest simply waned. And when he lost the fight, they dispersed without commenting on the match. There were few comments the next day. It was as though their identification took place simply at the point where his violence made an impact and disappeared at other times.

On another occasion the national television news showed Israeli armed forces. When the camera panned across a line of Israeli missiles, the dozen or so people watching the news began to imitate the sounds of missiles being launched. I thought at first that this was a sign of pro-Israeli support, or at least anti-Arab or anti-Muslim feeling. But they later told me when I asked them that they were anti-Israel, though their feelings were not particularly strong. Once again, however, identification had come just at the point of a potential impact, in this case overriding political sympathies.

Something like this occurs in the Sri Mulat scenes I have described. The ill-considered behavior of the master does not reflect on him as a sociological type. It is not the scandal of a master being really like a servant, lacking the refinement appropriate to his position, that is attractive. Rather, in this picture of a world where *Kromo* does not function to restrain thoughts, the attraction lies in saying whatever comes to mind regardless of who you are and to whom you are speaking. By this reasoning it is possible for women in the audience to identify with women on the stage who are jealous, not because they have felt jealousy or would like to cause it, not because they understand what it is to suffer in this way, but because they see the possibility of saying whatever comes to mind in this or any situation. And men who in life outside the theater are masters can enjoy seeing their equivalents reduced to unacceptable behavior, not because they would then understand what it is that they actually feel in such a situation, but simply because of the pleasure possible in saying whatever one wants to say, even the greatest nonsense, regardless of who they are. There is no attraction to any of the characters as characters, and no antipathy to any of the characters as characters; neither masters nor servants are the objects of sympathy or ill feelings. Identification comes, rather, at the point of unrestrained expression, regardless of who expresses it or who is its victim. The social world exists on the stage not as a reflection of things as they are, as they might be, or as they "really" are, but as the setting necessary for a certain sort of language to be expressed. Without the master and servant or their equivalents, there would be no way to understand what free language might be. Sri Mulat presents a world where masters imitate servants, where language escapes the boundaries of speech levels, where, in short, *Kromo* is spoken but does not function.

Neither Sri Mulat's founder nor the present members of the troupe intended to present a sociologically accurate picture. There is, instead, a conception underlying the comedy of Sri Mulat attributable to its present director, Teguh. One of his assistants explained that "there is no such thing as the comical [*lucu*] as such. Everything comical [*lucu*] is odd [*anéh*]. So for instance, 'A Corpse in Love' [the title of one evening's performance]: How can a corpse fall in love?" Teguh himself explained that "the comical comes later on. If someone says, 'that's funny,' that happens later. Players have to have odd [*anéh*] faces, odd movements, odd actions. If that happens, it's comical." The theater is built, then, on the notion of the "odd" (*anéh*), on what does not fit the rest of one's thoughts or what is not recognizable. The upsetting of the social world follows from the attempt to present what is out of place.

Though Sri Mulat actors have, if not routines, at least certain styles of comic action, to their eyes what they do is "spontaneous" (*spontan*). This word is the clue to the source of the *anéh*. Its meaning has to be placed in the context of the script and the actor's lives. The text of the script does not give the actor's lines, only the outlines of the story. The script is written in the afternoon before the performance, and the director-author reads it out to the actors just before the play begins. There is a carbon copy available if anyone wants to go over it. Members who have heard the roles they are to play often leave before the director has finished giving the story. Once they hear their own role they feel no need to understand the narrative as a whole. Their own performance, then, is not intended to contribute to the integration of the story. Nor is the story itself often a source of humor. The director and Teguh himself, however, are often after the actors to be sure to stay within the story lines. I believe the reason for this is largely political. Sri Mulat is resolutely apolitical. It has refused to be the vehicle for various government propaganda, something that is not the case for the *ludruk* troupes that tour the countryside around Solo. Sri Mulat avoids political subjects and political remarks. The reason given by one actor for insistence on following the story line was "the situation with the people" (*situasi rakjat*). There is not much trouble in getting actors to stay within the story. To them it means that if they do follow the plot they can be assured they will cause no trouble. They are thus given a certain space within which they can safely innovate.

The actors live in rude dormitories on the grounds of the amusement park in which they perform. The park is on the outskirts of the city. Days are spent in idleness; the actors frequently go for several days at a time without leaving the park grounds. As with other Javanese dramatic troupes, there is considerable intrigue amongst its members. The director claims that after writing the daily scripts, his biggest job is to make sure he doesn't put people on stage together who are at odds with each other. There are times when certain actors have refused to play together on the grounds that they were no longer speaking to each other. The rooms assigned the actors are too cramped and too hot for them to spend much time indoors during the day, and the grounds are too small to avoid other members of the troupe. Along with idleness, this leads to a fusion of life onstage and life offstage, a fact indicated by the general use of stage names for the actors offstage.

Time offstage is time spent waiting to act. One actor, asked how he spent his daylight hours said, "doing nothing" (*katah nggangur*). The actors do not talk about the performances. This, for some at least, is a conscious decision. I asked Basuki and some other actors what they thought about during the day: was it last night's performance, tonight's? "They don't think," he answered, speaking for everyone, "in order to be *spontan*." They thus spend their time waiting without thinking about what they are waiting for and without thinking about much else. This makes *spontan* not something that arises by itself at the moment of its expression, but the emergence of what has been avoided during the day. It is not that which comes instantly to mind, thus possibly connected with one's thoughts by associations. It rather comes from someplace other than the action on stage, to which it appears as a response. Its reference is a previous thought, but, since it is a thought that the actor has been avoiding, it is one that he recognizes only at the moment of its emergence. It comes in response to what another player says, but not in the way that Javanese responses should come, not as what is appropriate to the person to whom one speaks. It is also not what one intends to say. It rather contains a thought about which the actor, after having said it, might think, "So this is what I was not thinking about earlier." Its referent is nothing that the actor has learned and nothing that he has willed.

What emerges by itself without conformation to proper style is, of course, highly disvalued in Java. It is an image of *Ngoko* as it disrupts *Kromo*. It is, in fact, precisely what ordinary Javanese try to insure themselves against. Moreover, the disruptive energies on stage, *spontan* manifest, are, to the audience, the *anéh*, the odd. One thus sees how oddity in the world gets conflated with the disruptions of speech.

There are only a few sociological types in Sri Mulat: the master, the servant, the rich man, occasionally the university student, the nightwatch, the wife, the pretty girl. Actors tend to specialize in one or two of these figures. They heighten their recognizability with their exaggerated dress and make-up. One actor who plays a figure from Jakarta, for instance, frequently wears an open shirt with a giant medallion which swings from his neck. Whenever possible his words end in "e" in a burlesque of Jakarta-style Indonesian. He smiles incessantly. The incomprehensibility of his speech is the basis for his humor. In a performance on October 4, 1981, for instance, Gepeng, playing a member of the nightwatch, reported to Pak

Panggung that a man had shown up who "talks and talks
but can't be understood except that every once in a while
he says 'Panggung'." When the man from Jakarta came
on stage, Gepeng leaned against a wall, watching the man's
loose and broad un-Javanese gestures, occasionally mimicking them. After a long while, Gepeng spat. Other actors respond to the man from Jakarta with incomprehension and ridicule. The audience finds him hilarious; he
has only to swing his arm or say a sentence or two to be
greeted with derisive but enthusiastic laughter. He is unusual in several respects. He is not an ordinary member
of the Solo troop. He plays with the Jakarta troop, only
making occasional appearances in Solo, and he is the only
character who is laughable simply because of who he is.
He is an intrusion. The reaction to his appearance of foreignness alone indicates how thoroughly Javanese, even
Surakartan, Sri Mulat is in its Solo version.

Ridicule of gestures is a specialty of several actors. Sutikno, another actor who specialized in playing a member
of the nightwatch, or sometimes a servant, had a routine
in which he sat down in a chair and then crossed his legs,
raising one so high in the air, and so slowly, that one
could follow the motion first of his thigh, then of the
straightening of the shinbone. In reaction to this, someone across from Sutikno would grab his eye as though
something had been kicked into it or as though the sight
of such un-Javanese behavior itself hurt. Sometimes this
routine would continue, the person across from Sutikno
throwing the imaginary object plucked from his eye back
to Sutikno in an invisible game of catch.

Sutikno's distinctiveness lay in his extraordinary thin-
ness.[5] He frequently wore short pants, several sizes too
large for him, held up by a belt perhaps six inches in width.
In the minds of spectators this brought him to the edge
of being human. As he came on stage one night a woman
behind me commented, "A living corpse." This was a reaction that other actors played on. He would be met by

such remarks as, "What is it?" The freedom and energy of his body kept his unearthly appearance in the register of comedy. Given the reception his appearance evoked, he had even less need than others to justify his actions in accordance with any conception of the role he played in the story. For example, he often played opposite a fat woman with considerable décolletage. Quite apart from whatever action was occurring, he would raise himself as high as possible on his toes, stare down at her large breasts with dilated eyes and blurt out, "Suckle."

Tarsam is a very fat actor, 51 years of age in 1981. He might be called a straight man, not so much for his capacity to start off routines as for his ability to react to whatever is done to him. A favorite routine consists, in the midst of a wild chase, of someone stopping to suck his breasts. His reaction might be merely to open his mouth, moving no other part of his face or body. When his wife berates him, usually from jealousy, he smiles while the rest of his face and body stay motionless. He thus gives the impression of absorbing the energy of the action on stage into the bulk of his body, registering it as little as possible in the massiveness of his flesh. However, he is also capable of swift, deft movements, implying that his immobility, although it never leaves him at peace, at least shows that the wild motion of the stage can be soaked up without the need to react to it.

The capacity to detach energy from significance is also the forte of Basuki, a player in his twenties who usually acts the part of a servant. He begins with a pose, usually a stereotyped emotion: surprise, anger, sexual attraction. He seems to swell as he does this, sometimes rising up on his toes, or expanding his chest. Then feature by feature, in slow motion, his face relaxes and his body deflates. He seems to unwind, not emotionally but physically, releasing the energy coiled in his body. When he is through no particular expression is left. The pose thus breaks down into its component physiological parts. It is therefore displayed as a pose, as elements that taken together indicate an emotional state, but that taken separately are devoid of that state.

Pak Panggung has a similar talent. In a scene where he was being chased by Draculla he stopped, tilted his head up, widened his eyes, and raised his hands in the gesture that is part of Muslim daily prayers. His mouth worked rapidly though no words emerged from it. When he ran again, the motion of his mouth seemed to have been transferred to the regular, stylized lifting up and setting down of his feet.

In these scenes Basuki's and Pak Panggung's expressions are vastly exaggerated and stereotyped, often divorced from the narrative and sometimes without words. One has the sense that only the surface of the body is in motion, as though the body responds not to inner control but to something else, whatever it might be. The effect is that the actor is governed by a series of images rather than trying himself to make an impression.

When Draculla appears the reaction of the audience is extreme. Laughter mixes with screams. Some people curl up in their seats. A woman next to me once hooked her leg over mine while she grabbed her husband's arm with both hands. Spirits figured in other, older comedy forms. They became central to Sri Mulat, however. The extraordinary reactions they evoke and the important place they have in Sri Mulat makes it necessary to consider them further. No conflicts are resolved, no typical situations or particular fears result in the appearance of these spirits. Rather, spirits are a function of the imagery of the performance and of its motion. The word that is used to describe the plays in which spirits appear is *horor*, from the English rather than the Javanese word indicating fear. The difference is that the Javanese word for "fear" has theological connotations. *Wedi* we have seen to mean both respect and fear. It is the proper attitude to have toward spirits; expressed toward one's superiors, it results in an assured place in the social order. In Sri Mulat, however, there is not sufficient time nor a serious enough story to consolidate one's thoughts and feelings around the characters in such a way that fear or respect become attributes suitable to them. The story line is too loose, while comedy runs at right angles to it. To think about the action, to see why one scene should be connected to the next is neither interesting nor necessary, even if the pace made it possible. *Wedi* implies a certain anticipation that is not available given the insignificance of the narrative and the nature of the comedy in Sri Mulat. *Horor* implies being in the grip of what one sees, unable to locate it with respect to oneself in the way one can when one is *wedi*. The appearance of Draculla accelerates the pace further; there is always a chase. Nothing one knows about what one sees can distance one from the motion. Even when someone is killed they continue moving. Death in Sri Mulat simply means motion gone awry: Basuki, killed by Draculla, twisted his head with his hands, then continued the corkscrew motion down through his body; Bambang, another actor, stood on his head after he was dead; Begja was killed and the curtain closed leaving him outside, collapsed on the stage; he lifted his head and stared at the audience. And so on.

In other Javanese theatrical forms, the audience drifts in and out, watching what they please when they please. Comedy in the form Sri Mulat offers it, however, compels attention. One does not know what to expect next, but that is only part of the need to be attentive. The comedy theater is the only Javanese theatrical form that does not, in formal terms at least, repeat itself. Each night there is a new play, and each play contains "spontaneous" behavior. The attention of the audience is compelled by the possibility of seeing what they might not have seen before. The degree to which what they see seems to elude not only their expectations but their capacity to recognize it, to say what it is they are seeing and where they have seen it before, is the degree to which they feel the necessity to continue looking. Yet of course what they see is by no means completely new. It is merely outside of a definable context: not part of the story, not identifiable as behavior from life outside the theater. What makes spirits appropriate figures for Sri Mulat is not that they are eerie in themselves; they merely announce or consolidate a sense of eerieness already inherent in the comedy itself—inherent in the inability to say how it is that one actually does recognize what one sees, where it is that one has seen it before.

When Draculla first appears she evokes a terror in the audience alongside their laughter. Plays involving spirits always end with a chase; what happens, whether characters live or die, is irrelevant. What is important is that *horor* finally is transmuted into *wedi*. For Teguh, the manager of the companies, this is intentional. "The basis of laughter is the *anéh*," the odd. But for Teguh, *horor* too is based in the *anéh*. To the extent that the laughter of the audience can be consolidated as the *anéh* and given the form of a spirit, there is no longer a problem of recognition. Whatever is out of place, which is to say whatever is new in the sense of being unplaceable, is then given a place. The source of the *anéh* is behind the scenes, in the realm hidden behind whatever might be visible. The capacity of imagery to evoke the sense of the absence of its referent is thus drawn upon. The new, the unplaceable, is thereby given a place within the context of Javanese.

In Surabaya and Jakarta the audiences for Sri Mulat are different from those in Solo. Local actors frequently commented on the need to please local tastes, meaning that cruder, more direct forms of humor that would be acceptable in other places would not be acceptable in Solo, an indication of the greater refinement or "alusness" for which the Solonese are well known. But the difference in audiences extends beyond differences in taste. We could argue that in one sense, in the sense of a public body, there is no audience in Solo at all. The most accessible indication of this is that in Solo, unlike the other places where Sri Mulat troupes perform, there is no applause. When the play is over, people leave and do so quietly and with very little comment, either then or later. The question of the formation of the audience in Surabaya and Jakarta is one that, for lack of experience there, I cannot answer. In general, however, audiences in those places are seeing something they know about already. It is the Surabaya and Jakarta troupes that appear on television and that have become part of a national system of celebrity. Performers there put on display something that has become, if not exactly a tradition, then at least a public value. How well they perform becomes a question of how well they have expressed a public good. Applause then expresses not only the pleasure of the members of the audience but their appreciation.[6] It is by their appreciation that they constitute themselves as a public body. The "we" of the audience is the group of people who come into existence by virtue of having seen something, the value of which they share before the performance begins.

Such is not the case in Solo, where it is difficult, even with something as elementary as traffic regulations, to find people acting as members of a public. People buy tickets, but money can buy most things, and it is by no means clear what they are to get. The most they know before the performance is the title of the play. The picture on the hand-painted poster at the theater may well be misleading, having been made before the play was written. There is no list of players; one is handed only one's ticket and a broadside announcing the titles of the week's plays. One cannot be sure who will appear on stage; visiting players appear from other troupes when local players are sick, visiting relatives, or prevented from appearing by feuds with other actors. For the players, the script assures them of certain boundaries. For the audience the case is different. They may well be unaware that there is a script. Insofar as they are aware of it, its significance is not that something has been laid out that the actors must follow, but that for each performance there is a new script. What everyone is certain of is that they have not seen the play before. They do not expect to see it ever again, and they express no regret at this; they would no doubt be surprised were one to suggest that a performance might be repeated. They do not, then, expect what they see to become part of a treasury of cultural goods, to be brought out and appreciated whenever the occasion arises. Rather, buying a ticket to Sri Mulat in Solo is comparable to buying another favorite of Surakartans, lottery tickets.

The reactions of the audience are often extreme. Their laughter seems to be without reserve. It is seldom, however, that this occurs early in the performance. As the play gets underway, often with a monologue, the audience offers comments. When the action is slow, men in the front rows will sometimes throw packs of cigarettes onto the stage. These are invariably picked up and acknowledged—for instance, an actor might simply look at them and read the brand names aloud, or he might integrate them into the action. Throwing the cigarettes is a subtle way for members of the audience to indicate their impatience; things are not yet funny. So long as the action is rather dull and people do not have the option easily available to them of leaving and returning later, as they do in other forms of theater, they cannot ignore what happens onstage. They feel the need to comment on it, as if it were addressed to them and they must reply.

One sees this again in the verbal comments the audience makes. Sometimes such comments are addressed to the actors. Once, for instance, during the opening monologues, the actor mentioned he had taken a bus. A spectator shouted, "Did you pay?"; the actor replied that he had. The actors never ignore what the audience says or pretend that their theatrical reality is somehow enclosed and thus precludes direct communication with the audience. And the audience response does not depend on a notion of their own invisibility. The assumption is that there is single linguistic universe that allows anyone to enter the conversation.

As the action goes on, however, comments are directed less frequently at the actors or even at anyone at all. Such comments tend to be terse. In one performance, for instance, when something fell on the stage, the woman behind me made the onomatopoeic sound for something falling. Later, as one of the characters said he was "confused," she repeated the word. Or again, as a performer announced that someone "slipped," she repeated, "slipped." I never overheard extensive comments that either put some construction on the action or even summed it up. The latter type of commentary was common in the performances of *ketoprak* I saw. I recorded a village woman who seemed to me a typical member of the audience comment to the woman next to her after someone on stage had been killed: "That's fine. Revenge. His brother was killed; now he's killed." Or again: "He was enchanted by the man he killed. He killed him and the man he killed turned him into a monkey. He was a man, now he has the shape of a monkey."[7] Such comments were not explanations: the action was clear; the man was wearing a monkey costume and hopping across the stage as she spoke. It was rather a case of retelling what she was seeing, something that would not have seemed out of place if the action were not going on in front of her as she spoke. In the case of Sri Mulat, such retelling does not occur either during the performance or after. The comments one hears tend to actually repeat single words of the actors. They contrast with the *ketoprak* comments; the judgments of the *ketoprak* audience member ("That's fine") let us understand that there is a person who comments standing against what she is being shown. The summing up of the action is, from that perspective, her own version of what she is seeing. The repetition of the actors' words by the members of the audience watching Sri Mulat indicates something different: they seem compelled by what they are watching to the point where their behavior is like that of *latah* sufferers.

Commentary of any sort ceases, however, when the tempo picks up and the audience begins to laugh. Their laughter seems to be without reserve. It is comparable to the laughter one sometimes sees outside the theater when someone does something gauche. For instance, one day while walking down the street I turned to look at something and bumped my head on a low sign, provoking some drivers sitting nearby to laughter, the volume of which seemed equaled only by the extreme length of time it went on. On another occasion, a boy in his mid-teens was playing with some younger friends in the neighborhood alley. The game consisted of roller-skating as fast as possible up a small ramp and then flying down to the pavement without losing one's balance. Most boys succeeded. The older boy, however, was new at it and failed repeatedly, each time to the laughs and hoots not only of the other boys, but of the older people who were standing around. The older boy was embarrassed. Successful attempts aroused no reaction at all. Only failure stimulated reactions from the spectators, rather as though doing it right meant simply following the rules. Making an error, however, provoked embarrassment and allowed spectators to release bursts of energetic laughter that, under other circumstances, would have been held in.

Before we turn back to Sri Mulat we must note that in similar circumstances involving a person of high status it is extremely rare to find the gauche person laughed at. For instance in the case of a man of high status who knocked down his own privy, his fence, and his neighbor's porch wall because he could not yet drive, no one, even outside his presence, gave any indication that the incident was comical. What would have evoked gales of laughter if a mere chauffeur had done it was simply ignored as quickly as possible, the evidence hustled out of sight. The reason for the difference is clear from our considerations in Chapter One: the use of speech levels blocks one's "natural" reactions. Laughter is not only contrary to etiquette, it is easily restrained by the use of High Javanese. When a lower-class person or a child is involved (or a foreigner who is presumed not to be able to speak Javanese) there is no recourse to High Javanese, and the laughter pours out.

The laughter seems to mark the superiority of the people who laugh. Yet it is not the laughter itself, but rather the lack of restraint of those who laugh that is the sign of their social superiority—or better, the sign of their lack of need to restrain themselves before people who command no respect. Superiority may not be the correct word, however. I never witnessed such events consolidated into teasing or derision in the way that one would expect if social competitiveness were involved. The laughter is, rather, an identification with the gauche person. It does not so much say "I am better than you" as "I do not need to try to distinguish myself from you." It is comparable to the onomatopoeic sounds evoked by the sight of Israeli missiles, sounds that marked not a political identification but a sheer linguistic one. The language of the missile, if one can use that phrase, became the language of those who saw it. It is not the fate of the person who falls that is shared with those who laugh at him; they do not feel his pain. Rather, the freedom of a person to be gauche, his capacity to act without restraint, has spread to those who laugh at him, whereas one would not think of identifying with the *alus* language of a higher class person.

In the examples of embarrassment that occur outside the theater, the existence of High Javanese is always implicit. Because High Javanese can be evoked when it becomes appropriate, people can allow themselves the freedom to laugh on other occasions. Without High Javanese, the danger is that there would be nothing but laughter; structure would crumble, never to be rebuilt. As we have seen, Sri Mulat dramatizes a world where High Javanese is spoken but does not function. The Javanese rank their theatrical forms according to refinement of language. Sri Mulat is known for the coarseness of its language, the coarsest of all Javanese theatrical forms. It is indeed a theater that thrives on situations that in life outside the theater would provoke embarrassment. What, then, in the theater keeps laughter contained within the boundaries of the performance?

From the point of view of the audience, the question is how secure it feels in expressing its laughter. This points to the difference in Western and Javanese notions of spectator. The spectator in a Western audience who sees a play may see something he believes pertains to his own experience. So long as he remains aware of himself as spectator, however, he maintains a certain immunity from what he sees. The play is by convention a different linguistic universe than his; he cannot answer. His very perceptions of the play locate him outside of it. The spectator of Sri Mulat feels that he must answer what he hears, that the language of the performance is not closed off from his own language; he does not have immunity. There thus has to be something within shared language itself that puts a boundary on his reactions.

The existence of a boundary can be seen from the reactions of upper-class persons in the Sri Mulat audience— indeed, from their very presence. The sign of being upper-class is being in control of High Javanese in all circumstances. Such people are not likely to join in laughing at embarrassing situations outside the theater. To do so would indicate an unseemly lack of restraint. Yet in the theater they are free to laugh. Clearly theatrical convention has widened the scope of permissible reaction. But for just that reason, we must look also at the limitations that make reactions safe. (By safe, I mean that the audience is able to say that the master on stage is not the master in the audience.)

The skit itself shows a world in which language levels

do not function to produce respect. Yet in the scenery of the play, and in its accoutrements and gestures, the world of respect is very much present. The servant, for instance, always kneels when speaking to the master. It is, indeed, still the case in some Solo households that servants kneel as they speak with their masters or mistresses, but it is not usual. In Sri Mulat it is insisted upon. Furthermore, servants are referred to by the Javanese name *batur*, which evokes this gesture. By contrast, the name used outside the theater today is usually the Indonesian term *pelayan*, which considerably softens the relationship. A *pelayan* is unlikely to kneel; a *batur* always should. Similarly, male upper-class characters in Sri Mulat wear Javanese head-gear that was formerly a sign of class and that was worn twenty or thirty years ago, but that today is reserved for ceremonial occasions. These characters frequently wear *batik* cloths rather than trousers, the ordinary contemporary dress. The atmosphere that is invoked is one where class conventions strongly pertain; it is also one of a generation or two removed in time.

The cast, Teguh, and the audience do not, however, think of the action as being set in a previous time. Their statements all indicate that what they see they think con-temporary. It is precisely in their insistence that our ex-planation can be located. For a Surakartan to see and hear such things at Sri Mulat is at the same time to remember. But the substance of those memories is stereotyped. They are memories of the exaggerated forms of respect, the dress that was appropriate to certain social classes—things that were taught and that made one "Javanese." Though much of this has nearly disappeared from the contemporary scene, it reappears on the stage. When the audience says that such forms are not outdated, not part of a past, but are still extant, it means that what one might term their learned memory—the retention of that which has been consciously taught, as opposed to the memory of things whose origin can not be placed—is still valid. Experience would say that such memories belong to the past. But the perception of them on the stage seems to say that they exist regardless of what one might know by applying to one's own past or present. Against the uniquenesses of the script or the antics and wild language of the characters, all of which one can recognize without being able to say from where, there exist images that clearly originate outside oneself. To say that these images of the past are contemporary is to say that they are attributes of the world, not reminders of what was. The sight of them, or the hearing of them, means not that one remembers them but that they are there to be understood and that, referring as they do to hierarchy, the terms of their understanding is High Javanese.

The terms of hierarchy, its context, are always present. Even if these terms do not command deference at the moment, this does not mean their disappearance. It implies that even if respect is not currently a function of language, it nonetheless is not in ultimate jeopardy. If language does not work to produce respect now, it may later, at some point in the future. The nearest point in that future is just after the appearance of Draculla herself. At that point, one sees the failure of language to produce respect, the *horor* it evokes, and then the rehabilitation of language that produces respect.

The audience laughs at the actors just as they would at someone in a scene of embarrassment off the stage. The actors too, it must be pointed out, often laugh like the spectators, despite whatever contrary reaction might be called for by their roles. The audience's laughter thus does not bring its members into complicity with one another as they see something on stage that has a different meaning to the actors.

The relaxing of linguistic restraint within the theater should not conceal from us the nature of the audience's responses. The audience feels it must respond. The throwing of cigarettes, and the interchanges with the actors before the laughter begins, indicate this. It is not that the audience demands a certain level of performance from the actors but rather that, lacking the established role of an "audience" that expresses its judgment by the intensity of its reactions and by applause, what comes to the audience members as they hear and see the play seems directed at them as potential speakers. What is *anéh* or out of place produces the same reaction as in life: a certain identification with it, as though one were experiencing it oneself. The *latah*-like reactions that precede laughter give us our clue to the nature of that laughter. It is a release of one's "own" responses in reaction to what one sees. The new threatens one's ability to contain "oneself," to contain the *Ngoko* self (*aku*) that is constituted through the reservation felt in speaking High Javanese. The unrecognizable, the odd, the conflation of the *spontan* and the *anéh* produce laughter. And though, given the constant reminders of permanence of status, the audience feels it can allow itself to laugh, it does not do so because it chooses to, but because it has to. The trajectory of responses, from the interchange between audience and actors to the *latah*-like reactions to laughter, indicates this.

This trajectory becomes more apparent as we look at how Draculla is greeted. Her appearance always produces surprise and even shock. It also produces, after that, a certain relief, which can be sensed in the way that the audience enjoys its own reactions. Relief is not itself connected with the compelled quality of the reactions that precede Draculla's appearance, but since it occurs we must explain it. Whenever spirits are talked about, it is always in connection with something *anéh*; one connotation of spirits is "oddness." Draculla's appearance produces relief because it reverses the proposition. It is not only that spirits are "odd," but that the "odd," the *anéh*, can be attributed to spirits. Though it is not made explicit by the plot, Draculla makes it seem as though everything *anéh* that has occurred can be associated with spirits. If spirits are at work, there is no need to blame masters and servants for anything *anéh*.

Spirits confirm the world of hierarchy partly by being the ones on whom its disruption is blamed. Thus when the aristocrat drove his car through his privy, his fence, and his neighbor's porch, he was terribly embarrassed and disappeared inside his house within minutes of the event, not to emerge again for two days. When he did come out, however, he made it clear that a spirit had been at work, thus excusing his own unpardonably unrestrained behavior. He had put his foot on the brake and pressed, but the car kept on rolling. What happened was beyond his control, and what was beyond his control was not to be equated with whatever he did. Similarly, if all the antics on stage can be conflated with spirits, it means that hierarchical principles still work in ordinary circumstances. The audience can enjoy Draculla because she assures them that one does not have to worry about other causes. Thus she always has to appear at the end. If, as has happened, she appears at the end of the first act, the second act is distinctly flat. The *anéh* has already been accounted for and there is no need to laugh further; nothing is really out of place any longer.

It is more difficult, however, to explain the shock that greets Draculla. She does not come by surprise. The titles for the plays announce that she will appear. People come on Thursday nights particularly to see her. Nor is it that the audience thinks they have seen an actual spirit. Persistent questioning produced only the reply that what appeared on stage was to be distinguished from a real spirit. People are aware that they are seeing only the costume of Draculla, only an image of her. The real Draculla is elsewhere. To see the costume of the spirit is to know that the spirit is not there and if she is not there, she must be somewhere else.

Draculla is a spirit, but a new one. She seems to have been imported to answer the dilemma with which we began this chapter; how is the "new" to be accounted for when the linguistic and theatrical forms that had done so no longer functioned. Draculla indicates that there is something the audience does not yet know. She makes them aware of this and so accounts for the new. But she does so in a way that differs from ordinary spirits. The latter produce only *wedi*, fright and respect. The function of *wedi* in maintaining the social order is clear; to be frightened means to be respectful and therefore to engage in proper language. But Draculla produces something that the Javanese had only recently found a word for, *horor*. It is *horor* that produces shock. To the degree that *horor* is eventually converted into "respect" there is no problem. But the shock of the audience and their *latah*-like laughter indicates that each performance risks the possibility of this not happening. Draculla indicates the loosening of the connection between fear and respectful language.

By the end, the *latah*-like reactions and the laughter that are provoked by the performance are dismissed. After the last act they seem not to have happened at all if one judges by the lack of commentary of the audience on either the performance or on its own laughter. The audience has not forgotten its reactions but has made them into other thoughts. Draculla, in her domesticating function, has allowed the audience to see that, in retrospect, its laughter had a certain meaning. But it could be otherwise. Their laughter might be thought to be merely compelled. The failure of Draculla to domesticate would mean continued *horor*. Then the members of the audience might regain themselves by commenting on the performance—on the qualities of the master or the servant, for instance. To do so would put them on the path to sociological identification, to seeing the master as a "person" equatable in some way with themselves. The political significance of Sri Mulat is that this has yet to happen.

CHAPTER FIVE

Phantasm of Shock:
The Street and the House

RED LIGHTS are not reliable guides to the flow of Solo's traffic. Pedicabs, trucks, buses, bicycles, motorbikes, and some cars fill the main streets during the day. As loose-woven patches of these vehicles come to a stop light they seem to unravel. Some drivers stop, others make the corners, and some go straight on. Nor is there much use made of other signals; those for turning or changing lanes are not often given. There is one sign, however, that people heed. The right arm is extended straight ahead, the palm open and the fingers together. Made by a motorbike rider, a cyclist, a pedicab driver or even a pedestrian, this sign indicates not the direction of travel, but the determination of the signaler to take precedence. Seeing it, cars and trucks swerve out of the way, often into lanes the law reserves for oncoming traffic. They do so out of deference to intentions they have recognized. Public rules give way to the acknowledgment of individual determination.

The word used for "being determined" is *nékad*. It means not only that one is set on one's goals, but that one takes no heed of anyone else. The pedestrian's extended arm implies that ordinarily, when he does not so signal, not being *nékad*, he would give way to the truck. There is thus an unspoken acknowledgment of drivers and walkers that the signal allows us to understand. Ordinarily the cognizance that drivers take of each other means that bigger vehicles take precedence over smaller ones. This understanding is tempered by the assumption, sometimes false, that there is room for everyone, even if this means finding that room in areas the law allows only for those going the other direction. Rights on the street are not public rights, but conventions that extend the usual assumption of Surakartans in "public" places: the assumption that, though they may not know each other's names, each is knowable in the sense that anyone could speak to anyone else if they had to and would know their prerogatives as well. The ethnography of street and house that follows is intended to show how private intentions are constructed to ward off the *anéh*.

On the sidewalks that run in front of the Surakartan shops there are usually crowds. There, too, the assumption that no one is truly anonymous seems to hold. One indication that anonymity is not an assumption of Surakartan crowds is the attitude toward beggars. Walter Benjamin, in discussing the crowds in nineteenth-century Paris, quotes Brecht:

> "I well know," Peachum [in *The Threepenny Opera*] says to himself, "why people do not check the infirmities of beggars more carefully before giving. They are convinced there must be wounds where they have aimed blows! Shall none be ruined where they have done business? If they care for their families, must not families end up under the bridges? Everyone is convinced that in the face of his own mode of life, mortally wounded and unspeakable helpless people must everywhere creep about. Why take the trouble to check. For the few pence they are prepared to give!"[1]

Brecht points out that the bourgeoisie see beggars as the failed version of their own lives, evidence that they have struggled and built their lives themselves. Beggars in Java serve a different function. They are, to speak loosely, a "class" like others—nobles, for instance—but a class assumed not to have a history. They are present merely as an aspect of an unchanging structure. They can be simply

An example of the painting discussed on pp. 126-131. Note the edges of light running along the treetops that separate one plane from the next and the diverse sources of illumination.

ignored without anyone feeling remiss. Ignored long enough, a beggar will pass on, though he is soon replaced by others. Beggars gather wherever there are crowds, from which they get the worthless change of those who decide to notice them. Nothing can be bought with a five-rupiah piece, and little is to be had for Rp 25, which in 1981 was as much as anyone was likely to give. But if beggars accumulate enough of these coins they can, of course, spend them. To give to beggars is to give nothing; but beggars make money itself valuable by providing a function for worthless change. What one gets for one's money is simply negative: relief from beggars' soft, polite assault. When one gives they move on. If they are musicians, they stop their song the moment they receive a piece of change.

Beggars exist at the edge of Javanese society. They are the last people recognized in Javanese, or nearly the last. They mark the point where one need not even speak to the other. Even the lowest *Ngoko* is not called for. It is sufficient to simply put out one's hand and give away something valueless. Or one can merely ignore them. Beggars are still part of Javanese society; indeed, they make visible its limits.

But perhaps even below them are the mad and the wanderers (*gelandangan*) who earn their way as scavengers. In their rags and dirt these types are not always distinguishable from one another. They are people that no one feels the need to speak to or to give to. They float through the crowd without arousing either its hostility or its interest. The negative recognition given them—that one does not even have to ignore them—puts them in contrast with the rest of the crowd, all of whom are at the very least people one might move out of the way for.

On rare occasions one can see a pedestrian hurrying along the sidewalk extend his or her arm, warning others out of the way. As in the street, this gesture tells us that ordinarily the person takes cognizance of his or her fellows. The others on the sidewalk exist, in usual circumstances at least, as those she or he might potentially talk with. The crowd as a whole, then, is not a set of people one tries to ignore as though they impinge on one against one's will as one passes along. They are part of one's ordinary mental universe and are not excluded in favor of private imaginings.

What exists as part of one's ordinary mental world does not become the topic of much conversation in Java. Beggars, even wanderers and the mad, do not figure much in ordinary conversation. Their difference from other Javanese is merely one of rank: they are dismissable. Thus they arouse no more fantasy than they do hostility. Hierarchy functions in the same way to make the rest of the crowd uninteresting. The operation of deference, potentially at work in the assumption of lack of anonymity, means that everyone recognizable is different from oneself and that that difference can be managed in such a way as not to arouse the need for talk. Thus, for instance, transvestites are a common feature of Solo's streets. These men dressed as women come from various classes; some are beggars, but others are wealthy. They are recognizable as transvestites as they pass by. But they do not arouse the feelings of enmity that homosexuals sometimes arouse in the West, or even in Jakarta, Indonesia's capital. This is because no man recognizing them has to fear that he might be like them. The operations of Javanese speech, distinguishing the speaker from the person he addresses, preclude that.

On the other hand, the street is thought of as a dangerous place because of thieves, and thieves, as we have seen, arouse a great deal of interest. They are outside hierarchy and make people want to talk. In addition to thieves, there are "foreigners" (*landa*), meaning Westerners and sometimes Japanese. Foreigners are seen as incapable of speaking Javanese or Indonesian, and thus in a sense as incapable of language altogether. They are therefore without the first notion of proper behavior, and for that reason, they are fit objects of contempt. They are also, however, seen to be extremely attractive. Foreign women are thought to be without morals and thus appropriate sexual objects, whereas both men and women are assumed to be wealthy. As they pass on the street, male students, usually high-school students, shout "hello," "hallo, mister," or for some reason, "hallo, Mac," behavior that would be quite impolite to anyone in Javanese society. Foreign women particularly are targets. If they are alone, such women are likely to be treated to sexual gestures.

The contrast would be with the equivalent Javanese stranger who passes by without being addressed. This behavior follows from Javanese etiquette, which prescribes that under ordinary circumstances one not speak to those with whom one is not acquainted. Not to speak to strangers as they go by is thus also a form of recognition, a politeness that belongs to the realm of High Javanese. This silence might be seen to be elicited; whatever interest the stranger arouses is easily restrained. The exception comes with Javanese high-school girls, who are sometimes treated like foreigners, though less frequently and with less forcefulness. Since, however, this behavior is considered so crude, the result, boys say, is nearly always that the girl simply goes on without replying.

The result of addressing foreigners is not to include them but to exclude them. If a foreigner does not respond, or if he or she does say "hello" in return, the comment by the Javanese boys in either case is often, "Look, he does not speak Javanese." The boys are left in complicity with one another, while the stranger is left out.

The exclusion of those who arouse interest takes the form of speech in some cases and silence in others. The result is the maintenance of the tacit assumptions of Javanese society. Foreigners begin as indecipherable intrusions into territory where Javanese conventions pertain. As they pass by, the boys' taunts demonstrate that the foreigners' place is indeed not in Java. They are put where they belong, outside common discourse. The boys thus assign them to the place they otherwise would occupy only as a matter of accident.

In the case of the Javanese girls who are assailed on the street, the result is also to maintain the assumptions of Javanese discourse. One student told me that he only hangs out on the street when he doesn't have the money to visit a prostitute. This, indeed, is the attitude of most boys. The girls they address on the street, being mainly students from respectable families, are inappropriate objects for the boys. If the girls respond, they place themselves in the position of prostitutes. But, as I have said, they seldom answer the boys. The result for them is that, by passing by, they maintain their own position of respectability. The boys, however, have committed a solecism. They act this way only in small groups, usually of three or more. They are termed *nakal*, or mischievous, a type of behavior that is covertly allowed them and that strengthens their solidarity with one another.

The interior space usually created by deference has been breached for the boys when they inappropriately respond to the desire the girls arouse. What should be reserved has been blurted out. Only the ameliorating circumstances—the girl passes on, allowances are made for boys—make it possible for such behavior to be a regular part of the Surakartan street scene. Calling out to foreigners and girls is, in any case, a fairly recent practice, belonging only to the last decade according to the testimony of foreigners who lived in the city earlier.

One can find other instances of the breach of the space of respect. For example, one day in October 1980, a man came along the street of the gold dealers leading a monkey on a chain, slowly but regularly beating a drum. As he passed the gold dealers seated at small wooden tables, one of them began beating out a rhythm on his tabletop. He drummed on his table, however, not with the beat of the drum but in the interval between beats. Another dealer then divided the beat of his competitor, and a third divided the beat again. One can often see people beating time to the off beat as they listen to Javanese music. Indeed, the instruments of the Javanese orchestra do this to each other. However, something more than musical convention is involved when one sees such behavior on the street. For one thing, the division between music and other sounds is less strictly drawn. A bicycle repairman was banging on a bicycle frame with a steel hammer; a lounger nearby interspersed his beats by ringing a bicycle bell. A carpenter was pounding nails in the otherwise quiet courtyard of a hotel; a young woman, passing through, clapped her hands on the off beat. In these examples, the people beating syncopated time did not do so out of mere routine. They had first to discern a beat where otherwise there would have been only sound identified by the activity of the maker: repairing a bike, pounding nails, etc. A Westerner who heard a similar pulse would have repeated the beat, bringing himself in unison with it. The Javanese did not upset the tempo they heard. They did not try to add new rhythms alongside the first; their own drumming was played out in the center of the initial pulse. It thus was more a division of the beat than syncopation. It relied on the steadiness of the first beat in order to find within it an unmarked area. In that sense the second drummers had made a discovery.

When the gold dealers finished their emendations of the monkey owner's drummings, they let go a small cheer, while the monkey and the drummer continued steadily across their path, acknowledging nothing. Similarly, the bicycle repairmen ignored the bell ringer, and the carpenter did not respond to the young woman, who smiled to herself as she passed on through the courtyard. We are thus not dealing with a wish for some sort of connection that might transcend language. There was nonetheless a wishful component, as the pleasure of the second parties indicated. It was a pleasure that was satisfied by finding the rhythmic interval, the place where the main beat did not sound, where, in fact, "nothing" sounded until the second parties began their own drumming. Only those who discovered that interval, the second parties, showed that pleasure; the original drummers remained as they had been, merely going about their business.

Those who listened for the silence within the main beat thus put themselves in its place. The pleasure they expressed in doing so, the loud noises they made in public, emphasized their own low status. (The young woman was a clerk at the hotel; I do not know who the man was who rang the bicycle bell, but his bearing indicated he was not from the upper classes.) By Javanese standards, they betrayed an unbecoming lack of restraint. Indeed, one can see in these reactions something close to *latah*. As often is the case in *latah*, loud noises set off the incidents. But their reactions saved these people from *latah*. Dividing the beat meant finding a center within it. Their "own" drummings thus occurred in a manufactured absence, a place where they heard "nothing." This "empty" space was "their" space, as opposed to the place where the initial drummings occurred. A structure of statement and response was thus established. On the one hand, the coarseness of replying at all indicated that their acts were quite possibly compelled. On the other hand, the structure of response established boundaries between the parties that the shock of the loud noise seemed about to disrupt. One sees the logic of this by comparison with *latah*, where a surprise merely sets off repetition of the same words without any pretense at reply. Nonetheless, the element of mimicry, which often occurs in *latah*, occurs in the shock administered on the street as well. Without the structuring of the mimicked sounds one would, in fact, have *latah*.

A similar sort of structuring can be seen when we turn back to the mimicked foreigner. Actually, Javanese youths, not foreigners, ordinarily speak first. The shock here is the appearance of the foreigner on the Surakartan street.

He or she is someone who seems to come from nowhere and whose appearance goes unexplained, there as yet being no developed tourist industry, for instance, which would furnish an explanation for his or her appearance. Such foreigners are outside the discourse of Javanese; there is no way to speak to them properly. Like the "replies" to the drumbeats, the boys' shouts would not be tolerable in anyone who pretended to refined behavior.

The boys' "hello" or "hallo" often represents all the English at their command. It is in that sense an imitation of what they think foreigners say rather than the initiation of an interchange that, for linguistic reasons alone, in most cases could not go farther. In any case, the boys' intentions are clear from their frequent comment that the foreigner who does respond does not speak Javanese. They imitate the stranger's utterances, but again it is imitation that is positioned as reply. It is once more the structuring of mimicry that distinguishes such incidents from the compelled taking-on of the sounds of the other that is one form of *latah*.

The streets of Solo describe the boundaries of vast residential neighborhoods. Alleyways that run off the main streets penetrate these neighborhoods. The architecture of the residential areas manifests strong concern for safety. Its distinguishing feature is the prevalence of walls that surround houseyards, occasionally reaching twenty feet in height. The purposes of these walls are description of property boundaries and protection against thieves and whatever else undesirable might enter. They help to achieve the tone of calm and security that often prevails inside Javanese households. One might speculate that they work to create the same tone on the street. Javanese neighborhoods, especially those in the center of the city, are not homogeneous. They contain the palaces of the wealthy and the noble as well as the shanties of the poor, and also, often, small factories, repair shops, and other businesses. The walls, then, hide what they protect, and they protect a great variety. To someone who is not familiar with the neighborhood, what is behind the walls is unknown. They create a pervasive sense of a "somewhere else" of the sort we have already seen in speaking of the theater, a pleasant mystification. The walls may physically exclude the passer-by, but they include him within the psychic ambiance of Javanese hierarchy. These walls can create the same effect whether seen from within or without.

That the same tones, the same mixture of voices, prevail on the street as in the household is because the dominant idiom in both is that of respect and hierarchy, of which kinship is merely derivative. Thus in Sri Mulat the family is present in the roles of the characters, but it is respect, not kinship, that furnishes the issue of the drama. Here the contrast might be with the shadow-puppet theater, whose stories, drawn as they are from the Indian epics, are in the idiom of kinship. They dramatize stories of conflicting loyalties, of family set against family, and so on. In Sri Mulat, the family is present merely because of the setting of the play. The same setting, the front room of a Western-style house, occurs in all performances. Draculla invades this space. The house is a place of security that becomes vulnerable.

The conception of the security of the house can be seen via a picture. It is the most common picture found in Java today, available as it usually is on the streets of any Javanese city of even moderate size. It can often be found inside village and city houses alike. It is the picture likely to be produced by school children when asked to draw, but it has also been painted by such sophisticated Javanese painters as R. M. Sayid.

The picture shows a mountain in the background, trees on both sides in the foreground, and either rice fields or a body of water in the middle. The mountain is depicted, not with volume, but as though it were two-dimensional.

The trees in the foreground exist in a single plane and have a rather flat appearance. It is thus easy to see the picture as a series of planes, one in front of the other. An edge of light extends over the tops of the trees on the middle plane and seems to indicate a gap between these trees and the foot of the mountain. The trees of the foreground are separated from the next line of trees by water or rice fields.

The idea of a framed picture meant to be hung on a wall is clearly imported from the West.[2] Indeed, nineteenth-century Javanese painting contained clear imitations of Western-style landscapes. As such landscapes gained in popularity, however, they took on their own spatial arrangements. The spatial sense of our picture can thus best be understood by comparison with that of the Javanese shadow-puppet theater. The elementary facts of the Javanese shadow play (*wayang*) are that it consists of flat puppets manipulated on a screen. What is important for our purpose is the superficial quality of the *wayang*, using "superficial" in the Javanese sense. Surface, *lumah*, in Javanese does not contrast with interior or with depth. The word means "front" as well as "surface." The usual opposite of *lumah* is *kureb*, meaning "back." "Surface" in *wayang* is constituted not merely by the screen, however; the screen of a *wayang* performance has a front and a back, thus taking on the full meaning of *lumah* only with the presence of puppets. Only then is one side of the screen distinguished from the other. In the same way, it is often thought that puppets off the screen cannot truly embody their characters. It is only on the screen that the play can be enacted. Puppets plus screen form a surface with two sides, though without depth.

The notion of surface is developed further in *wayang beber*, the form of *wayang* in which puppets are painted on cloth, which is unrolled as the story is told. In *wayang beber*, the puppets are not painted on the cloth as though they occupied real space. Instead, they are painted over one another just as puppets in *wayang kulit* (the shadow-puppet theater) sometimes overlap each other. Their flat character is thus preserved. But more important to us here, the superficial character of the cloth is also preserved. In no sense does the cloth develop into a place on which an illusion of depth can be created. The tendency in *wayang beber* seems to have been to preserve the sense of surface. Originally the space between the figures was left blank. As time went on, however, it became filled with ornaments, again promoting the superficial character of *wayang beber* by bringing the surface itself to prominence; what was ornamented was not the action, not the characters, and not the setting, but simply the surface itself. The ornaments are placed in the space where the characters are not, that is, on the surface of the cloth.

Wayang beber uses only one side of the cloth. "Front" and "back" metamorphose into the extension of the cloth as it is unrolled. What is in "front" is what is to come. Functionally, the similarity with *wayang kulit* consists of the use of the surface to both display and conceal. In *wayang kulit*, one sees only one surface and knows that there is another that is not visible. In *wayang beber*, the exposure of a particular portion of the surface means that there is more out of sight ahead or behind, since the cloth is re-rolled as the story is told.

We can now turn back to our picture. The canvas of the picture cannot be compared to the screen of either form of *wayang* we have discussed. Rather, the planes within the picture take over the function of the screen, seeming to confront the viewer and therefore to suggest something on the other side. The construction of these planes consists first in lining up objects in a row, as I have pointed out. The suggestion of these planes as "surfaces" (*lumah*) is furthered in our picture by the use of light. There is no single source of light in the picture, nor is there what can properly be called shadow. The edge of darkness on the top of the second plane is used to suggest the furthest point back, the plane itself. Whatever is lighter is set in front of the plane. To equate light with foreground and dark with background, the light source has to be variable. Thus the tree to the right of the house is lit from the left and above, whereas the house itself is illuminated from a point in front of the picture and to the right. The effect in both cases is to make objects rest not on the ground but in front of the plane. Were the house to be illuminated from the same direction as the tree, from the left, the upper side would also be light, making the house seem to extend in two directions: at right angles directly out to the plane (the roof) and parallel to it. The upper side of the house would also be illuminated and would seem to form part of the support of the roof. As it stands now, the roof does not appear to be supported by the walls, but seems rather to be suspended from the ridge pole which is in turn attached to the plane. The darkness inside the house seems to be an opening onto the plane. Because this plane runs at an angle to the canvas, the effect of layering of objects over a surface is not so apparent as in *wayang beber*, but it is the same conception of objects in space.

In *wayang kulit* and *wayang beber*, the movement of the story with the constant replacement of puppets or the progressive rolling and rerolling of the cloth maintains a continuous interest in the surface of the screen. By the convention borrowed from the West with its attendant function of wall decoration, the picture is bounded by its frame. What replaces the change of surface is the multiplication of planes. The planes of the picture gape open in front and close up toward the back: The lines formed by the opening of the planes thus recede, creating a sense of distance. But this recession never reaches the vanishing point. Instead of being drawn into the picture, the viewer thus bumps up against a plane confronting him.

My reaction is that the mood of the painting is tranquil. Javanese viewers tend to confirm this impression, though it was very difficult to elicit any reactions at all to the painting. The painting was termed *saé*, or "nice." But certain spots in it, such as the blackness showing through the trees, were called *serem*, "terrifying," and others, such as the waterfall, were called *anéh*. The latter places are those where the interval between the planes, what is hidden, seems about to reveal itself. To have this mixture of moods in the painting is not terribly surprising. The scene of wilderness in the mountains is always taken as the realm of spirits. The sense of something hidden implied by the planes of the picture merely doubles that impression. But as we have said, fear produces respect, and respect produces reserve and safety. The tranquillity (*tenteram*) of this scene is the result of reserve and safety. No one commented much on the activities of the people in the pictures. People were always shown engaged in everyday tasks of making a living: farming, washing, drawing water. The picture suggests not opulence but sufficiency. The well-being of the people depicted is shown in proximity to places of fearfulness; this seems quite intentional.

The mountain picture is not valued for its beauty nor for what it portrays. Its value lies, rather, in its ability to generate a sense of something that lies beyond it, something on the other side of the mountains and on this side as well. It is seldom gazed at—never, in my experience. This does not, however, mean that it is ignored, any more than the view it pictures is ignored. Surakartans frequently talk about the view from the mountains. Some even make expeditions, *piknik*, to the mountains to enjoy the view. But though I went along on several such trips, I never saw anyone take a prolonged look at the scenery. Even when I tried to prompt them to do so, no one seemed willing. To gaze at the view would stir thoughts within the viewer, whereas the purpose of the view—which is, after all, also the abode of the spirits—is to put such stray thinking to rest. The view is valued because the viewer knows there is a faraway place where spirits live, from which they could emerge. And, even when they themselves are in the mountains, that place is itself separated from the viewer. Knowing that the view is there is enough.

The picture amplifies the sense that the walls around the house evoke. The wished-for safety that the walls convey is produced by keeping fear always in the background, but always in mind. The multiplication of planes in the painting implies that what is to be feared is elsewhere, outside the picture's boundaries. By showing the tranquil, the well-off, and the safe, but at the same time indicating the hidden areas of fearfulness, the picture implies that, at some point in time, something might intrude.

It is by portraying the imminence of shock that those in the picture are integrated into the scene. Their tranquillity and the ideal orderliness of their activities—they do what people who live in the countryside are supposed to do—results from the fear (*wedi*) that comes from living near the spirits. So, too, those who look at the picture or simply know it is there are brought in touch with the potential disruption of spirits. In the sense that there is, then, not only experienced shock, but also the imagining of its potential occurrence, one can speak of a phantasm of shock.

The *latah*-like reactions that come in response to shock on the street prevent *latah* by becoming the language of the startled person. It is as though the person who claps in response to a drum is not compelled to imitate, but rather intends to do so. The *latah* sufferer is different: she remains in the grip of the person she imitates. The mimic not only conforms her response to what has intruded on her; she also says that she already knew she was compelled to utter—that, in effect, she wanted to utter it. The strength of mimicry in preventing *latah* comes just at that point.

Why cannot the *latah* sufferer do the same? Both, after all, imitate. I have pointed to the positioning of mimicry as reply as the difference between the two situations. This formal distinction makes clear the difference between the imitator and the source of the shock delivered to her. The person who escapes being *latah* through mimicry, when she "means" to imitate, makes her utterance seem to originate within her. The degree to which she controls her sounds can be seen in their positioning.

The reason the *latah* sufferer cannot control her sounds, we have seen, is that she does not control High Javanese. She cannot respond as she ought to. For her, it seems that High Javanese might as well be English or French or some other language that she does not know. This makes her no different than the boys who accost strangers with the single word of English they are able to mouth. There is, however, a distinction between the two cases. The boys know that the strangers are not Javanese, that they belong to the category "stranger" or "European" (*landa*). Their problem is that this is a murky category for them, just as the difference between themselves and the girls they shout at is a difficult one for them to control. Their actions put the strangers or the girls in their place "outside" discourse, as people who cannot speak Javanese in the case of strangers, and as people with whom they will not speak in the case of the girls. They make firm the distinction between Javanese discourse and what lies outside it.

The *latah* sufferer who has only a poor knowledge of High Javanese cannot do this. She cannot control the High Javanese that would take the place of her inappropriate outpourings, whether they are obscene words or repetitions of what someone else says or does. Nor can she position her utterances in relation to the person who startles her, as the people on the street do. It is as though she cannot find intervals in their language because she does not recognize that what they say is language at all—as though her problem with High Javanese, not knowing if a form is High Javanese, Low Javanese, English, or nonsense, extends to the rest of language once she is startled. The *latah* sufferer seems not to understand what is language and what is not. For her, there is nothing outside of discourse, since her capacity to recognize language at all seems to have temporarily collapsed.

With this in mind, we can turn back to our picture. The painting confirms the existence of an "outside" from which the spirits, who are always *anéh* and who always startle, originate. In front of such a place one can be fearful (*wedi*) and, in being so, restore order, since fear is the basis of respect.

A person who suffers from *latah*, in our analysis, is not startled from someplace outside of discourse. She is startled in a way that is not *anéh*. Having no identifiable source, there is no way to recoup the startling stimulus, through repetition or otherwise. There is no even marginally appropriate response to being startled for the *latah* sufferer, since what startles her is beyond being even "odd" or *anéh*.

The mountain picture guards against just such a possibility. It creates a sense of security by indicating a fearful place. But it says in effect that everything that one fears comes from there, that there is no fearful place that is not *anéh*. It thus tries to take account of oddities that might otherwise not be thought of as such. We can see in another picture, however, that oddities of this sort do exist.

The painting is not the only decoration Surakartans hang on their walls, of course. There are also posters, many of them photographic enlargements, and calendars, again usually featuring large photos. One such poster is reproduced here. It shows an actor and actress from the Surakarta *wayang orang* theater. *Wayang orang* is the theatrical form, based on the Javanese shadow-puppet theater, in which humans replace puppets. None of the Javanese with whom I spoke had any difficulty in identifying (without solicitation) the play involved or the actors. In each case, the clue used was the mountain greenery, the locale of the play being the mountains. Though one of the sixteen people I asked about this picture identified a particular scene from the play, others disagreed with him and would

Wayang orang players in a setting meant to duplicate the scene
of a play. Note how easy it would have been to remove the
cornstalk that, it was agreed, "should not be there."

speak only about the play itself without being able to locate the action in any precise way. To identify the photo
meant to name the play and tell its entire story.

What is important to us here is that the photograph of
the mountain has, in the telling of the commentators, been
turned into the backdrop for the play. For instance, one
person, asked what he thought about the picture, replied,
"The colors are wrong," explaining that there should be
no brown. His response implies that what in the original
scene of the photograph is a garden plot has, in his mind,
been turned into a stage set, raising the question of its
appropriate color. There is no garden plot in the play, but
to this informant the scene appears not as an anomalous

locale, but as a patch of brown where there "ought" to be green.

The historical referent of the photo was ignored by the commentators. No one knew or was interested in where precisely the photo was taken. Nor did anyone think that this was a picture of an actual performance. The pose itself was declared never to occur in the play. Why it was used in the photo was unknown and was a question of no interest to the commentators. In that sense the photograph differs from, say, Italian photo stories, in which the story gains realism from the series of pictures, which represent distinct events. The pose of the Javanese picture functions like an emblem that brings to mind the entire play. The question, "What happened in the picture?" which we might assume could be asked of any photograph, cannot be asked of this one.

One might compare the picture to the tableaux popular in Europe (and Indonesia) at the turn of the century. But photographs of tableaux were taken to record a particular event, a moment when certain people dressed in costume. A photo was intended to commemorate the occasion. In such Javanese photos, made to be duplicated for sale, the original event, the moment of the taking of the picture, is of almost no importance. It has disappeared along with the reference of the colors and shapes to any particular setting in nature.

The denial of the power of the *wayang orang* photograph to refer to the occasion of its taking is seen again in the question of the beauty of the actress. Everyone I asked declared, when asked, that she was beautiful (*ayu*), but agreed too that she was too large and too old. Only one person, when pressed, could conjure up an aspect of her beauty that referred to anything in the photo itself (her eyes). In all cases people told the story of how the actress ran off with the actor and the scandal that ensued. What people identified as her beauty was, then, her beauty as it was years before the photo was taken. The "identifica-tion" of the actress was thus like the "identification" of the scenery; rather than the notion of an original of the photo functioning to limit what might be said about it, photographed images were the beginnings of stories that denied the character of the originals as they existed when the picture was taken.

Whether one thinks of the setting in the mountains, of a moment in a play, or of the presence of the actors them-selves before the camera, whatever might have been ac-tually before the camera when the picture was taken is denied—whatever was in front of the lens when the pho-tograph was made does not seem to adhere to it, as Barthes says it does in the Western photograph.[3] Precisely be-cause it is thought not to, the photograph evokes a sense of absence. It is not the historic absence of something that had been present when the picture was taken but is known to have since disappeared, but a conventional absence. As if the picture suddenly materialized on the photographic paper from the "elsewhere" that is the site of spirits and the unknown.

The photographic poster thus shares a common meta-physical or perhaps religious space with the mountain picture. It goes beyond it, however, in including images that have no place in this conception. In the poster, for instance, there is a cornstalk. Invariably when I asked about it, the reply was that "it should not be there." In other posters there were also anomalous details, such as a bit of a modern building included when one *wayang orang* scene was taken on the grounds of a hotel, or bits of grass growing between the rocks of the ruin of a temple that, in the play, is supposed to be intact. The responses to my questions about all such out-of-place details were the same: they "shouldn't be there."

People were able to say that such details "should not be there" because they did not fit into the narratives of the play or the stories of the players' real lives. They were there simply because the camera sees indiscriminately. They do not appear as manifestations of the *anéh*, the materialization of a someplace else that is, nonetheless, still hidden. The *anéh* is reserved for what appears by chance. But chance is defined in advance as having a certain locus. What merely appears before one's eyes does not generate fear. Being wholly unanticipated, it is simply ignored. It is not a manifestation of the unknown; no one knows that such an appearance is unexplained. Called to attention, it generates only the response, it "should not be there." Accident, the *anéh*, is thus a considerably smaller category than the appearance of the unexplained. The *anéh* means only what one knows to be not understood. The popularity of the mountain picture needs to be explained against the possibilities raised by the photograph; the mountain picture shows the possibility of things that do not belong, are not *anéh*, and could, at some time or other, shock.

CHAPTER SIX

Phantasm of Shock: The Classroom

IF THERE IS a pervasive archaizing in present-day Sura-karta, there is also one place where the new is recognized as such without being confined, ignored, or assigned to the realm of the *anéh*. Students, those studying in the public schools, are seen as having access to the new in their studies. In this chapter I want to show how this "new-ness" is conceived and what it has to do with Javanese modes of learning. Before I can turn to that, however, I must sketch the status of youth in society.

B.R.O'G. Anderson has pointed out that the sudden emergence of youth into prominence during the revolu-tion was based on the status of youth in traditional Ja-vanese society. Anderson points out that "youth" was both a stage in the life arc and the place where that arc was transcended. It was the time when males left their fami-lies to roam the countryside, often studying at religious schools or gaining esoteric religious knowledge in other ways. "Throughout Javanese history there were always . . . self-contained pools of single males, within or be-tween [religious schools], or attached to [local teachers]: some of them were boys going through their rites of pas-sage into adulthood, while others were older men for whom the esoteric wandering life, mediating between the natural and invisible world, was permanently appealing. It was in these pools that the utopian, voluntarist and transcendent elements of traditional Javanese thought found their most ardent adherents."[1] In his book on the role of youth in the revolution, Anderson traces the fo-cusing of youthful efforts into modern forms during the Japanese period.

Within the city of Surakarta itself it is still common to meet youths who have found local *guru* to teach them skills of invulnerability or other forms of mystical learning. But the real heirs of the religious schools are the public schools; it is there that youths today acquire a moral education. Schools are the subject of anxiety: there are not enough places in the public schools for everyone, and the expenses of attending school are more than some can afford. (Indeed, when school fees become due, one notices how many fewer people there are in the markets. Even newspaper sales decline as people scrape together whatever they can for school fees.) Whatever their inadequacies, there can be no doubt that schools today are the places where sentiments of nationalism are centered; when people view youth in terms of the future, as they do frequently and fervently, it is the schools they think about. In a society where secular education on any scale is recent, students are seen as having access to knowledge that was denied to their parents. If things are to be different, it is presumed that students will make them so. Just what will differ, however, is not clear in the minds of most. Nonetheless it is still the case that students are seen to bear a special responsibility for the transformation of society.

A word commonly used to mean "to learn" in Indonesian and Javanese, *apal*, is usually translated into English as "to memorize." Indeed, watching an Indonesian high-school class at work, one believes that "memorize" with its sense of rote learning is the correct interpretation. What brings about this impression is the lack of explanation and the amount of repetition. For instance, in a history class the teacher told the biography of the prophet Mohammed. At certain points she would pause and students would fill in the missing word. When she finished, she had the class open their books while she read the same narrative in the same words that were in italics in the book. As she read the text, students once again filled these in.

Occasionally a student would read a paragraph. Occasionally, too, the teacher would explain one of these terms. At those points students would make notes. At the end of the hour, the teacher instructed the students to "first read, then learn [*apal*] carefully the names and dates." Her attitude was that of a person somewhat removed and not responsive to the moods of the class. This was probably intentional. This attitude displayed the most admired trait of Indonesian teachers, namely, patience. The teacher was someone who, like the other teachers in the school, saw herself as having a body of information that students did not yet have. Her reserve meant that her mind was on that body of information, thus not in touch with the students, and that she was willing to keep her thoughts there as long as necessary. The lack of change of tone in her voice throughout the hour was therefore not a lack of interest in the students themselves, or at least in their welfare. It meant that, by not responding to what we shall see to be the students' own volatile moods, she was doing everything she could for them. Thus in no class I observed were there any personal remarks between students and teachers. No answer betrayed the teacher's awareness of a special difficulty that a particular student might have. When the teacher thought something was unclear, she repeated what she had already said. In the history class there were no questions and no way of actually knowing whether students had grasped the material. In the mathematics classes, however, it became apparent that some students could not solve the problems. The teacher then merely did the entire example over again.

The mathematics classes thus followed the same pedagogic method. As the teacher drew a graph on the blackboard, her students called out to her what to draw. The graph she drew was one contained in their textbooks. The students, then, did not so much join her in following in the logic of the problem as in repeating with her what was already in the book. In one class, when the teacher asked for questions, as she did off and on throughout the hour, she only once got a reply. This was not a general lack of responsiveness, however. Whenever there was a pause, students were eager to fill it in for her. And when she called several students to the board to work out a problem they did so with no reluctance. She watched as they put their work on the board. If a student made an error she corrected him, giving him the right answer. She did this, again, in a voice that might be called "official," that is, it contained no special feeling of her own. It did not express disappointment with the student, for instance. It showed her willingness to say what needed to be said, but without acknowledging the subjective state of the student, neither his possible nervousness nor any particular difficulty he might have reached at the point in the problem where she intervened. When they were finished the teacher went over the problem again, and again the students filled in the answers as she spoke. When she was finished, she said, "Is it clear? Whoever wants to ask a question, do so." But, as I have said, only once was there a question. The teacher's reply was to repeat the problem.

The basis of Indonesian teaching methodology might, in fact, be said to be that of repeating the book. The point of this repetition is not to make the written text clearer by enriching it with vocal modulations. The opposite is more nearly the case: the teacher's voice is drained of inflection as if he or she is not responsible for the words. Teachers try to add nothing to the book; to elaborate, in their view, would not be an addition but a deviation. Thus the history teacher would occasionally smile as she read. Her smile, however, was not an indication of her own pleasure with the book or with the reaction it evoked in the students. It came, always, at the end of a phrase, and it was never directed at anyone in particular. It said, in effect, "That's the way it is," and so served as a form of punctuation mark, a period embodied by a twist of the mouth.

It is not the Indonesian teacher's purpose to enter a process of exchange of ideas in which at least one party will have his or her mind changed. Thus teachers made no attempt to draw out their students beyond asking for questions. Thus too, in the repetition of a problem, as I have said, the teacher never gave any clue as to the difficult parts. To do so would be to acknowledge that he had at one time solved it himself and might have himself fumbled at that point. By repeating the entire problem, he acted as though he took no notice of the trials and false starts of the students. For him they were not worth acknowledgment.

In order to give a more detailed description of the classroom atmosphere I must quote directly from notes. Class had just begun, and the history teacher had gone through the names of the caliphs:

7:30. Caliphs' names given and repeated. Half the students have their heads raised, half have their heads resting on desks. No doodling.

7:35. Starting to fidget. Movements in chairs; picking at eyes; picking at face. She [teacher] starts with fill-in-the-blank, but answers herself: "E. . . . ropa." Asks them to turn to book, page 28. She reads. They begin talking amongst themselves. But they also answer.

7:45. Lots of fill-in-the-blank. Boy taking apart a ballpoint pen, but also shouting answers. Finishes and takes out eraser to play with. Lots of foot-tapping, moving of pages.

The history class tended to be quieter than the mathematics class. The noise in the math class was of two sorts. When the answer was called for, many students responded. They did not do so simultaneously, however.

And they often accompanied their answers with gestures, writing in the air or shaking their ballpoint pens. The other sort of noise occurred between students. Much of it was talking about subjects that had nothing to do with mathematics. When the teacher assigned the class a problem to do in class, the volume of noise increased greatly. Students divided into sections of boys and girls. When they were given the problem, they broke up into small groups of the same gender. As Indonesian students frequently do, they huddled together, arms around each other, with lots of movement: caresses, tugs, and pulls at each other. They leaned over each other to look at the book, pulling it back and forth. Talk here was not so much exchange as ejaculation; students seemed to arrive at the answer not through the following of a method, but by mutual contradiction and shouting out what to put down.

The dispersion of the students' energies was readily apparent in their shifts of postures, their talking, their sporadic attention to their books. There seemed to be no moment when they were absorbed with the learning at hand and with nothing else. The answers they came out with arose from a jumbled sort of attention, or even, it sometimes seemed, despite a lack of attention. Thus a boy who was apparently asleep in a Javanese class was the first to interject a reply when the teacher paused for someone to fill in the missing word. The girls sitting on either side of me in an Indonesian language class were animatedly asking me for souvenirs. But one, in the midst of a sentence to me, filled in the word the teacher had paused for, then went on with her sentence. As they whispered or even talked aloud to one another, passed each other notes, borrowed pens and paper, they also came up with the answer, without noticeable confusion in either activity. It was, of course, an example of the rapid switching of tones between language levels that we have already seen.

One might take this extraordinary restlessness as the boredom that naturally follows from the method of teaching. However, the students lack the listless and dull feeling that accompanies boredom. They are responsive whenever the teacher calls for a response. They seem to have too much energy, or, perhaps better, a great deal of energy that is not channeled to any particular purpose. This does not present a problem for either student or teachers. This does not interfere with students' performances; they come up with the answers when they are needed. Nor are the teachers fazed by the many currents of energy that strike their classrooms. That this is the case is best explained in terms of speech levels. The language of the students to each other is *Ngoko*; the language they share with their teachers is Indonesian. In this context, Indonesian functions like High Javanese. It is the language of respect, whereas the language of familiarity is Low Javanese. There is no feeling of boredom because there is not expected to be integration of all of a student's energy. What goes on in Low Javanese is clouded by that language's peculiar invisibility. It is not worthy of the teacher's notice, though of course she actually sees what goes on and no doubt understands what is happening before her. Had students been expected to focus their entire attention on the teacher, no doubt it would have resulted in unbearable boredom. Free, however, to concentrate partially, or perhaps only at certain moments, the monotony of the classroom is quite bearable.

This apparent (I will argue later it is only apparent) discontinuity between the *Ngoko* restlessness of the students and their answers in Indonesian is the framework within which whatever is discovered in the school is made into something already inherent in Indonesian tradition. Whatever students come across as new to them in, for instance, learning how to solve an equation cannot appear as their own discovery. Should they come up with the correct solution and tell it to the teacher in Low Javanese, it would be unacceptable and in that sense wrong. What the teacher says flatly, in the tones of the book, is discovered by the students for themselves. Their discovery does not make it "theirs" if that means it becomes part of their own minds integrated with the rest of their thoughts. It is not "correct" until it has been given back to the teacher in Indonesian, a process that is more than merely code-switching. The "correct" answer is not the solution that students have discovered for themselves, but the use of an idiom different from that which they employed to work out the solution for themselves.

Most things that one can say in Javanese one could say in Indonesian. The change of idiom means as well that none of the students' restlessness, which goes on in Javanese, is acknowledged as having anything to do with finding the answer. The relation of the answer to the rest of their thoughts is one of separation. Rather than being made part of the rest of their thoughts, the answer becomes part of the set of knowledge contained in textbooks and activated when speaking Indonesian. Any discovery of the students' own is thus either not allowed, since it does not match what the book calls for, or, if it does match, appears as the reaching of a point that exists somewhere apart from their own Low Javanese churnings.

Of course, students learn much that is alien to their usual lives. In place of the recognition of only those elements one is sure one has seen before and the disregard of all else, as in *soré*, a great deal that is new is given to the students. It nonetheless takes on the appearance of a tradition. It is already inherent in the language of the books and the teacher. What gives this knowledge a moral and even perhaps a religious tinge is that it is set within the context of speech levels, but in a way alien to Javanese itself.

Students, in speaking Indonesian to their teachers, suppress the *Ngoko* in which they usually converse and which comes normally to them. The Indonesian language in that sense stands in the place of High Javanese. But in a formal sense, Indonesian is free of hierarchical significance.

It is often the language used to avoid reference to status. However, in the classroom one speaks Indonesian not only to show respect for the teacher, but because the school is a national, not a Javanese, institution, and Indonesian is the language appropriate to it. Hierarchical concerns are reintroduced, but with a difference. A teacher replies to the students in the national language. But in doing so, he shows them no particular respect. The flatness of his voice indicates that he takes no account of what goes on in their minds. In that regard, he speaks to them as though he were using Low Javanese. Nonetheless, for him too, Indonesian stands in the place of High Javanese in a sense. High Javanese is widely asssumed to be imperfectly understood and to be the language of high culture. It is conflated with literary and court languages, languages desirable to know and thought to contain the wisdom of Java. Low Javanese, on the other hand, is thought to be transparent. When a teacher intones Indonesian to the students as the voice of the book, his language takes on the mystery of High Javanese. It is also a second language, and, although it is not thought difficult in the way that High Javanese is, it nonetheless is not one's natural language. The mystery of learning is thus turned toward the pupils, in a way that would be impossible were the only language Javanese and the teacher obliged to speak to students in *Ngoko*. If the tone of the teacher's voice takes no account of who pupils are, it nonetheless directs unknown subjects and a sense of something hidden or not perfectly transparent toward them. When the teacher addresses students in Indonesian, they are in the presence of something that they have not yet had access to.

If students speak as the teacher does when they answer, they nonetheless cannot be said to put themselves in his place. Each time they speak to him in Indonesian they indicate their respect for him, hence their difference from him. It does not matter if they learn all that he knows; as long as they express their learning to him in Indonesian while they speak *Ngoko* among themselves they remain in an inferior position. It is this fact that gives students a connotation of futurity. Adults may recognize whatever there is to be recognized and ignore the rest, as they do, for instance, during *soré*. Teachers, too, are guardians of tradition. But students are thought to have special access to the new, not so much because of any specific knowledge or skill they are expected to learn, but simply because they are always standing before a mystery. In their own eyes, and in the eyes of most other people, they have a privileged access to the future.

But to say this is to glide over the sense in which "future" is a matter of chance in Indonesian and Javanese. One sees this in the classroom. The probability of students knowing what they will have to contend with is rather lower than for Western students. Take, for instance, the question of what the teacher will call for next. In the Surakartan classroom, this is determined by the book and implemented by the teacher. The same may be true in an American classroom. But the mental horizon given by *Ngoko* discourse precludes anticipating what is coming next. Student *Ngoko* thought and conversation is concerned with almost any topic other than what the teacher is teaching. What the teacher directs to them, then, comes as chance, not as anything they have worked to foresee. What is foreseen is only that they will, at some point, have to respond.

When students reply by deferring, by changing codes, they sever the connection with the discourse that goes on between them. Two mental worlds exist side by side. As elements from one world, that of the teacher, enter the world of the students, students deal with them by giving them back. Their response is one that allows them to continue their own chatter with little disturbance. This does not mean that they never learn anything; it means instead that what they learn is put somewhere apart from the world that pertains between themselves. But they anticipate the future, expecting always to be struck by the new. Their parents, in contrast, when assaulted by something outside their understanding, find Javanism revalidated.

We have said that, due to the operations of speech levels, whatever students learn turns out to be not their discovery but the property of "tradition," that is, something already formulated. At the same time, this tradition turns out to be the source of the future. The contrast with *soré* shows how this is possible. In *soré* there is never anything new. Whatever intrudes is recognized only to the degree that one knew it before. On the street, to continue the comparison, whatever is new is placed outside Javanese discourse. The classroom contrasts as well with the picture of the mountain. The picture, like the classroom, confronts the viewer with a certain mystery. Again, however, the mystery would emerge as unassimilable disruption. In the classroom, the new is taken in and seen to be Indonesian. Thus "Indonesian" becomes the source of the future.

The classroom exposes students to a barrage of the new. So long as the students return what they learn to the teacher in the form of deference, everything remains under control. But the problem that learning poses comes precisely at the point of deferral. There are two textures of speech in the schoolroom. We have named the teacher's voice as the voice of the book. His principal task is to repeat what the book says. He is the instrument by which the subject matter of the book is made into rote learning. Through his repeated voicing of the book, students can learn what the book says routinely, without needing to take the book's contents apart and rejoin the pieces with the rest of their thought. The teacher's repetitions enter the students' world as something discontinuous. It is as if the reassuring quiet behind the planes of the mountain picture were to erupt with a barrage of mortar fire. Students are assaulted by the new. Peace is disrupted, and they can not respond by simply saying that they have seen it all before. Nor can they attribute the assault to the *anéh* and expect to see Draculla, as in the theater.

A rather lengthy comparison will help us understand the threat to the operation of deference. In their mathematics classes, students are confronted with a series of numbers, which they are expected to transform into a second set. There is a close parallel to this in Javanese gambling. The national lottery is held every three weeks.[2] A great many men and women, including most of those I knew except for strict Muslims, buy chances on the last two or three digits. Some people play every lottery. Others play only when they feel especially sure that they have come across winning numbers. There is, of course, no sure source of winning numbers, but there are places to look. One might, for instance, go to one of the many people known to have supernatural powers, some of whom have reputations for handing out winning numbers. Such people have connections with the *anéh* in that they have something odd about them and that they have connections with spirits. One person with such powers, for example, lives in a house in which every room is filled with miscellaneous objects he has hoarded for nearly fifty years. This he calls his "museum," though in its miscellany it resembles the collections of a miser. He does not give out numbers in any obvious fashion. Returning home, you have to think hard for clues to the numbers. It might have been the number of times he shook hands with you or perhaps something you noticed on one of his numerous calendars hanging on the walls, which extend back for many years. There is also a boy who lives in the remote countryside several hours from Solo. Many Surakartans come to see him. He was born with truncated arms and legs, and for that reason he never attended school. Nonetheless, when he was about 8 years old, he picked up a pencil with the stumps of his arms and wrote out a number. This number won the lottery. One can also buy numbers in the market. Usually these numbers come with systems attached to them. In one case, one is given a number that appears again on a chart. One counts up three and down three to get two more numbers. It is these numbers that one uses in figuring out what to bet. What matters in all cases is that the numbers seem somehow *anéh* or odd. Thus, if one should dream of a number, that would be sufficiently odd to cause one to place a bet.

The comparison with the mathematics problem comes, however, not in the finding of the initial numbers, but in the systems that are used to convert the numbers one might find into a number to bet. I never came across anyone who bet the number he or she first stumbled across. It is, for instance, quite usual for the initial numbers to be converted into several others through use of two sets of equivalents, called "new style" and "old style." In these sets, each number from 1 to 9 has an equivalent. One does not choose between sets, however. Thus the number 29 is the equivalent of 56 in the old style and 63 in the new style. But the numbers can also be interchanged to yield 53 and 66. They can also be reversed to give 65, 36 and 35. To bet all permutations, one would spend more than the return. Consequently, people bet only certain combinations. They are unable to explain why they reject some possibilities, but they can always tell you the method by which they arrived at the ones they ended up with.

Many people have their own methods. One woman, for instance, told me that a dream someone had had two months earlier was true. The girl had dreamt the number 29. "Take 29 and add the digits," she said. "You get 11. Then add 1 and subtract 1, giving 12 and 10. Reverse these, giving 21 and 01." In fact, the winning number was 01. She added that the girl had had the dream in June, but it only came true later. That, she explained, is because June is the 6th month, whereas the number came out in September, the 9th month, and 9 is 6 upside-down.

In this case, the idiosyncracy of the woman's method

REJEKI. ANDA. seri: ①

No.	Value	No.	Value	No.	Value	No.	Value
00	6.94	26	2.5.9	52	0.5.2	78	94.7
01	53.0	27	7.6.7	53	9.1.9	79	80.2
02	1.9.9	28	3.8.1	54	94.9	80	4.5.5
03	1.4.5	29	3.8.0	55	9.2.1	81	50.3
04	2.76	30	37.5	56	6.9.8	82	7.98
05	87.2	31	74.8	57	1.2.0	83	82.6
06	91.2	32	2.7.3	58	0.5.5	84	94.7
07	37.0	33	5.5.2	59	90.6	85	81.6
08	27.5	34	7.9.9	60	0.82	86	4.7.5
09	9.1.7	35	2.2.7	61	3.7.8	87	80.3
10	5.8.1	36	0.29	62	9.5.0	88	8.18
11	4.5.9	37	2.3.0	63	5.7.1	89	3.2.1
12	9.0.1	38	0.64	64	1.2.1	90	6.36
13	14.9	39	3.4.3	65	0.3.0	91	1.3.0
14	88.5	40	14.5	66	6.65	92	2.7.2
15	9.0.8	41	24.4	67	6.1.5	93	0.7.3
16	5.8.6	42	4.8.9	68	1.2.5	94	0.1.2
17	49.8	43	2.3.6	69	9.9.5	95	65.0
18	82.6	44	1.3.0	70	0.9.3	96	5.4.7
19	94.7	45	8.7.7	71	82.6	97	2.7.0
20	75.0	46	9.4.7	72	90.8	98	8.44
21	0.6.8	47	6.5.2	73	5.0.0	99	8.0.5
22	81.6	48	1.6.4	74	3.98		
23	47.5	49	4.5.9	75	2.9.8		
24	0.7.6	50	6.9.4	76	5.4.3		
25	3.5.2	51	8.7.4	77	8.0.9		

CARA²NJA
3 x. NAIK.
3 xMENURIN
+ + + + +

The instructions in this numerical system sold on the street read, "Go up three and down three." If the reader believes 66, for example, to be his number, he should count down to 69 to find the numbers 9, 9, and 5, and count up to 63 to obtain 5, 7, and 1. It is the second series of numbers that he should bet. The title translates as "Your Good Fortune."

This slip of paper furnishes the buyer with a series of numbers to bet. He or she is told to bet the bottom numbers last. The bettor is likely to convert the numbers into others using the system in Illustration 3 or some other process, despite being told that the numbers 25-6-86 are already "screened" or "filtered." Under the picture of the woman, the price is advertised as Rp 1000, though it sold for only a tenth of that.

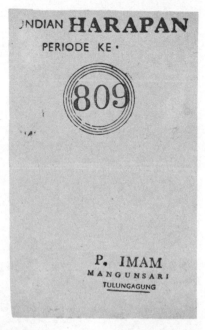

A simpler version of Illustration 4. It advertises itself as "Lottery Chance, period . . . ," the period left blank. The presumed originator of the number and his address appear below.

might be explained because she did her figuring after the event. But idiosyncratic method is in fact the rule. No one can ever justify why they follow only some of the possibilities of the permutations of the "old" and "new" styles. An example of pure idiosyncratic method was given to me by a man who said that he rejected these "styles" because they were too complicated and tended to confuse him. In their place, he simply used the serial number on whatever rupiah note he happened to come across. He gave me this example: The serial number was 4389-48. He added the first four digits to get 24 and subtracted this from his age. He apparently used his age, 49, because it was suggested by the next two numbers of the bill, 48.

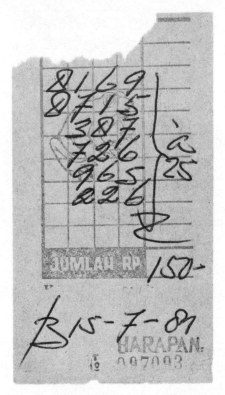

Slip given out by an illegal lottery agent. The numbers on the left (8169, etc.) were each bet at Rp 25 apiece.

Subtracting, he came up with 25. The last time that the numbers came out he was one off. Therefore he subtracted 1, getting 24. Since he already had arrived at 24 in his earlier calculations, he added 1 and subtracted 1, giving him 23 and 25, and bet these numbers.

It is clear from the fact that people do not bet the numbers that they come across initially that the same initial number can win for some people and lose for others. There is no absolute quality to these numbers, therefore. They are valuable because people see in them certain possibili-

Numbers given out by a seer to one of his visitors. It is left to the bettor to understand the relation of 9 and 7. 491 are said to be "excellent"; the bettor nonetheless put them through a system (and lost). The numbers were written out in the buyer's presence.

ties. They are intended "for one," though they are not yet one's "own" until one reads in them other numbers. The numbers always have an *anéh* quality. That is, they seem to come from nowhere explicable. They are made explicable by finding in them other numbers that are meant for the reader or figurer. What the numbers have in common is not a referent that is the same for anyone, but rather a certain anomalous position in the mind of the person who, precisely because of that anomaly, feels that the numbers are meant for him or her, and who is therefore moved to calculate.

One might ask why people never seem to bet the number as it is given to them. Particularly because there is a religious element to some numbers, since some of them come from prognosticators thought to have special relations with spirits, one might think such numbers would be treated as "blessings" (*pangestu*) and bet in their original form. But it is only in following the "rules" of transformation that the number comes to belong to the bettor. The initial number is a shock. The "rules" gamblers follow are the traces of that shock as it spreads through their minds. In its original form, the number is merely anomalous; it has no place in the bettor's thinking. The application of a hallucinatory reason says to the person, in effect, that he had been thinking of just that number all along. It confirms that he had always had it in mind. It is for this reason that bettors never needed to justify not playing all the possibilities of their systems. The other possibilities are not what the bettors had in mind.

It is strange that there is no secrecy about systems nor any attempts to devise new and private systems of transformation. What excites bettors is not new systems, but stumbling across anomalous numbers: hearing of a dream or learning that someone visited a prognosticator. Rules seem self-evidently reasonable and are thought of as general property. No comparisons are made between systems, and no system is debunked. Though there is a great deal of chicanery in the selling of numbers, no one seems to proceed with suspicion. Thus the chart in Illustration 3 turned out to contain only numbers that had already won. This was taken as an indication of its reliability rather than as an attempt to play on bettors' gullability.

When the wild associations set off by the initial numbers are viewed as systems, one can see the comparison to the operation of speech levels. To reply in High Javanese is to prevent oneself from blurting out whatever first comes to mind in Low Javanese. One might, in coming across a promising number, say the next number that comes to mind. Instead, one follows a train of associations but thinks of them as a system. A system is necessarily something unspontaneous. In retrospect at least, it seems to the bettor not as though he said the first thing that came to mind but rather as though he transformed his impulse into generally acceptable language. To think one is following a system is to believe that one is subjecting one's spontaneous impulses to a pattern imposed from without. Thus comes the wish to believe that "systems" really are that: fixed processes, hence outside of the intentional speech of a deceiving swindler. Systems are not speech at all, just language. And thus they are at the disposal of the bettor.

The final number, the one the bettor bets, places him in a hallucinatory structure of speech. He has kept back his own impulses and followed instead the language given to him. He has seen his "own" thoughts appear, first in the concealing form of the initial number, then in the number bet. His thoughts take shape only in displaced form. They become visible in a guise that leaves unsaid the major part of his thinking. Only in this way do his thoughts come to be significative; he thus can hope to win, that is to say, to get a return. Accident is transformed into gift and return-gift.

The gambler's recitation of his process of winning numbers leaves out a great deal. If the initial number sets off trains of associations, there is no reason to think that these are restricted to numbers, yet little besides numbers appear in the rehearsals of "systems." When the teacher sets students a problem and they huddle together, one sees them arrive at an answer in a process that includes tugging at each other, pulling the book back and forth, calling each other names, caressing each other, and talking about other subjects altogether. All of this follows the teacher's initial numbers, and, in that it is part of the mental process used to arrive at the answer, one can say it follows "from" the teacher's initial numbers.

Students are obliged to see the answer, the correct reply, in the teacher's words, as gamblers see the winning numbers in the figures they come across accidentally. But it is not obligation alone that sets off this squandering of student speech. The doubleness of textures I have already mentioned means that what is rote from the teacher's point of view, comes to students as intrusion. Their discourse excludes the teacher's voice. To the extent that they are engaged in their own discourse, they are unprepared for his setting of the problem. It comes as surprise or shock, not as something already seen.

Students do not, however, have the gambler's privilege of naming their own interior procedures "systems" or "styles." What is taught in the mathematics classes is, after all, standard procedure. Students cannot assume that what goes on in their minds is what is generally true without the teacher catching them out. What "rules" or "systems" do for the gambler, a change of register does for students. When they answer the teacher, they do so in his language. Nothing of what they have gone through appears in their answer. As the gambler feels that he has not said the first thing that came to mind in response to the initial number, so students replace the discourse in which they are currently engaged with another that leaves the first discourse behind. The answer is acceptable only if they do so. A "correct" answer given in *Ngoko* would not register. By this means, like the gambler, they convert shock into restraint and signification.

With this process, students make the schoolroom continuous with the house. They create a blankness that is also the space of hierarchy and safety. Their answers, indeed, appear in the blankness created by the gap in the teacher's voice. Students seldom generate questions on their own, as I have pointed out. Their responses, then, seem not to be voluntary. Responses are not initiated by the students but are shocked out of them by the teacher, who first intrudes on them, then gives them a space in which their answers can appear. Their answers appear in his idiom. This, however, gives them space for themselves. It reserves for them everything that, it is apparent to the observer, has already been expended. Between expenditure and reserve there is no difference if one is only counting what goes on. It is solely in the formation of signification that the difference appears. How phantasmagorical this formation is can be heard when listening to student responses. The answers come as often before and after the gaps in the teacher's voice as within the blankness he provides. The students themselves manufacture the teacher's blanks.

Javanese gambling can be an entirely solitary proposition. One might walk along the street, see a number, and think it *anéh*. A Javanese can use a method of transformation that belongs to him alone. Only when he places his bet does he have to turn to another person. The agent with whom he places his bet is, however, merely an agent. In the bettor's mind he bets with the future, conceived of as the possibility of eliciting a reply from a party unknown. Taking place solitarily, perhaps internally, the formulation of the bet shows us the operations that precede speech. One sees first anomalous bits of language, numbers themselves rather than numbers of something, that do not fit with the rest of thought and therefore are labeled *anéh*. The calculations to which these numbers are subjected show that they have barely entered the linguistic process; they remain only calculations, not conjoining themselves with other thoughts.

Being operations performed in solitude, the calculations are outside speech levels—a form of talking to oneself, but in the hope of a reply. Benjamin has called gambling a "phantasmagoria of time."[3] I take this to mean that gambling is a series of shifting scenes of what might occur. The particular hope in Javanese gambling is that language will signify and picture what is to come. And for that to happen, the equivalent of speech levels is generated through the invention of systems, by which anomalous bits of language are converted into a form of thought in order to be made acceptable to a fantasized other. However, these are not truly systems, since they never become generally adopted. Consequently new systems continually appear, which is to say that gambling remains a form of talking to oneself—a form of talk that tries to enter discourse but does so only when it is talked about. It is language that only the future can redeem.

The *anéh* is the consolidation of this linguistic process, the attempt to bring it within social discourse by first giving untranslatable language—the initial numbers—an origin, and by being as well the source of a reply. Indonesian schools are in rivalry with gambling. It is not that they spread a rationalist mentality and banish experiences of the anomalous. It is rather that by the systematization of learning, the schools attempt to relocate the anomalous within discourse. They thereby claim that the systematization of shock in the school yields the sole clues to the future. The processors of learning thus become the processors of the future, equivalent to the spirits.

PART THREE

Money, or The Failure of the *Anéh*

CHAPTER SEVEN

Money: Its Domesticated Forms

JAVANESE GAMBLING can be seen as the insistence that the circulation of money takes place within boundaries established by deference. So long as money exchange does not exceed forms of respect, it causes Javanese speakers only minor concern—though, as we shall see, even in daily shopping, worries take shape, as do defenses against them. When the boundaries of deference are exceeded or are unclear, as in the lottery, the *anéh* is invoked. In November 1980, an anti-Chinese riot broke out in Solo that involved notions of money and the *anéh*. It is of particular interest to us because ideas of the *anéh* were insufficient to account for wild monetary circulation.

In this section I want first to describe the major domesticated forms of monetary exchange, and then to show the special place of students in Solo; it was students who were the principal rioters in 1980. The last chapter of Part Three accounts for the riot as an event in search of a form and turns on questions of circulation.

MARKETS AND STORES

In the Surakartan post office, lines form in front of the stamp windows, but they rapidly dissolve into amorphous crowds. People insinuate bodies, arms, and hands past those ahead of them as they thrust their rupiah notes toward the stamp seller. The idea that those who were there first have priority no matter who they might be does not hold for long. This contrasts with the polite behavior of High Javanese, where each person urges the other to go first. In the post office, possession of money seems to create the feeling that one is entitled to immediate service. It corrodes not only notions of public right, but also those of hierarchy.

Talking with a bank teller one day, I noticed a stack of bank notes. "That's lots of money," I said. "You have to have discipline," she answered, using the English-derived *disiplin*, perhaps to refer to me as well as herself. She meant that you have to keep your wits about you; tellers are responsible for any losses from their cash drawers. She also meant that she felt obliged to keep her distance, that money had a certain attractive power that might result in theft or, more probably, in daydreaming, which could have unlooked-for and unwanted consequences. There is, indeed, a wariness about money, which is not to be confused with an aversion to it, but which acknowledges that the desire it arouses can be dangerous.

In the marketplace, one sees again the danger of money. Women, not men, are more likely to be the handlers of money. Women frequently earn more than their husbands, particularly if their husbands have jobs in government service. Such positions are prestigious, but they pay little. Even when both spouses work in the private sector, women frequently earn more. It is not for this reason alone, however, that women control money. From the men's viewpoint, their prestige is protected if women handle the money and allot them small sums for cigarettes. If women are in charge of money, then they must do the shopping. The language of the marketplace is notoriously crude; the phrase "market language" is, in fact, a synonym for crude language. In making this judgment, lack of general linguistic ability is conflated with the language of bargaining and the overall quality of utterances in the market. In contrast with the stores, which are almost all owned by Chinese, the market is mainly in the hands of Javanese market women. Whereas stores stock manufactured goods at fixed prices, markets furnish daily essentials to be had only through bargaining. Stores enhance the attractiveness of their goods: merchandise is often under glass and separated from the presence of the owners or sales clerks. In the markets, each type of good is sold in a section of the market that is devoted exclusively to it: first bananas, then coconuts, and so on, with the owners next to them. Sales clerks in stores wear Western-style clothing; market women are swathed in Javanese cloth, though often with generous décolletage, their money tucked away somewhere in the depths of their dress. In the crowded market space, as they crouch between piles of fruit, the boundaries between these women and their goods are not always apparent. The women solicit customers in crude fashion, shouting "sweet" or another appropriate adjective at the prospective shopper.

The advantage of the seller in bargaining is that she knows what she will accept for the goods. The defense against this, of course, is for the buyer to know how much she will spend. The asset that both try to maintain is inscrutability, putting the other party in the position of having to judge and thus cater to their intentions. At this point alone, status considerations can be reversed.

Javanese bargaining involves very little beyond an exchange of numbers. The buyer, for instance, is reluctant to disparage the seller's goods because it might offend the seller. The seller makes no appeal to the person of the buyer, this being considered too forward. Numbers are not exempt from speech levels, and to that extent the status of the buyer and the seller is recognized apart from their possession of money. But the speech level used is usually very low, sometimes almost undistinguishable from pure Low Javanese. What drives the levels so low is that bargaining contradicts the usual working of Javanese. Ordinarily the purpose of speaking Javanese is to leave one's desires behind, outside of speech. But there can be no disguise of the purpose of bargaining: it is a frank acknowledgment of wants.

It is not the goods or the specific amount of money involved that lends bargaining its particularly corrosive quality, however. It is rather that status considerations leave numbers isolated as the chief rhetorical figures of exchange. In the register of money, as number responds to number with little other rhetorical reference, it seems as though the language of number is momentarily freed from the rest of language or thoughts. Thus the curve of emotion in bargaining peaks before the bargain is struck. The conclusion of the bargain, as goods and money change hands, seems always a matter of indifference to either party. It is the sometimes heated exchange of numbers in speech, not the concluding exchange of goods and money, that is laden with effect.

One sees here why men, more protective of their status than women, avoid the market. They are addressed in a language lower than they often feel they deserve. But perhaps worse than that is having to attend to the mental calculations of someone whom they could otherwise disregard, and in the process, having to respond with language they would prefer to keep to themselves.

The domestication of money takes various forms. In the house, the commodity nature of household items is not entirely transformed into use value. Practically anything in the house might at some time be sold, perhaps to the wandering merchants who come by seeking used items. Indeed, there is a group of traders in Kemlayan whose specialty is the buying, rebuilding, and reselling of used shoes. Newspapers, bottles, and other useless items are also sold out of the household. Items that retain their usefulness, for instance furniture, are not as likely to disappear. Nonetheless the purchase price is remembered, often for many years.

It is quite within the bounds of etiquette to ask the price of items in the household. Labelling by price makes any item seem potentially to disappear. Familiar items are not likely to serve as momentoes, or if they are, they are willingly given up nonetheless. Still, there is a nostalgia or pathos connected with domestic objects. The nostalgia comes not from familiarity built out of the experiences they evoke, but from the sense of imminent loss they stimulate. This also applies to the decoration of Javanese houses. Things—pictures, furniture—are often moved around. Yet their arrangement seems independent of their setting. Thus a table and chairs can appear in any part of the room and in any relation to the walls. In some households, chairs are stacked on top of each other during the day while the room is used for domestic work. When the furniture is set up again, there is no effort made to reproduce the arrangement of the previous day. In such a situation, a room is not a homogeneous environment evoking a single mood, but an empty space in which individual pieces of furniture appear and disappear. This is, of course, wholly congruent with the retention of price names designating the furniture's possible replacement.

Certain goods, usually expensive luxury items, are more prominent than others. For instance, one of my neighbors had in his living room a refrigerator with an electric fan set on top of it. Neither was plugged in during the year I lived there. There was not much need for the refrigerator since people shopped daily. Javanese dislike wind, and so the fan was never used. Both items, however, were expensive and were on display. Items that are not used but are merely displayed become images of themselves. The fan was not a functioning fan but a reminder that somewhere else there was such a thing. So, too, the refrigerator. It is by making commodities into images or into indications of their potential disappearance that they are fit into a spatial structure analogous to that of the mountain picture. It is for this reason that it would be a mistake to see them as merely vulgar displays of wealth. They show

how money is converted into the idiom of status. By doing so, they help to preserve the space of the household as a space for the functioning of respect.

The items sold in stores are treated in similar ways. For instance, there is a strong tendency to use brand names instead of generic names. It is brand names that are featured in neon signs. One cannot ask for a felt-tip pen; one has to ask for a "Boxy-Riter" or a "Snowman," though generically they are the same. In this way the use value of the item is obscured behind its designation in the market. Its value is its money value. Bargaining, the adjustment of price, is usually not possible in stores. Combined with the obscuring of use values, this makes price seem to be part of the definition of items.

Money does not lead the shopper into a realistic connection with goods but into a fantasy much like that of the household scene. One sees this in the use of glass. Most stores have glass display cases, usually stuffed with goods in such a way that one gets a sense of their great number. After coming from the market, where goods are heaped up in the aisles, one feels cut off from merchandise in stores. Nor is there much of a connection furnished by the shop clerks. Their function is mainly to pull the goods out of their display cases and write up a sales slip, which the buyer takes to a cashier. Market women always seem to know what they are doing. Store clerks display no knowledge about what they sell aside from whether or not the item is stocked. Toward customers they are passive. They are not accustomed to tending to people based on their possession of money, whereas considerations of deference prevent them from empathically understanding customers' needs.

Most Surakartan stores have open fronts with metal shutters that pull shut when the shops are closed. Recently, however, there has been a tendency to close in the front of the shops with display windows. In October 1980, I surveyed the shop area. There were 150 stores without glass and 36 with. Of the latter, precisely half, 18, had glass fronts that were not used for display. These included restaurants, Chinese dentist offices, optical dispensaries, a photo store, a store that sold paintings, and a motorbike dealer. These stores used glass as a means of blocking vision. In most cases, such as restaurants, barbershops, and dentist offices, the glass, either painted or already black, furnished valued privacy. It thus solicited viewers' interest by the fact that it was, after all, glass, ordinarily transparent, marking an opening, only to refuse the viewer visual entrance. It announced that it hid something.

The display windows of the remaining 18 stores had in common that their goods did not seem arranged with the viewer in mind. In the case of a musical instrument store, for instance, in a window eight feet across there were 2 sets of drums, 2 electric amplifiers, an electric-guitar case, an electric organ and, since they also sold sporting goods, an exercycle. There was no space left to be filled; instruments were stacked behind other instruments, partially out of sight. There was no special lighting in these store windows. Usually an overhead fluorescent light, of the same sort used inside the store, was the only light source. There was no backdrop that set an imaginary scene for the goods.

One might want to say that there was no coherence to these displays. Yet judging from the fact that pedestrians, although they did not gaze into the windows, did notice them in passing by, the windows exercised a certain attraction. Without the attempt to make the goods attractive in themselves, they functioned as signboards, announcing that more goods like these were available inside. Rather than being an opening into the store, an imaginary view of what it might be like inside, and rather than attempting to stimulate fantasies that would put the viewer in the picture, these windows implied only that if one wanted the things displayed there was another place, behind the window, where they were available. The cramped quality of the display when goods filled the whole space and the fact that one's eye, travelling into the window, usually came up against a barrier separating the window from the store, seemed to me to flatten the goods displayed. The windows thus achieved a layered effect, somewhat like the mountain picture or the shadow theater.

Windows and glass cases, the general inarticulateness of shop clerks, and the lack of a rhetoric for commodities work to separate the shopper from the goods, leaving only a visual connection. Commodities are turned into items in a display, things to be looked at. And people did tend to look at goods in a fashion that suited the sort of display offered. It was not unusual to see people wander into the stores, particularly the larger ones, look at all of the showcases, often not missing a single one, then wander out. They did this, however, without gazing long at any particular case, and often at a pace that meant they could not attend to specific items. They were not so much directing their attention to commodities as feeling themselves to be in their presence, treating the space of commodities as though it were the space of the household.

The phantasmatic character that the Chinese store shares with the Javanese house is enhanced by the refusal of the shopkeepers to bargain. The imagistic effect, associated with respect and refinement, is more easily maintained when it is not undercut by the need to anticipate the calculations of the seller. But the absence of bargaining makes itself felt in various ways. Most strongly, there is the contrast with the market; in some cases—cloth, for instance, or certain smaller items—the same things are available in the market. The chance is that one might get them for less. But it is also often repeated that one takes a strong risk of overpaying if one is not skilled at bargaining. There is also the fact that, though the transactions in the larger stores are handled by clerks—mere agents of the owner who insulate buyers from him rather than taking any initiative on his behalf—nonetheless the owner's presence is still felt. Shopkeepers most often live above their stores. One sees photographs of them and sometimes of their ancestors in the store. And often, rather than having a separate office, their desks, with letters, cash drawers, and so on, are clearly visible. It is thus possible to visualize or to see directly the calculation that occurs. Unlike the market, one cannot share in it. But behind the imagistic character of the commodities, the realm of calculation announces itself.

We could summarize the place of commodities in Javanese discourse by saying that to the greatest possible degree commodities are taken out of discourse. In bargaining in the market, any attempt by the seller to suggest the uses of her product for the buyer would be presumptuous. The use value of the goods is therefore not part of their conversation, which is instead limited to price. There is thus no attempt to multiply the meanings of products for the potential buyer. This is left entirely to the buyers themselves. It is most appropriately part of *Ngoko* discourse, and that is what people in the market try to avoid. The interchange of numbers alone, with its implied linkage to desire, is already sufficiently hazardous.

Commodities sold in stores, by being made into images, frequently become thought of in terms of status. Their transformation back into imagery comes about through the use of price. As I have said, price designates the disappearance of commodities and their replacement, and this alone is sufficiently close to conceptions of the spirit world in its relation to the everyday world to assimilate commodities to Javanese religious thinking. The limitation of rhetoric is also important. The use of brand names, I have pointed out, prevents a rhetoric of usage from developing and links the definition of objects to their prices. Price could be the linkage to another rhetoric; one might think of all the things one might do with the money that one spends for any particular product. But brand names and price in Surakarta are not part of a larger rhetorical system that stimulates wishfulness. Instead, commodity objects, thought of as money, become things one cannot talk about. They become removed from language, and thereby suggest the source of the *anéh*, the "elsewhere." Javanese, we have seen, do not dwell on commodities displayed in either homes or stores. There is nothing to extend their interest. Thinking of commodities as absence in Javanese terms in fact checks curiosity. It is at this point that commodities become images.

WORK AND WAGES

The singers that perform before the comedy of Sri Mulat begins, whether their music is "pop" or one of the various forms of Javanese music, are alike in their use of highly exaggerated gestures. Their wide, slow arm movements, the anguish in their facial expressions, seem to indicate intense sincerity. Sitting in the front row, however, one can see that their eye movements, as they appraise the audience, are unrelated to their gestures or their music. They do not try to conceal this from those in the audience who sit close enough to observe it. Their eyes may meet those of the audience without either turning away or giving any indication of complicity. Seeing this, one might feel that their performance is formal or even mechanical. But one never hears complaints of lack of sincerity or praise for seriousness of feeling.

The singers are doing what they are supposed to be doing. They are performing, presenting something for which they get paid. When they are through singing, they bow, even if this is before the orchestra is finished playing. Their "performance" has nothing to do with their internalization of the music and their ability to express it. Their gestures, their rhythms, like the music itself, are things given to them to embody, in the way that the teacher voices the text in the classroom. It is not supposed to be infused with his or her "own" feelings. Singing for a paying audience is a form of work, and work means doing what is given to the worker to do.

One sees this pattern again in small batik factories, usually owned, these days, by Javanese. Batik is a method of lost-wax dying. The workers who apply the wax by hand, thus covering areas to be reserved when the cloth is dyed, are Javanese women, often from villages on Solo's outskirts. After the dying, the wax is removed by melting, the pattern revealing itself in the undyed areas. The patterns are highly repetitious. The same elements are repeated over the entire length of cloth, an area long enough to be wrapped several times around the body and wide enough to reach from waist to ground. When the women apply the wax, they trace in parts of the design one at a time. The usual method is to create oppositions and then fill in the blanks in-between. For instance in one element, about one-half-inch in length, it was common for a woman to break the design into five segments drawn in from opposite directions (see figure, p. 174). Another method was for the front part of a line (4) to be drawn in before the segment that preceded it spatially (3).

After the design has been laid down on the cloth, it is often filled in with various figures. A common one is a series of dots. To form one figure that consists of an enclosure of several sides with a small circle in the center, these dots are commonly put in around the inside of the perimeter of the larger enclosure first, then another layer is added around the outside perimeter of the small circle, and so on alternately. Elements inserted with this method seem to suggest their doubles somewhere else on the cloth; the entire design element is not conceived as a whole. Another example of this is the making of what is known as *parang*, a slanting design. In the design on p. 175, one sees that first the straight slanted lines are put in, then

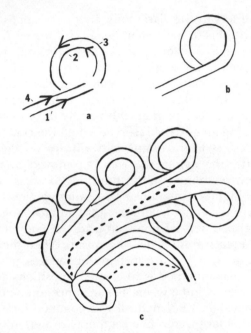

The making of an ornament for batik cloth. The sequence of strokes used is shown in (a). The numbers indicate the order of the strokes. Note that the figure is drawn not as a whole but in opposing sections. The completed ornament is seen in (b), while (c) shows its position in a design known as *Peksi Rawa*. (Part [c] is abstracted by Jodi Woody from an illustration in N. Tirtaamidjaja and B.R.O'G. Anderson, *Batik: Pola dan Tjorak—Pattern and Motif* [Jakarta: Penerbit Djambatan, 1966], Illustration 52.) The drawing is approximately five times actual size.

the flower elements are drawn on alternating sides. After this the leaves are added, again not by drawing in all the leaves of a single flower, but by alternating leaves between opposing stems.

By breaking the line into segments, the worker did not so much draw a design as follow a procedure, the repetition of which resulted in a design. When these workers

This design is usually made not as a whole, but element by element. First several flower stems are drawn, then the leaves for these stems, alternating from one side of a stem to the next. The design is called *Parang Kusuma*. (From J. E. Jasper and Mas Pirngadie, *De Inlandsch Kunstnijverheid in Nederlandsch Indië*, vol. 3 [The Hague: Mouton & Co., 1916], 161.)

receive the cloth, it often has the design sketched on it in pencil. However, I never saw a batik worker wax directly over the design. When I asked why, they usually had no interest in telling me the answer, saying at most that it (the design) was "not right." Their job is to do the design over in wax. They are said to *apal*, to have memorized, the designs, which they see as their duty to repeat in the same way that the singer behaves as a singer should behave, rather than singing expressively. The batik workers follow a procedure, which they equate with what they have learned. Simply to express the vague pencil markings in the definite lines of the wax is not how they see their job. The lines are disregarded in favor of a mechanical procedure that only in the end "says" the intention of the pencil lines.

Most tasks in Java are thought to have a correct procedure—wringing out clothes, sweeping the floor, tying a package, are all thought to be done correctly in a certain way and incorrectly in another, even if the result is the same. The odd thing is that this "correct way" is often not standardized. Each worker feels that he or she is doing a task "correctly," that is, following a procedure that he or she has learned, or "memorized." Batiking is no different. It is not merely that workers offer their labor to their employers, it is also that in doing what they do, even if it is only for themselves, they feel that they are following an authority inherent in the procedure. They submit themselves to their work.

When authority is inherent in this procedure, workers' labor for their employers becomes a form of respect. What they offer their bosses is neither simple labor nor a product, but a form of deference. The sense of authoritative procedure is the structure for the relationship between bosses and employers. Its existence is the reason that the Javanese, unlike most other Indonesian peoples, have firms with employees.

Workers are paid either by the day or by the piece. In either case, the schedule of work is erratic. It is common practice in factories that pay by the day to offer a bonus to those who show up every day for the week. Some workers spend the night in the factory. If they are paid by the piece, these women are likely to work off and on during the night, but to start work late the next day and gradually work for longer periods as the hours pass. In one sense, the schedule of work is the workers', but in another, the workers seem out of control of that schedule.

They seem to work only when they feel the pressure to do so. When they work, they fill an obligation given them rather than doing what they feel like doing.

Work stands opposed to their restlessness. Though I asked frequently, I could not get any worker to say that work bored her. The repetitious quality of the labor is not thought of as being contrary to workers' own feelings. Workers may not like the work, finding it "tiring," but never boring.

One reply I got when I asked a woman if batiking bored her was, "How could I be bored; there's money." Working for money is precisely what bores Western workers, who find that they then are not working for their own ends. Boredom as affect is potential energy that finds no expression; it arises when one works for ends other than those one has made one's own. It is because Javanese workers, like Javanese students, do not expect work to result in an internal integration that they claim not to be bored. It is also because in a sense they do not work for money, if working for money means that they exchange their labor for money in a bargain concluded on payday. Rather, Javanese traditional work is a form of deference in which wages become a type of gift. The return for deference is a relation with the person to whom one defers, part of which includes a gift of money. Batiking as I have described it is considered "refined" (*alus*), an equivalent of High Javanese. In jobs where the work is considered "crude" (*kasar*), workers are more likely to express dissatisfaction. Nonetheless, even when discontent arises—and it does arise—work procedures, no matter how crude, still contain an element of authority. It is this concept of procedure that domesticates money at the point of wages.

FASHION

The sense of appropriateness that governs Javanese social intercourse is also apparent in dress and its concomitant, fashion. At the city-wide contest for the best *keroncong* performers (*keroncong* is a type of song), the performers felt they had to dress for the occasion. In some cases this took the form of identical batik shirts for the men, a sort of uniform. But where there was no uniform, performers were left to dress as they saw fit. This meant a variety of styles. Male singers usually wore suits or sport coats. These were never ordinary; one was pale green, another pink. One had extra-wide lapels of a shiny material recalling tuxedo lapels. Women who did not wear traditional dress wore Western-style costumes with features recalling fashions of the past: padded shoulders, extra-long hems, and so on. The indication that this was not meant to be dress that expressed the individual whims of the musicians but dress appropriate to the occasion is the quotation of period features. It was as though each contestant tried to recall what might be right for such an occasion. There existed no precise model. Seen together, these costumes looked eccentric rather than appropriate.

The attempt to be appropriate can become eccentric on other occasions as well. An elderly musician had the habit of taking a daily stroll. For this occasion he purchased a suit coat and a flat cap, though the temperature was in the 90s, and carried a walking stick. Such attempts turn into fashion, however, when there is a group that finds itself in similar circumstances. Within a period of a few months, many pedicab drivers, for instance, began wearing knee socks and berets with large pompons, both items having recently appeared in the market. The group that seemed most vulnerable to fashion were students, who sometimes read fashion magazines and who have definite styles in jeans and T-shirts. School officials say that it is in order to be sure there is no "unhealthy competition" that they insist on school uniforms. This may also be one reason for the insistence on uniforms in large businesses such as banks and government offices, though the question of esprit is also important there. It is necessary, then, to distinguish the inappropriateness of student fashion from the dress of the *keroncong* singers.

Money and fashion are, of course, closely intertwined. Price works both to rule out certain possibilities and to open certain areas of permissiveness. Women who are invited to ceremonies such as weddings and do not wear traditional dress are likely to wear dresses of synthetic materials, even though in the pervasive heat synthetic materials are more uncomfortable than cotton. The reason they wear such dresses, according to one woman, is that cotton is cheap. To wear it would be disrespectful. Once one has spent enough for fabric that shows its price, however, there is latitude allowed for cut.

It is a noteworthy aspect of Javanese fashion—in dress as well as other matters, such as music—that one seldom hears complaints of anything being out-of-style. There are, for instance, several kinds of music to be heard in Solo: popular music, the music of the traditional gamelan orchestra (*karawitan*), and *keroncong* as mentioned above are a few. However, people who like *karawitan* only occasionally complain about being in the unavoidable presence of popular music in the way that Westerners who like classical music might complain about rock. Similarly, I never heard remarks about any particular dress being outmoded. The reasons are that in Javanese, the subject, the "I," takes its social identity from the person it confronts. Since the "I" is not considered the source of its own language, the repository of a defining subjectivity, it is not soiled by being filled by sounds alien to it. In the case of dress, anything that looks as though it is old not in age but in memory, as though it has been experienced or learned about in the past, belongs to the immutable residue of culture that is valid precisely because it is thought not to originate in oneself.

Questions of fashion, recognizability, and money come together in *alus* or refined batik, of the sort we have discussed. There are thought to be a definite number of batik

patterns. Each of these is named, often with the color of
its background. These designs are said never to go out of
style and always to be salable. They are used in the high-
est-priced batik materials, for traditional dress. One sees
here the nature of Javanese fashion. The patterns are said
not to change, yet small variations are introduced into
them. These consist of varying the *isèn*, the decorations,
within a pattern. The *isèn* are also named. The batik authorities Jasper and Pirngadie list them. One of the *isèn*
might be substituted for another. Or they might be moved
from one design element to another. Or the batik boss
might decide that colors should be exchanged between
design elements. The highest-quality batik uses only one
of two colors besides the yellowish or white space left undyed. It is again a matter of varying old, recognizable elements rather than introducing new ones. A large change
might consist of introducing a design element from one
particular pattern into another in which it was not previously used.

These small changes can create sudden demand for the
cloths that display them. Batik manufacturers keep a very
close watch on the market. Any successful design is shortly
repeated by other manufacturers. Batik entrepreneurs
complain about this, but in a resigned way, knowing that
there is little that can be done about it, though recently
there have been attempts, unsuccessful, to protect designs. In any case, the operations of fashion in batik can
be dated from the middle of the nineteenth century, even
though at the time certain designs were reserved for particular social ranks and probably existed before that. Variation thus probably consisted of small changes within
permitted patterns then as well as now.

The purpose of making these small changes is, according to one batik entrepreneur, to make the consumer say,
" 'There's a difference, it's nice.' But they will not know,
often, what the difference is." This means that something
has to strike the buyer as being anomalous, though he or

she may not be able to say just what. This sense of anomaly attracts buyers. What makes them buy, according to their statements, however, is the feeling that the batik is *alus* or refined. *Alus* batik is always handmade rather than printed with metal stamps or other means. "Alusness" is primarily a feature of workmanship and is recognized not through the large designs but through the small elements. The regularity in the application of dots and the grace of the curves of the small lines are important, as are very slight variations between repeated design elements. To recognize "refinement" in batik, however, takes a special talent called *rasa*, which some Javanese readily admit they lack. One batik manufacturer, for instance, told me that he did not have it; for that reason his wife, who did possess it, made the decisions about design. When one asks people about "alusness," one quickly reaches a point where people can no longer say what it is that makes the batik *alus*. *Rasa* is a notion that is embedded in Javanese religious philosophical notions. If it is to be translated simply, it is usually as "feeling." It refers to something that surpasses language. It takes *rasa* to know "alusness," which means that one cannot say what one knows. Refinement in batik, like refinement in language, is thus, in its appreciation, associated with a moment when one is prevented from speaking.

Batik fashion is always a matter of pattern, never of cut. In traditional clothes, the cloth is wrapped around the body, forming a second surface. Removed, it retains nothing of the body's shape. There is thus no embarrassment about showing one's clothes to others while the clothes are off one's body, or about lending others batik for their own wear. The interest people show when choosing batik is an interest in surface, in pattern by itself. The great batik expert G. P. Rouffaer pointed out that, unlike the Indian batik from which it is possibly derived, Javanese *alus* batik always covers both sides of the cloth.[1] This is despite the fact that only one side is visible, and despite the great extra expense of tracing the design a second time on the reverse side. Each element of the design is duplicated out of sight, on the side of the cloth hidden from the viewer. Javanese thinking on this subject is revealed by a slip they sometimes make. Speaking on the "background" or "ground" (*latar*) of the design, on several occasions people used the word *tembok*. *Tembok* is the term for the wax put over the background to preserve it from being dyed. Its meaning in ordinary discourse is "wall." The "back" of the pattern is thus conceived as something that hits the eye, preventing one from seeing further, suggesting, as with the mountain picture, a space hidden from view. Since the design is repeated on the other side, each cloth has two patterns, separated from one another by "walls," implying a space between them.

The sense of a reserved space is, of course, apparent in the colors themselves, since Javanese understand that each design has been formed by covering it with wax to keep it from being colored. It is only through a process of reservation analogous to that of Javanese speech that there is a pattern at all. The formation of this pattern, indeed, is known in High Javanese as "writing" (*nyerat*). Batik is only considered *alus* if, as with language, it produces a feeling that one has in mind more than one can say. In batik this feeling of "alusness" is induced by the small changes that instigate fashion. It results in the desire to buy today.

But fashion is also a form of standardization. That certain patterns are popular means that others, equally possible, are not. One pattern is no longer precisely the equivalent of another; it is better. Others are of less interest. The possibilities of other designs brought to mind when the buyer identifies one design, finding in it the small changes the manufacturer has put there, are put out of mind. The phantasmatic character of Javanese fashion, however, by which whatever is put out of mind is accompanied by the designation of a place where it might recur, occurs in batik with the implication of the hidden side of the cloth.

Batik is a commodity, traded in the market. Of the various forms of batik, *alus* batik is the most expensive. The association of batik with wealth occurs via its price. The more *alus* the batik, the longer it is said to have taken to make it, the more respect it commands, and the higher its price. At one time certain patterns were reserved for specific social ranks. This is no longer the case. That money can now buy respect does not seem to have diminished the general validity of hierarchy, however. Money is concealed by the legitimizing facade batik furnishes. As speech level usage has broadened to accommodate new social ranks, so too has the wearing of batik. The respect batik commands is enhanced by the sense that it has continued to survive. To Javanese the antiqueness, not of actual batik cloth but of batik patterns, testifies to batik's continued validity, even divorced from the social hierarchy that prevailed in the colonial era.

The validity of recognition of "alusness," the sense that it generates respect, comes with the acknowledgment that those who wear batik today are different from those who wore it previously. This is not acknowledged censoriously, as though it brings with it an erosion of Javanese values. If anything, the opposite is the case; there is a certain pride that *alus* batik can still command so much respect, as proven by its high price. Yet some batik manufacturers understand also that the market works independently of aesthetic values. One manufacturer, for instance, was in charge of a cooperative that marketed its batik in Jakarta as well as Solo. The same batik in Jakarta often brought considerably higher prices than in Solo. This manufacturer's reasoning about this runs as follows: Both Javanese and non-Javanese buy batik in Jakarta, whereas the market in Solo is dominated by Javanese. It is the Javanese who have *rasa*, "feeling." If high price can be equated with "alusness," it is because buyers, on the whole, possess a sense of "alusness." *Rasa*, a sense of "alusness," as we have seen, means the sensation that accompanies respect, the feeling of something being reserved. At the point of buying, of spending, money thus becomes assimilated to the payment of respect. Money enters the framework of hierarchy by becoming a token of deference, not to the batik worker, her boss, or the seller, but to the *alus* language commanded by batik. It becomes once again a form of gift or sacrifice.

The entering of money into hierarchy as a type of gift or sacrifice suggests that it has a double form. When money is equated with a gift or sacrifice as a token of respect, it is assimilated also to the speaking of High Javanese. As such it implies its reserved self, a form that manifests itself in the dissolution of the post office lines.

The assimilation of money to hierarchy can be seen again in the nature of Javanese business. It is a peculiar feature of Javanese business that, as owners grow older and their children mature, they do not prepare their offspring to replace them. Traditionally traders stood outside the rankings of Javanese society. Today most traders would prefer that their children be educated to become bureaucrats. Though they may not encourage their children to follow their line of work, they do not necessarily discourage them, either, in my experience. One batik entrepreneur, himself the son of a retired thread manufacturer, said he did not particularly want his children to do batik. He wanted them to do well in school, but also to understand batik. Later, after they get a degree, should they want to work in batik, it would be all right. "But it's very hard to guide children," he added.

Even when it's clear that the children do want to go on in batik, they are unlikely to do so in their parents' firms. One trader who, with his wife, had once had quite a sizable enterprise, had a son who wanted to become a trader.

He took him into the firm as an assistant, teaching him the trade and introducing him to people in the market he would have to deal with, arranging for him to get credit. The son then began his own business, using capital his parents had lent him. The parents, meanwhile, growing older and feeling unable any longer to manage a large enterprise, gradually cut it down in scale, until it yielded only enough for their needs. The reason for not taking the son into the business, the father said, was that if one did so, or if one actually gave him money, the son would feel that he would always be taken care of and would show no enterprise of his own.

It is, indeed, commonplace that firms that have descended to the second generation gradually decline in profitability. An example is a manufacturer and retail seller of the Javanese cloth called *lurik*. *Lurik* is handloomed striped cotton. As in batik, there are a large number of patterns and continual innovation that brings out small changes within them, changes that, again as in batik, are quickly copied by other manufacturers. This particular firm was founded in the 1930s with five looms. It grew until in the 1950s it had 50 looms and 200 workers. The parents died in the late 1950s, leaving the business to their two daughters, one of whom runs the retail store and the other the factory. There are now only four working looms. The remaining machinery is mostly still in place, but idle. The store still looks as it did in the 1950s—the same furnishings, the same signs—giving it a spectral look. Most tellingly, today's owners still produce the same designs as their parents, having added no new ones. Such stories could be repeated many times.

The market for *lurik* as a whole has declined considerably in the last decade, although not to the degree of the enterprise I have described. What is missing in this particular business that is present in first-generation *lurik* and batik firms is a sense of pressure. There is a general listlessness about the present owners. They exemplify what the batik entrepreneur who refused to take his son into his business feared: a sense on the part of heirs that they will be taken care of. This sense of passivity is not one of depression. The *lurik* enterprise was frozen at the time of the death of the parents. It stands as a constant reminder of them. But this means not a sense of loss, but of potential well-being. The feeling that one will be cared for accompanies the general notion of death, that it is not absolute loss. Those who die, we have seen, are merely out of sight. By the logic of Javanese death, the dead are in a position to yield *pangestu*, blessings. Without a sense of loss, there can be no attempt at replacement. Each generation, then, has to begin for itself rather than taking its parents' places if it is to be economically successful.

Notions of hierarchy that give Javanese business its corporateness thus also limit its continuity through time. It makes wealth into something hidden that can descend on one from nowhere. Javanese business tends to equate wealth with restraint and deference, making it a form of gift from beyond that comes with sacrifice rather than enterprise. When wealth is thought to come if it is put out of mind, however, it tends to return through unorthodox means. Thus, when an entrepreneur does succeed to an unusual extent, it is common to hear that he did so via the supernatural: that he received unpredictable mystical good fortune, or that he meditated in seclusion for 40 days, and so on. Business in turn often becomes not a source of steady investment but the chance to become wealthy. For instance, the absence of a daily newspaper in Solo is sometimes laid to the fact that the men who ran Solo's papers in the 1950s gave them up, though in some cases they were profitable, when batik began suddenly to thrive, exchanging a steady return for the hopes of enormous fortune.

When work procedures alone can make money take the form of a gift, the boss, the real authority, does not have to be present, as indeed he or she usually is not in Javanese batik factories. The sense of an authority who is not here but who is somewhere else is inherent in Javanese notions, which are ultimately validated by reference to the spirit world, to an invisible force that is always elsewhere. The condition for making wages into a gift, for inheritance that precludes succession, is thus illustrated by such Javanese products as batik and by the Javanese notion of commodities as images. This is the domestication of money. By concealing and temporizing desire, domestication ameliorates the fears of squandering shared by men and women alike, fears that we will address in the following section.

MONEY AND GENDER

We have already noticed that commodities, including money, have an association with gender. It is Javanese women who handle money, who manage family finances, who become market traders, who manage wages and accounts in many batik firms and in shops—who handle all possible commercial negotiations. The marking of money by gender is not unusual in Indonesian ethnological perspective. In Aceh, in Sumatra, for instance, men are expected to earn money in trade or commercial agriculture. Women traders are few. Women are important in the domestic economy, however, managing family lands where crops are grown mainly for domestic consumption.[2]

The specialization of one gender in money matters in other Indonesian societies, however, does not mean that one explanation for gender marking pertains everywhere. When men handle money in one society and women in another, all one knows is that "money" and "gender" are important categories. The way in which they become associated cannot be taken to be identical when one sees that the associations are reversed from one society to the next.

To see how money comes to have a connotation of gender in Java, we have to understand the specifically Javanese characteristics of descent and sexuality. Genealogical descent in Java is of limited importance. Genealogies are shallow. No one in Kemlayan, including those of noble line, could trace their ancestors further than three generations back. Noble titles descend a grade each generation for four generations. The issue is not the length of time that a family has held its title, but how far removed it is from the original holder. The reasoning is that the title was granted by the Sunan or the Mangkunegara (the senior and junior royal figures of Surakarta); the first holder was closest to the ruler and those after him are further removed. Noble descent, then, is marked by attrition; lineage in general is not traced far back into preceding generations.

Moreover, biological connection is only one consideration in figuring genealogical descent. Adoption, as in other places in Java and, indeed, throughout Oceania, is widespread. The subject is complicated because there are various forms of adoption. One is the type whereby the adopted child becomes entitled to inherit from his adoptive parents. But the issue of inheritance after death is of little importance since the distribution of property to children before death is frequently practiced. The adopted child, whether legally adopted or not, is often included in this distribution. Inheritance is thus not seen as a problem. In most forms of adoption, a child is eligible to inherit from his real parents but has no intrinsic right to inherit from those who brought him up. However, a child raised by someone else may have property settled on him before the death of the guardian in order to avoid conflict with the guardian's descendants.

From the point of view of those involved, the question of adoption is not one of legal rights. According to Hildred Geertz, "There is one primary concern of the parent and adopting person, kinsman or otherwise: When the child is adult, whom will he support in their old age? The duty of the child to support his parent in old age is the aspect of the parent-child relationship which is most emphasized both in discussions of general relationships and in critical gossip."[3] One sees in this comment the importance of the household as an economic unit.

Descent is traced bilaterally. The question of biological connection complicates matters. The father's sexuality in the Javanese notion of power, as B.R.O'G. Anderson describes it, is substantively conceived. It is acquired often through mystical practices and results in the ability to command deference and obedience from others. "The human seed," says Anderson, "and especially the seed of a man of Power, is itself a concentration of Power and a means of its transmission."[4] The man of Power has the capacity to distribute his seed to a range of women. It is remarkable, given this belief, that questions of true paternity seldom seem to be discussed in Javanese society. Indeed, if semen is an attribute of mystical power, to trace descent is to trace the *anéh*. It is to see oneself on the one hand at a remove (descended) from the *anéh* and on the other as embodying it. Legitimacy, the right to be the person one claims to be, comes not from biological or even sociological descent, but from the taming of the *anéh* one inherits. That taming occurs first in the family.

In order to see the nature of the Javanese household, it is useful to look at its most characteristic product, cooked food. Eating is a complicated matter in Java. The ethnologist Teruo Sekimoto has said of the Javanese ritual feast, the *selamatan*, that it consists mainly of passing food from person to person.[5] Often, indeed, the food is packed up, taken home, and eaten there. The Javanese ritual feast can, then, be a feast without eating.

When Javanese do not eat together, eating itself is somehow removed from social intercourse. The ethnologist Robert Jay says that "each guest on being served excuses himself to those on either side of him and, turning to one side, eats straight through as though temporarily absent from the company."[6]

Eating is no less complicated on ordinary occasions. I could not find a single family in my neighborhood who ate together. Jay again has described daily eating habits:

> No space is set aside specifically for dining, since among the villagers family members do not join for daily meals. Each returns to the family hearth for food, especially in the middle of the day, when the main meal is served, but comes in his own time, collects a plate of food, and retires alone to eat it. The wife usually eats as she has time in the kitchen; the children, each by himself, also eat in the kitchen or in a corner of the front room, while the father usually eats alone at the table in the front room (although I have seen men also eating off to one side in the kitchen). Eating is felt to be a highly personal act requiring privacy.[7]

Jay's description of rural practices matches my experience in the city of Surakarta. Only a few of the more Indonesianized middle-class families I knew ate together.

Javanese food itself differs considerably from other Indonesian cuisines. In the first place, it lacks both visual contrast and flavor contrast. Minangkabau or Acehnese food, for instance, contains various curry dishes. The color of the sauce, however, is often different from that of the meat or fish. One thus recognizes the different ingredients before one eats. Such Javanese dishes as *sekol liwet* or *gudeg* cover all ingredients with a single hue, leaving only contrasts of shape. Javanese are also averse to strong flavors, so their food is more bland than Sumatran food. Javanese food has little aroma and leaves little aftertaste, both being called "unpleasant" by several Javanese I questioned. There is little attempt, then, to stimulate appetite through either the odors or the sights that precede taste; at the same time, lack of aftertaste means that stimulation of memory by food is avoided.

Lack of appetite is thought of not as a question of food

but of the state of the body. Thus if one is too thin or not in good health and is without the desire to eat, certain medicines are available. However, many Javanese like to eat the same thing every day. None of these people thought that altering their diet would increase their appetite. In any case, appetite is too discordant a topic for most Javanese to discuss. Eating is shameful because it acknowledges personal desire; it is better not to have too large an appetite.

The impulse to eat the same thing every day is expressed again in the tendency of Surakartan households each to have a characteristic flavor that is unvaried from day to day, even from season to season. When one dish substitutes for another, the use of the same seasoning prevents a change of taste.

These characteristics of food and eating reflect the complicated way in which food becomes entangled in questions of status. The refined person who knows how to act properly is supposed to curb his appetite. He should eat lightly. His awareness of the needs of others means that he should defer by passing dishes on rather than helping himself.

Passing the food to the next person in a ritual feast implies in effect, "You want it; I can hold out." It thus marks the passer as refined, as one who acknowledges the desires of others while holding his own in check. Passing the food, acknowledging the desire of the next person, also confirms the desirability of the food. It is the wish of the person passing the food along that the next person's desires be satisfied. His intention is only capable of full expression if it is assumed that the food is itself valuable to both parties. As the food continues on down the row of guests, each act of passing it onward makes it into a token of desirability and an acknowledgment of the next person's appetite. Refusal to eat it makes the food taste good only by definition. It thus passes into the register of High Javanese.

In the everyday life of the household, matters are different. The lack of family meals means that the food is not passed. "Each [person] . . . in his own time, collects a plate of food," as Jay accurately remarked.[8] Eating separately acknowledges that, in eating, the consumer gives in to his desires, perhaps more than refinement would allow. If feasts put food into the register of High Javanese, acknowledging the desires of others and the suppression of one's own desires, then the household, being the site of consumption, puts food into the register of the Low Javanese.

But we have already seen that Low Javanese can be made into a form of High Javanese; it can, that is, be made to show that desire has been suppressed. The lack of distinctiveness in household food, the fact that it is made to taste the same on every occasion, is the means to do this. The tasting of the same flavor every day is like seeing the same sights every afternoon. It is the occasion for a certain sort of recognition. The recognition that whatever one tastes is precisely the same as what one tasted the day before. The interest in this repetition of the same is that the food could be different. It could have contrasts; it could have a flavor that one might not recognize. But so long as household food has a single flavor, this is not the case. Daily recognition of the same acknowledges that desire for difference is possible, that it exists within the person, and that it has been refused. Low Javanese is thus made into High Javanese.

That the food always has the same flavor is the work of the mother. She either does the cooking or supervises her daughter's or servant's work. Her food is a guarantee of a certain negativity, much like the production of negativity by women batik workers. Even without communal meals, without serving of any sort, hence without the convention of passing or giving over, food in the Javanese household is known to come from the mother. Its unique flavor attests to that. Its uniqueness is also the guarantee of blandness. A guarantee that nothing else will arise in the place of the particular blandness of the food of any particular Javanese household. The mother assures consistent flavor and consistent blandness. The two have the same effect; that the food is always the same means that nothing else, no other possibility, will occur. The mother as originator of cooked food guarantees her household of this negativity.

Eating itself, however, indicates the inadequate suppression of desire. Eating food that comes from the mother indicates that she is the origin of its desirability. But she is also the author of the negative qualities of the food, its consistent flavor and its blandness. These negative qualities themselves raise the possibility of the food being potentially desirable. To say this much is to say nothing that could not be said about the speaking of *Kromo*. There, too, suppression is detectable and, we have seen, often becomes the object of complicity between people who speak *Kromo* to each other. *Kromo* speakers, we have seen, delight in the fact that they share a secret that they tacitly acknowledge to each other. The negativity of Javanese food, however, makes such an occasion impossible. It marks the peculiar position of the mother. She is the one adult to whom a child is likely to almost never show respect. She remains the source of a pleasure or desire—one that, we will see, is not returned. Without reciprocity, the mother maintains herself as an origin, the center of the household.

The security the Javanese household offers is not that of privacy. Privacy in the Western household means that within the family, individuals can hold idiosyncratic notions unchallenged by public criticism. Javanese families are in fact full of idiosyncrasies, as the wide divergence between families in the flavor of the same dishes would suggest. These are not considered to be idiosyncrasies, however. The Javanese family operates as a generator of acceptable meanings in the way I have described previously. It is able to do so because of the role of wife-mother. In the production of signs within the family she holds the position of an origin, equatable both with emotions and feelings that need to be suppressed to act properly and with the means to generate that suppression.

To perceive the special position of the wife-mother in the generation of deference, we can schematically trace the progress of children in learning to speak High Javanese. Here I rely primarily on the work of Hildred Geertz, Robert Jay, and Ward Keeler. My own observations on the subject were unsystematic; nothing I saw, however, contradicts their reports. Before the age of about 5 or 6, children are close to both parents. Until that age, they are considered "not yet Javanese," meaning they do not yet know how to behave properly. As children begin to be taught respect, the close relation to the father ends. Geertz says that the shift is "from one of affection and warmth to one of distance and reserve" and, though it is "only one step . . . by which the child learns the specific Javanese concepts of self-control and respect, [it] is probably the most significant. . . ."[9]

Geertz does not specifically describe the teaching of language usage. The primary inculcators of respectful language, however, are the mother and the older sisters. I have already described how the mother will speak in place of the child, speaking as the child ought to speak, particularly toward the father. Geertz points out that "in the Javanese family the mother exerts the real authority, but the father receives the 'respect'."[10] The father, in fact, ordinarily refrains from correcting children. Jay reports that "few fathers actually use any direct authority in their relations with their sons." (In my experience the same is true of their practice toward daughters.) The rationale is that the child is so submissive to his father's authority that the latter must use it only with great caution. For example, a son might, it was argued, "continue to perform a task the father has set for him so conscientiously as to wear himself out, endangering his health." (Jay mentions this in regard to adolescent sons, but the same is true of fathers' behavior toward younger children.) The father is considered to be a figure that denies children's wishes. When mothers want to deny their children anything, they often do so in the name of the father.[11]

As this process continues and children reach adolescence, boys have less to do with. their mothers, though their attitude toward their mothers remains warm. I have often seen adolescent boys being rebuffed by their mothers when they wanted to act toward them with the familiar attitude their sisters display. At the same time, however, they usually persist in addressing their mothers in ordinary Low Javanese. By contrast, they are likely to use respectful pronouns at the very least in addressing and referring to their fathers.

Making the father into a figure of denial and authority towards whom the boy shows respect allows the boy to constitute himself against his father. He shows himself to be a person capable of deference, hence worthy of respect himself. As he distances himself from his father, his use of High Javanese indicates his difference from his father. The consolidation of himself as a figure separate from his father allows him to become an adult.[12] One always must add the caveat that there is no final consolidation since, given the nature of the language levels, there is always the possibility of a slip into a position of lack of separation.

By contrast children do not ordinarily use respectful language toward their mothers. Mothers, therefore, remain sources of indulgence and attraction. Without the movement of separation that is generated in the use of respectful language, mothers can become powerful sources of the dissolution of self.

The difference in the roles of father and mother in this process of learning respect is critical. The child is corrected and denied in the name of the father. The mother, however, continues to be a figure of indulgence. ("Children turn to the mother with assurance that they will get what the father has denied only to find that the mother, if she does not want to grant them their wishes, does so by referring the children to their father. . . ."[13]) Boys become separated from their mothers at adolescence, but this separation differs from the distance they experience in regard to their fathers at an earlier age. Distance from the father is the condition for the generation of respect. The boy's distance is itself a mark of respect; the father's removal of himself and his metamorphosis into a figure of denial make him into an authority. That the authority is actually exercised by the mother only protects it from possible diminishment through being challenged. In contrast, the boy's separation from his mother does not mark a diminishment of affection or of feelings of closeness, which often continue into adult life. It is only a question of a physical separation, usually, in my observations, instigated by the mother herself.

By being "mothers," women come to threaten the process of separation. This threat is not inherent in their biological nature but in their position as indulgers vis à vis the denial of the father. They act as authorities not in their own name but in the name of the father; what a child does properly, he or she does in the name of the father. Being "mother" may not even entail giving birth since adoption is so common. Mothers, rather, are fixed within the economy of respect as figures of gratification.

There are a great number of families without fathers present in Java. Nonetheless to be a "mother" in such a family still entails the acknowledgment of social convention and the education of children in the name of that convention. The fact that fathers so rarely risk their authority by actually giving orders makes their actual absence no great inconvenience.

Sexual standards for women are higher than for men in Java. Nonetheless prostitutes also have families without,

apparently, the question of paternity ever becoming bur-
densome. It is not the issue of the reservation of sexual
rights to the husband that is crucial. It is rather the issue
of incest, specifically mother-child incest, which is the
question of the limitation of indulgence, of the mother's
instigation of a separation from her son and her insistence
that her daughter fulfill household tasks. It also is the issue of her capability of acting in the name of convention.
A woman who does not understand respect would be a
person incapable of withholding her indulgence to anyone. Since "mother" is a term that stands in relation to
children, and since her children are not necessarily those
the women has borne but those she educates in respect,
such understanding of respect and practice of restraint is
crucial. Without it, there would be no boundaries of indulgence of mothers toward their children.

The separation of boys from their mothers at adolescence is not repeated with girls. They not only remain
emotionally close, but also frequently remain in close daily
association. However, despite the fact that they often take
over many tasks from their mothers, including care of the
younger siblings, daughters are not exempt from a certain
dependency. Even when they have their own families,
dependency continues, according to Geertz.[14] Simply doing
what their mothers do is not enough to make them adult.
Like their brothers they need to learn respect vis-à-vis their
fathers in order to become mothers themselves; it is thus
not technical performance but the respect that entails reserve that allows them to become mothers in their own
right, independent of their own mothers.

It is in this context that we can again raise the question
of *latah*. *Latah* usually affects women, though men too can
become *latah*. Yet none of the literature reports that men
are obliged by those who tease them to expose themselves. Nor is it reported that they blurt out obscenities as
women *latah* sufferers usually do. A female's inability to
be reserved means an inability to be sexually reserved. In

the case of women, loss of self, complete identification with the other, results in exposure. Exposure and the utterance of obscenities has been interpreted as the return of repressed sexuality. This is no doubt the case. But it is also regression to the state before the self was formed by separation. That this state takes the form of sexual exposure for women indicates the importance of sexual reserve for them. Without it, their central role, "mother," would not be possible. Thus accession to respectful language, to adult roles, and to sexual reserve come, if not at the same time, then as a single bundle. It is not women as sexually functioning beings, but women as sexually reserved beings who are able to become mothers.

With all of this in mind we can turn back to the relation of money to gender. "Financial authority," says Jay, belongs to women: "In children care and practical discipline, in everything connected with the kitchen and the food supply, in sales of the harvests and purchases of clothing and household equipment, and in cash expenditures for wages, labor exchanges, and social celebrations women come to make most of the daily decisions."[15] Geertz supports him: "Most Javanese rely on their wives' financial judgment rather than their own, feeling themselves freed of an unpleasant responsibility."[16] There are, of course, exceptions. Geertz cites the case of a successful trader whose first wife was financially incompetent. He therefore handled the money. But his second wife "was an excellent manager, and he let her handle all the finances completely, conferring with her only on major decisions."[17]

Geertz's example shows that even men who are adept at handling money hand the management of finances over to their wives if possible. And this is so not only in household matters but also in business. It is often the case that batik firms in Solo, for instance, are managed mainly by women. Even when their husbands are capable businessmen, women frequently handle the accounts, the buying and selling of the goods in the market, and the negotiation of wages with employees. Men often deprive themselves even of pocket money. One batik trader who had become quite wealthy told me, "What does it matter if you have to ask your wife for money for cigarettes?"

Observers agree on the attitude of men toward money. Geertz says:

Men frequently express the belief that they are incapable of handling money carefully, whereas women are supposed to have thrift and foresight; for this reason most men give all or the greater part of their earnings to their wives and are forced to ask for spending money as they need it.[18]

Again Jay reports the same thing:

Women in general are convinced that men are chronically incompetent in the handling of money. Women, their conviction goes, can be trusted to put family interest and the desires of their children first, while men can be expected to squander any money they may get their hands on for extravagant purchases, treats for each other in coffee shops and gambling. There is some substance to these charges; men are prone to such spending, and there are many more spendthrifts among them than among women. Men among my informants were unwilling to challenge this argument except occasionally in reference to specific instances. Many of them indeed seemed comfortable with the conception.[19]

Ward Keeler says that Javanese men "are generally thought to be unable to handle money well. Rather than a real failing this incompetence shows that they are above materialist calculation."[20]

Again all that they say I have confirmed in Solo. Men do sometimes squander money. One man and his mother lived in a shack behind one of the better houses of the neighborhood. The house had once been theirs but had been lost by the woman's husband, a compulsive gambler. Such stories magnify the fear of squandering, which, however, often has nothing to do with the actual capacity to handle money. Jay adds that "many men are thoroughly competent to invest their funds with care and skill, and the family achieves success as much through the managerial skill of the husband as of the wife."[21] But it is not a question of competence. Many competent traders nonetheless turn the handling of money over to their wives whenever possible.

The reason for this practice is not hard to find. We have seen already how money is a danger to the maintenance of status in bargaining, since it means acknowledging desire and leaves a man open to the charge of lacking *iklas* ("detachment"). It threatens the detachment necessary to the maintenance of proper behavior. The charge of squandering is an accusation of behavior improper by the standards of hierarchy. In the register of money, men are threatened with a lack of reserve. They are threatened, thus, with a state like *latah*: with helplessness and loss of self. Surrendering their money to their wives does not diminish them, therefore; it protects them. The risk now belongs to their wives.

Men hand their money over to their wives. They do so because they fear squandering it. But of course they need it. They give it to their wives, rather than to anyone else, so that they can get it back. Women accept it because they, even more than men, fear men will squander their resources. They fear that men's spending will endanger their families.

"One older women who had had fifteen children said that she did not care what her husband did as long as he gave her the major portion of his salary every month."[22] Women believe they, "can be trusted to put family interests and the desires of their children first while men can be expected to squander any money they may get their

hands on. . . . ."[23] Without the possibility of women using
money for children (that is, for production), and thus con-
serving their husbands' resources, it would not seem possible for them to accept this money with the stigma attached to it.

Women thus come to control the resource that would
allow men to breach decorum and dissolve the boundaries of the self. In doing so women come to embody what
men fear most. If women were thought to be only the
source of fear, however, they would be a source of danger
for Javanese men. They would evoke an earlier state in
which the mother fulfilled desire and did so without the
use of speech levels. But the assignment of that fear to
women is also the means to domesticate it. Women become its source and also the agents of its control. Women
become "mothers," the source of unrestrained pleasure
and hence of behavior in a single register. But also, as
"wives," they are controllers of the means to limit pleasure in later life.

Children's experience of indulgence is not frightening;
rather the contrary. However, the thought of adult squandering, of behavior in a single register, produces fear, even
though that squandering is in the pursuit of pleasure.
Money becomes associated with women because the same
experience, unrestrained pleasure, is experienced again in
the context of hierarchy. It is dangerous the second time
because questions of hierarchy and separation are present
that were not present initially. The second experience may
not have to do with women. It may only have to do with
gambling or with buying, for instance. But the assignment of the fear to women makes women seem to be the
source of an initial pleasure. It thus domesticates fear by
giving the social self a locus of its fears of relapse. And in
doing so it constitutes the Javanese family.

It is because money is an idiom of difference and the
dissolution of difference that it becomes linked to gender.
And it is also because it is an idiom of difference that it

needs to be tamed when it is used in relation to work, wages, and the exchange of commodities. We can glimpse what Javanese life would be like without such domestication by returning to the *gelandangan*, the homeless scavengers we have already described. Surakartans distinguish *gelandangan* from beggars. With beggars, money is assimilated to speech as it is handed over—a gift, resulting in the cessation of the beggar's refined imploring, that ratifies their use of High Javanese and makes them part of the recognized world. *Galandangan* live by scavenging and selling their findings. They collect refuse, of no value at all to those who discard it. But, they are ignored. No one seems to notice them or the sometimes naked madmen and madwomen who also occupy the sidewalks. No one moves out of the way for them, for instance, though they seem somehow never to collide with them either. The transformation of what has been discarded is not attended to; the productivity of the *gelandangan* remains invisible, and they remain outside discourse. Indeed, *gelandangan* are often confused with the "insane."

CHAPTER EIGHT

Topchords Pop Music Society: School, Music, and Clothes

THERE IS a conception of fashion that prevails amongst students other than the one we have described. Students' notion of fashion as it affects clothes and music approximates the workings of fashion in the West, though the notions are not identical.

It is music and not clothing that is the major subject of teenage fashion rhetoric. There is a magazine called *Topchords* that caters to teenage tastes. The bulk of the publication consists of lyrics and guitar chords for both Indonesian and Western popular music. It also publishes articles on Western and Indonesian musicians and sells clothing. It contains a "Centerfold," sometimes also referred to as a "Poster" (both in English) with photos of male and female models wearing clothing that can be ordered from the magazine or bought locally from agents. The March 1980 issue lists 47 agents in 33 Indonesian cities. The prices for these items, mostly between $5.00 and $8.00, give some notion of the readership to which the magazine caters: not the upper-class wealthy but the middle-class and barely middle-class kids. The letter column indicates that although some are from Jakarta, the nation's metropolis, most are from provincial cities. The magazine itself is published in Salatiga, a small city three-quarters of an hour from Solo.

The importance of this magazine is that it marks the emergence of a new social type, the *remaja*, perhaps best translated as "teenager," perhaps as "adolescent," on the Indonesian scene. *Remaja* can be equated with high-school and junior high-school students. To say "student," however, is to give an organizational affiliation. To say *remaja* is to name a social persona. It is precisely the difficulty of saying that anyone of a particular age or institutional affiliation is ipso facto a *remaja* that makes magazines such as *Topchords*, which express the tastes of this new group, important. A person may be a student, but he cannot be sure if he is a *remaja*. It is by having certain "tastes" (*selera*) and certain aspirations that one is or is not a *remaja*. One of the letters to the editors of *Topchords* says, "Most of us [meaning most *Topchords* readers] are students [*pelajar*, high school, including junior high-school students, and *mahasiswa*, university students], right? Therefore we respectfully request that *Topchords* really think about our needs." The editors replied saying "that has been our thought" and that they had therefore "realized [*menrealisirnya*]" among other things a "Sing a Song Bag" and a "Notebook" (both in English) "printed in deluxe style with a price that is sufficiently cheapppppp.*[1] Despite the emphasis on price, the goods are presented as having a certain decorative quality and thus take on the characteristic of being luxuries. They fill tastes more than needs, and, indeed, the editors speak frequently of "taste." "For you who have taste [*berselera*]" is the heading of one "Centerfold."[2]

Here is a typical *Topchords* letter:

> I am one of your fans, fanatic [in English] enough about your creations.
>
> Most recently this was the way it was with the appearance of your Indianapolis style [referring to a shirt or blouse]. As soon as I saw it I sent off a postal order

---

*It is the habit of both editors and letter writers to add extra letters, as often as not unpronounceable, as an element of slang. They thus stress that access to becoming a *remaja* is limited to the literate, that is, to students.

This particular editorial reply continues with the unabashed hucksterism characteristic of the magazine. "Go on and read the 'buy-by-mail' page. And for your attention . . . [*sic*] thanksssss."

to your headquarters. But . . . [*sic*] I have waited and waited for its arrival but it still hasn't showed up. What is it with your service, bung [a familiar term of address]? Has it started to go bad? So much for now and thanks.[3]

On the same topic another says:

Could we meet [the centerfold models]???? And if we could, how and what are their addresses? Many, many thanks in advance, Bung [a familiar term of address] [Edi]tor, for your consideration.[4]

This, as with all letters printed, was answered. In this case, the editors told the writer to simply send his letters to the models to the magazine. In the following letter of that issue a writer wanted the addresses of his "favorite singers," though he did not specify who they were. The editors listed the addresses of 14 prominent singers.[5]

A girl writes: "Does *Topchords* not have a plan to create something neat?????" They answer that they "hope to satisfy their fans, especially the chicks who are . . . . [*sic*] antiqueeeeeeeeeeE!!!! So, for the moment you can enjoy the rock Vest . . . . . . , [*sic*] Grease Pant Trousers!!!!!"[6]

Another reader complains that many of the songs published are "superannuated and musty." The editors tell him, "We try as hard as possible to satisfy *Topchord* fans."[7]

If one can judge from internal evidence, the letter column is genuinely popular. There are many requests for it to be expanded, and the editors keep advising those whose letters may not have appeared to be patient. One might suspect this of being the sort of hucksterism with which the editors are wont to peddle their own goods. But the range of styles of the letter writers attests to the letters not being written by the editors and to the strength of feeling of the writers. I therefore feel that the "Pos Topchords" feature, as it is labelled, is one of the important sections of the magazine.

If the language of the letters is not standardized, the topics are. What one has is a series of messages about music, fashion, and singers that are more or less alike, but repeated by different writers in their own styles. Each letter is answered by the editors. But, in contrast to the letter columns of such Indonesian magazines as *Tempo*, one does not come across comment by one letter writer on the opinions of a predecessor. Letters are always intended for the editor and never via the editor for someone else. Exchange therefore never opens up into a conversation that includes others. Furthermore, no letter writer ever seems to answer an editor's remarks on his or her letter. A letter writer thus sees his or her sentiments, which match those of other fans, appear in print above his or her name. This makes it seem as though the real purpose of the letter column is to register oneself as a fan, a member of the "Topchords Pop Music Society" as readers are sometimes called. "We and the whole crew [in English] say welcome to the pop music society family," the editor said to one correspondent.[8]

Each letter appears beneath a heading that indicates its contents. A spectacle is created. Acceptance into the pop music society is put on display to be witnessed by the magazine's readers. One might see one's own name in print framed by captions above and below it; one then has to imagine others reading the letters. But only a small proportion of readers can ever be able to see their names in print. It is not the letter writers themselves who are important to us, then, but the readers. They see the interchange of editor and writer and know that they are not included. Their possible inclusion could come by writing a letter themselves or by buying the fashions the editors tout or by playing or listening to the music.

Topchords is a fan magazine and so features articles on musicians. These articles are biographical rather than musical. They focus on the stars' rise to success but have little to say about their lives presently. The vocabulary of these articles heavily borrows from the West. Words such as *sukses*, (or "success") and *karier* (that is, "career") figure prominently. One article begins:

> "Jakarta, Jakarta . . . . . [*sic*] Jakarta," such are the hopes of every musical artist desiring success in the metropolis. They feel that in Jakarta they will have the opportunity to develop their talents and their careers. . . . Such were the hopes of Toar Tangkau when he roamed [*merantau*] for three years from one city to the next . . . trying to develop his talent [*bakat*] as singer. Finally, he too chose Jakarta.[9]

Such articles tend to be standardized and feature the "talent" (*bakat*) of the musician. Thus one girl who went on to win a national and then an international contest revealed an ability to play the *electrone* (electric organ) at the age of five. She watched her older sister play and insisted on playing herself. "It was in that way that the Danuwidjaja family became aware that one of their children had musical talent." Such talent is "natural"; it is sometimes called *bakat alam* or "natural talent." It comes by descent or simply reveals itself. It can be accompanied by "inspiration"—at least, that is the way one is obliged to translate the word *ilham*, which comes from Arabic and previously had been used to designate divine inspiration. Thus the girl was "inspired" to write a song called "Bajing Melompat," or "Jumping Squirrel," by a visit to the zoo. Her talent manifested itself suddenly:

> As Yani herself says, the inspiration to compose sometimes comes to her suddenly. Her feelings [the English word is used] are extraordinarily acute; she becomes exceedingly sensitive to something. For example, when she toured Yogyakarta with her mother and sister Yani needed only ten minutes to record within herself in the

form of a composition something that later bore the title, "Yogyakarta."[10]

These biographies tell of critical points that come about
accidentally. Thus Toar Tangkau "from the time he was
small wanted to be a sailor." We are not told what in particular prevented him from doing so, only that events
turned out differently for reasons that seem to have been
unintended by Toar himself. The article goes on, "But
. . . . [sic] God clearly wanted something different. Finally he came across his life's path as a singer himself."[11] In the case of a teenage singer named Astri Ivo,
accident was crucial to her "career."

> At that time in her neighborhood there was a Lebaran
> celebration [a festival at the end of the fasting month].
> By chance Achi [her nickname] was asked to fill in the
> program even though she was not wholly prepared in
> the way the important singers were. Well! It was from
> that moment that the same small girl with the pretty
> face went into orbit.[12]

Her lack of preparation reveals the extent of her talent,
whereas her opportunity came accidentally.

The stars insist that hard work is a necessity; one must
be prepared. And talent can be sensed even before it is
expressed. Thus *Topchords* says of the singer and drummer Reynold that "he began mainly with the natural talent bequeathed by his parents" and that "from the time
he was a boy his talent pushed up against him but he did
not seriously feel it. He only knew that inside him was a
sort of power which might be channeled who knows
where." As a result he used to assemble pots and pans
and beat them, often arousing his father's anger. He formed
several bands in his native city. In this account as in the
others, no matter how much talent and how much hard
work, "success," which often comes with being "sent into
orbit" (*diorbitkan*), happens without one knowing how.

Thus Reynold's story continues; he worked with several bands in a provincial city, went to Malaysia where he was apparently unsuccessful, and finally came to Jakarta where "he was seized by a certain record producer" who put out his first album. "With that the name Mercy's [the band he formed; Mercy is the nickname for the Mercedes automobile] became better and better known by the public."[13] The article gives the impression that talent was there from the beginning. It never mentions the development of Reynold's music and so gives the impression that "success" comes by being "seized," that is, as a surprise.

Toar, commenting on his "career," said, "It is very difficult to emerge onto the music scene; there are others who are already popular. But no matter how good the music, how fine, how enchanting the songs, it's no guarantee of success on the Indonesian pop music market, because there is always FAKTOR X [in English in bold letters in original] which has a hand in determining things."[14]

Talent (*bakat*) is linked with surprise because talent is natural and therefore always at odds with social circumstances until it has manifested itself in the world. The moment when the "career" is put into orbit thus has to have an element of chance to it. It is this notion of chance that is central to generating a conception of biography. It has been noted before that biography is not an Indonesian genre.[15] One can get a notion of why this is by looking at the idea of *rantau*, which *Topchords* often invokes. Toar, for instance, is said to have "*merantau* [the verb form of *rantau*] from one city to the next," which I translated as Toar having "roamed" between cities. In its traditional usage, *rantau* is the practice of young men leaving home to study or work in far-off places. In most cases it is expected that they will return and marry, though in some cases men settle permanently away from home. The *rantau* is expected to be a time of varied experiences, often experiences not available at home. But the end of the *rantau*, settlement, is known.

Experiences while away do not change the course of one's life. *Rantau*, as it is used with Toar, however, results in a play of chance that gives him a career. The notion of *rantau* can drop out altogether, as with the girl who at age five suddenly played the electric organ. What is important to us is that "chance" intersecting with "talent" results in a "career." There is then a record of a life in which what happens to one, the events that are recorded, are no longer isolated occurrences that one merely witnessed. Experience is now used, and the direction of life changes.

Many of these stories contain elements that in the context of life in Surakarta would be considered *anéh*, the sort of oddities that indicates the intervention of spirits. Thus the five-year-old organ player can "quickly record a voice in her mind and brain and later express [*mengexpresikan*] it on the organ keys."[16] Her phenomenal memory is the type of bizarre talent that in another context would make her into a curer or a prognosticator of lottery numbers. However, the status of *dukun*, magical curer, and sometimes of prognosticator, is not equivalent to a "career." There is only one option to someone who embodies the *anéh*. But a career could have outcomes other than musical ones. One's talents might equally well carry one in another direction. The notion of "chance" implies not only that talent might or might not develop, but also that one's life could have various outcomes.

Furthermore, a person who becomes a *dukun* often does so against his or her will. But it is not something anyone can strive for or against, and it is certainly not anything that someone can choose. Though "talent" pushes one, nonetheless it requires "work," which means choice; one might not work and thus not be a success, though such cases do not appear in *Topchords*. The notion of chance as it is used in *Topchords* implies the one almost missed becoming successful. It might easily have been otherwise except for a combination of circumstances that, though they always contain an element of chance, always are given a historical ring.

Surprise is also a feature of the *anéh*. One understands that the supernatural has intervened through being surprised (*kaget*). Precisely for this reason Javanese guard against the unexpected. To be surprised means always to be thrown off-base or upset in some way. Even though the intervention of spirits may have good consequences, still the disturbance of calm that comes with chance in the context of Javanese is not wanted.

By contrast, the surprise that comes with the emergence of talent never seems to throw anyone off-base. It merely occurs unexpectedly. The first sign of Reynold's talent came when he began to beat his parents' pots and pans. This development, however, surprised no one at the time. It only became surprising in retrospect. But we do not hear of anyone being astonished in the *Topchords* accounts. Until Reynold became a star, no one could be sure he had talent, so that only with hindsight could the sign of his talent be recognized. So too with "FAKTOR X," which can only be known by the success it produces later. Surprise so firmly located in the past can have no shock value.

There are no failures in *Topchords*. No stories of people without talent and, especially, no stories of talented people who did not become a success. By contrast, stories of the *anéh* are generally stories that have no repercussions. The *anéh* is precisely that which has no place in the world. It can, therefore, become the basis of success only by means that are suspect. Wealth often, but not always, arouses stories of the *anéh*. A newly successful business man is often said to have become successful through supernatural methods, some of them, at least, considered to be asocial. But in *Topchords*, success always implies money, and this is not a matter of concern. Money in *Topchords* is always benign. Stories of scandalous lives of singers (except for Western singers who are understood to be amoral in any case) do not appear. The notions of "talent" and "career" imply that something that does not belong to the social world initially really can be made to belong. "Success" ("Good studying and success," the *Topchords* editors sometimes wish the letter writers) means winning a place in the world (which includes having money); it means having a biography.

Musical celebrities, in fact celebrities of any sort as opposed to heroes, are new on the Indonesian scene. On any scale, they are a New Order phenomenon. Many of the pop musicians are also film actors. In contemporary Indonesian movies this view of money is played out again. These movies tend to be full of soap opera-like complications that always resolve themselves in the end. In the movie "Seputih Hatinya, Semerah Bibirnya" (Her lips as red as her heart is white), a son marries someone other than custom allows and lives apart from his family. After a number of episodes, for no particular reason, the son, his wife, and their baby are reconciled with the son's family. In "Dibalik Kelambu" (Behind the mosquito net) a man lives with his in-laws. His brother-in-law is considerably more successful than he is. He himself does not make enough to move out to his own house. This movie, too, ends with all families reconciled. In these movies and most others, catastrophe follows catastrophe, but in the end everything works out. In this first movie, the son and his family move back into his original household; in the second, the daughter and her husband move out. It does not matter what the substance of the reconciliation is. Nor does anything in the plot justify the rectification of so many complications. What apparently makes everything seem reasonable is that the parts are played by celebrities. These are people who are known in their own lives to have achieved "success," that is, to have the means to live as they wish. One has only to posit the conflation of the actor and his role to understand people to say, "If that is Rano Karno [an actor], things can't go wrong."

Talent implies the sort of direct expression (*mengespriskan*) that would be forbidden in Javanese. The outpouring of emotion that one sees in popular music is not far removed from the direct expression of emotion in greed and squandering that makes money such a difficult subject for Javanese men. In contemporary Indonesia, bringing wealth more fully into the acceptable social world depends on the sort of reformulation of emotions within language that the popular music scene furnishes. But it depends as well on presenting wealth as benign, as not, for instance, being at the expense of the poor or of the autonomous identity of persons. These questions are evaded on the pop scene.

The huckstering of the editors seldom seems to make *Topchords* readers think that the magazine is put out for money and not for worthier causes. The closest any published letter comes to expressing such an idea is a letter we shall take up later from someone who called himself a "cynical ex-detester" who thought it was impossible to play the guitar by the method *Topchords* offered and considered anyone who bought the magazine "stupid"[17]— "stupid," presumably, for wasting their time and their money and getting nothing in return. But to claim that the organizers of the "Topchords Pop Music Society" were in it for the money would seem to arouse no sense of outrage. In the world of *Topchords*, success and money are unthinkable without each other.

Western and Indonesian popular music are listed under separate headings in the *Topchords* tables of contents. Similarly there are separate rubrics for Indonesian and Western musicians. Until March 1980, Western songs were listed first. At that time the number of Indonesian songs was increased, and they were given first place in the listings. Still, the hierarchy that pertains and that determines the position of *Topchords* itself was in no way upset. Western popular music is sometimes a model, but it is more often treated as an influence. Indonesian songs are not supposed to be identical to Western ones, but rather to absorb external influences and pass them along to the fans. Next down the hierarchy come the fans themselves, who are often called a "barometer." They are said to "accept" musical efforts, the indication of which of course is the number of cassettes sold.

An album is "put into orbit" or "thrown onto the market." One does not hear of failures in *Topchords*. Whatever is sent orbiting seems always to stay up. *Topchords* publishes a list of "World Hits," but it publishes no equivalent for Indonesian music. The "fierce competition" that it reports in Jakarta is not reflected in monthly standings. And even the "World Hits" column gives only current ratings, so that tendencies could only be traced on the initiative of individual readers.

One reason for not ranking Indonesian songs is probably lack of sales figures. The editors claim that they publish the songs readers write to them about, though considering the absence of song titles in published letters that seems a little hard to believe. In place of rankings, *Topchords* features a few songs in the "Hallo Fans" column adjacent to the table of contents. However, the editors do not seem to try to be arbiters of what is currently popular or about to become so. Nor do they give much inside information about the stars. They present themselves rather as registers of their fans' likes, the barometer made visible. But also, by listing current Western hits, they track the weather conditions, as it were, that will send the barometer up later. (It never goes down.)

One sees the results in statements such as that of Reynold:

The public evaluates. But I have tried to find a distinctive style in music too. For instance by inserting a drum synthesizer in the middle of songs. This was indeed my intention because in the West this instrument is at the moment at the very top, especially in disco.[18]

Reynold finds his style by being influenced from abroad. In doing so he indicates the way in which the popular music scene is thought of as a national scene. As in school curricula, the content may be largely international. But there is communication on a national scale in which something is passed in one direction. It is this line of communication between national stars and national fans that makes people feel that pop music is national music today.[19]

The authority of the *Topchords* editors comes from making themselves the place where communication between stars and fans becomes visible. It is not a question of individuals liking certain songs available on the market, but of their seeing that their tastes collectively make them fit a social category and thereby make them actors on the popular music scene. They may buy a cassette or play the guitar. But reading *Topchords* they see that such acts have a certain power over the stars themselves. They determine what songs will stay in orbit.

This schema, however, depends on innovation having a locus. It should come from the stars, as they themselves turn to foreign influences. Some popular movements, however, especially the musical style known as *dangdut*, threaten to disrupt the hierarchy. *Dangdut*, known sometimes as *Orkes Melayu*, began to be popular in the early 1970s. It was and is considered "hickish" or low-class (*kampongan*). The very label meant that it was not "national." It might be (but it is not the case) that in every village in Indonesia villagers like to listen to *dangdut*. But that would only have made it more confined to villages and thus not "national." To become "national," it had to enter the pop music circuit, as it since has.

The entry of *dangdut* into the "music scene" (*blantika musik*) was perhaps most furthered by a Muslim singer named Rhoma Irama, who tends to compose and sing songs with a heavy "religious" content.[20] He became known as "King Dangdut" as his songs became immensely popular. It should not be thought that Rhoma Irama simply sang what villagers were already hearing. He insists, according to *Topchords*, that he revived the *dangdut* genre by infusing it with foreign elements. When he first began playing the music, according to him, *dangdut* was "almost dead." *Topchords* comments that Rhoma Irama tried "to energize the music and made it dynamic." Rhoma Irama himself is quoted as saying, "I and my friends mixed in hard or rock music to preserve that music. And thanks be to God the public accepted my sort of music."[21]

Public acceptance did not make the music less popular in villages or neighborhoods; rather the reverse. But it came about only when "that music" was transformed into "my sort of music" by the addition of Western forms. *Dangdut* became part of the circuit of stars and fans when someone who became the agent of foreign influences made it so.

It perhaps could not have been otherwise. For a star to be a star, which means to "express" his "talent," he must add something new. The significance of "the West" is that it is outside national boundaries and thus a convenient source of what is not yet Indonesian, of what is "new." The musician seems to find something inside himself: "It flashed through his marrow," *Topchords* reports about Rhoma Irama, "that he would break down [*mendobrak*] that music [*dangdut*] with other character and forms."[22] He is the site of inspiration; "other character and forms" come to him from outside, from "the West."

Nothing less traditional could be imagined. But when *Topchords* asked him why he turned to *dangdut*, he replied that it was "about to die," and that he wanted to "preserve this music."[23] ("*Melestarikan*," "preserve," is the same word used for the preservation of the environment.) One thus has the spectacle of a traditional form being torn down and infused with foreign elements in the interest of pre-

serving it. This, however, is not a paradox; it is not ethnological preservation but preservation by being kept as
(actually made part of) a national interchange. And to
achieve this it had first to be made to seem to come from
outside. In this way, pop music is national music, part of
a "heritage" that is passed down. It is passed down, that
is, so long as it is recognized as being influenced from
some other place. What makes it "national" music is the
boundary that is drawn between the circuit of communication of singers and fans on the one side and the source
of that influence, across national borders, on the other.

This boundary also governs the notion of success. *Topchords*, as I have said, reports little about the current lives
of stars. It does, however, have a gossip column that tells
fans about the lives of Western singers, implying sex
changes, drug scandals, etc. I do not believe that readers
are supposed to infer that Indonesian stars are no different. Rather, following the common belief of provincial *remaja*, foreigners have no morals. On the foreign side of
the line is wildness; on the national side, success. The
conversion of one into the other is the interplay of talent
and chance.

One senses the unease *dangdut* caused by not originating from abroad but from inside Indonesia; it provoked a
good deal of concern about the motivation of the singers.
The article on Reynold begins:

> It is not just small fry singers who have begun to jump
> into the *dangdut* cauldron. Recently it has also been sev-
> eral pop/rock big fish who have begun to plunge in.
> This indeed is not the fault of anyone; it's surely merely
> individual character. But as a layman of course you can
> only guess at the background which made him flee there.
> Popularity, money, or are there other motivations?[24]

It is not conceivable that a pop singer who began singing
in a Western genre would awaken such suspicion. It would
merely be taken as the chance that awakens talent.

But if *dangdut* is upsetting to the people in *Topchords* who depend on the stability of the terms that define hierarchy to have a place of their own, popular music in turn might be a threat to the culture that produces not only *dangdut* but other peasant forms.

It is by no means clear that *Orkes Melayu* was "almost dead" before Rhoma Irama (and others) transformed it into *dangdut*. Frederick, citing John Goldsworthy, notes that "the Melayu tradition had continued to develop, far from the capital and its critics."[25] The strength of these popular forms is itself a challenge to the notion of "national" music. Their continued viability makes them the target of "nationalization." The nature of the conflict is clear: popular music, like public education, sets up a system in which knowledge and forms of expression are nationalized. In doing so, there is an implicit claim that the "new" takes shape in the interaction of talent, foreign influences, and chance. This contrasts with Javanese notions, which imply that everything that does not belong within the social hierarchy stems from the realm of the spirits. We have seen that Sri Mulat features "Mrs. Draculla from Abroad" and thereby pulls the foreign into the *anéh*. The continued strength of popular forms that are not part of the circuit of fans and celebrities seems to deny the claims of "talent."[26]

We can continue to trace the popular music circuit by turning back to the letter from the "ex-detester" of *Topchords*. The complete letter, including the editor's heading, reads:

I used to hate the *Topchords*, But now . . . . . . I can't waittttt
I am an ex-detester of *Topchords* and it used to be I was cynical [*sinis*] whenever anyone would buy *Topchords* because in my opinion, that buyer was stupid. Couldn't even look for the chords [much less find them]. But

gradually I bumped into [was able to play] songs with strange chords. I began leafing through friends' *Topchords* and it turned out I was struck by the with-it-ness of [you] my elder brothers [at *Topchords*] in listening for and searching out the chords of a song.

We say thanks loads for your consideration and for publishing my letter. Arban-sma loyala Semarang.[27]

The word he used, *ketanggar*, which I have translated "bumped . . . into," means in fact "to bump into something while reaching for something else." He had made certain sounds, the sounds of the songs; merely by striking the guitar he came up with "strange" (*anéh-anéh*) sounds. What makes them *anéh-anéh* is that in retrospect they turn out to be the intended chords of the *Topchords* diagram. What is strange is not the sounds, but that, without at first knowing how he was doing it, he found what *Topchords* intended him to find. Between his knowledge and intentions and the instructions of *Topchords* there was initially no connection. Accidentally a connection occurred; he could then read the chords.

The implication of his letter is that before he learned to read the diagrams he was alone with his own thoughts. These thoughts were unclear to him. But he struggled to bring them to expression. When he learned to read the chords, he turned from a "detester" to a *Topchords* fan. In his mind, he was not by himself at all as he learned his new skill. The fact of his letter to *Topchords* indicates that he felt that he learned to read chord diagrams with *Topchords* as an audience. It is as though when his thoughts crystallized and he could play the guitar, he expected *Topchords* to hear him. That is why he wanted *Topchords* to know about it.

Without *Topchords* he would be merely blundering. His chords, accidental or not, would have corresponded to little, the way one's casual humming does not mean much. He might have struck the same chords that appear in the magazine, but without his possession of *Topchords* or something like it (such as confirmed knowledge of the song), he would merely be making motions that would not register, because he would have no way of knowing if they were right. He is a former detester of *Topchords* because he remembers a moment of embarrassment, of not having the sounds he produced register with anyone, himself included, and thinking, nonetheless, that in some way he was present in the eyes of *Topchords*. He would have thought of himself as talking to himself, but of doing so in the presence of someone else. Having learned to read the chord diagrams, he feels that he is no longer talking to himself, but that he still is within *Topchords'* range of view.

Topchords is a fan magazine. It is therefore not obvious why the bulk of its pages should be taken up with chord diagrams, which, to one reader at least, take up too much space.[28] But the chord diagrams, more than the lyrics alone, make *Topchords* into the place where the musical language that pertains between stars and fans appears. The listings of songs and the fan letters make visible the "barometer" of popularity frequently mentioned by the musicians. Musicians "launch" or "toss out" recordings. They are shown to create a reaction, not merely with sales figures, but by having their music and themselves appear in *Topchords*. When fans learn to play the guitar and to follow the magazine's diagrams, they too make sounds that register within the popular music hierarchy. The chords make the pop hierarchy appear to be a circuit in which fans not only hear music but produce what otherwise might only wander vaguely through their minds. Fans thus produce a circuit between themselves and stars, a circuit that is assumed when fans write in for the addresses of stars and of fashion models or when, at the end of articles about musicians, *Topchords* gives their addresses.

"I used to be cynical when someone bought *Topchords* because in my opinion that buyer was stupid."[29] The buyer was stupid not because he could not learn how to read diagrams, but because *Topchords* could not help him to do so. He was "stupid" in the sense that he got nothing for his money; he squandered it. But if the buyer is not stupid, he learns to play the guitar, become a *remaja*, and see himself favorably in the eyes of others. The possibility of this not happening is the separation of money from exchange (nothing is gotten back) and the emergence of talking to oneself in the presence of others (as one tries unsuccessfully to match one's efforts to the diagrams), all occurring at once.

No one accuses *Topchords* of doing what they do only for the money. Nor would an accusation that by doing what they do the editors get rich seem to have any weight. To make such an accusation would raise the possibility that, whether one is listening or singing, one is doing so futilely—that one is really talking to oneself.

Fashion plays a part in the circuit of stars and fans. Musicians' fashionable looks are the subject of commentary. When Reynold played for The Mercy's his hair was "scattered over his forehead." He is furthermore said to be "unusually warm, with handsome features and an athletic, pop-style (*ngepop*) body."[30] Photographs show the dress of the stars, but this is little commented on. For a magazine that sells clothing, there is very little in the way of description. At most the anonymous column on the first page that announces the featured songs of the month also announces featured fashions:

> Hallo fans . . . . . Topchords Fashion this time sends ten new models into orbit; among them the Monte Carlo Jacket which we crown "Top Fashion of the Month" [in English]. A jet-set creation ala Shaun Cassidy made of shiny parasit-acrylic. It's popular in formula racing in the world racing arena, Monte Carlo.[31]

The "Centerfold" containing colored photos of these styles, however, often does not attempt to play on the connotations of the names. Underneath each photo is the name of the article and a description of the sort that might appear in an American mail-order catalogue. There is a list of these articles and others for sale under the rubric "Buy by Money Order":

Acapulco Shirt: Material: delicate burn-out [in English] Model: Singapore combination collar, flying bird sleeves, zebra-cross motif. Colors: blue, brown, black. Price Rp 3900 (Jakarta Rp 4290).

T-Shirt Jean Belle: Material: Delicate TC. Model: split personality [in English followed by an Indonesian approximation] Dr. Jekyll and [in English] Mr. Hyde, belted. Color: black-white, dark orange-white. Price: Rp 2850 (Jakarta Rp 3135).[32]

There are about fifty articles listed for sale in each issue of *Topchords*, most of them the same as in the previous issue. About a third of the fashion names are place names, all of them foreign. The others refer to music (O'Dolly, Gilbert O'Sullivan), or to clothes (Jacket VIP), fashion (Elegance, Charmant, Chic '78 [this in issues from 1980], Stylistic) or such miscellaneous names as Coca-Hash and Don't Touch II.

These names, like the clothing itself, at least to my eyes, have an indeterminant character. They refer in nearly every case to something or someplace foreign that is unlikely to be known to the reader of *Topchords*. For that reason, there is no attempt to correct such anomalies as noting that the Acapulco shirt has a "Singapore collar" or that the "Wembly T Shirt" is "Amsterdam Pop," or to disentangle such agglomerations as Charles Da Vinci. Foreign words, even when translated, are likely to remain meaningless, as with "split personality," which is followed by "Dr. Jekyll and Mr. Hyde." Similarly the photographs themselves are mostly without context. Usually there is no identifiable location. Occasionally, however, the "location" of the photos will be named. In such cases it is a place of some prestige such as the "Mangkunegaran Palace Hotel" in Solo.[33] But there is no recognizable feature of this hotel in the photos. The corridor shown in one picture, for instance, is without distinguishing marks.

Remaja fashions are not presented as appropriate for any particular setting. One should keep in mind that Indonesian students are required to wear uniforms in school, so that the most common setting for the wearing of student fashions has been eliminated. The reason usually given for the requirement to wear uniforms is that otherwise the wealthy would shame the poor. This reasoning is somewhat spurious in that the requirement to buy uniforms works a great deal of hardship on the less well-off, even keeping some out of school. The logic, however, is related to the Indonesian fear of what they call "unhealthy competition," that is, the display of agonistic individuality.

One sees in *remaja* fashions what is suppressed in school. But fashion amongst *remaja* is less standardized than in similar Western circles; the question is not so much what is out of fashion as what is in. There is individualism with less competition than one might expect. It is true that *remaja* might accuse each other of being "out-of-date" (*kuno; ketinggalan jaman*). But *Topchords* does not pretend that everything they sell is new with that issue. There is a stock of fashions available so that an item might be featured in each issue for six months or more, while some items have been listed for more than a year.

The seeds for a more highly competitive situation exist. That is does not actually evolve is due to the lack of a clear standard of what is fashionable and what is not. This, in turn, has to do with the lack of clear models. We have seen that the appearance of the stars is described. It is therefore surprising that little or nothing is said about their clothes. The list of fashions in *Topchords* occasionally includes the names of certain stars, but these are invariably Western. (Indianapolis . . . Model: maskulin ala Steven McQueen" or "Alpine Blouse . . . Model: Vivien de Maupassant" or the "Monte Carlo Jacket, Shawn Cassidy model.") In no issue of *Topchords* available to me does an Indonesian star appear as a "model." Furthermore, the names of Western "models" are not always known to *Topchords* readers. One wonders about Vivien de Maupassant, Maurice Valency, Jean Belle, Dino Rossi, Alain Sarazin, Guy Marchais, Julien Meinard, or Niki Lauda. What all these names indicate is simply that the model comes from somewhere that the wearers know nothing about. If the clothes are meant merely to come from the outside, they need only be recognizable for their strangeness. This allows for a great deal of variation.

The lack of metaphoric description and absence of pictorial context suggest that fashions do not get linked to elaborate fantasies. They remain foreign entities that simply "show up" (*muncul* or *nongol*) in the pages of *Topchords* or in the city's store windows. Their "context" is always to seem to have come from elsewhere. In the sense that *remaja* simply come across them "by chance," fashions fit in their lives somewhat the way that "chance" or "FAKTOR X" does in the lives of the stars. No matter what their plans, something seems to happen accidentally, and it is always beneficial. In that sense, the fantasy that is attached to clothes is not the fantasy of being a star oneself, which explains why so very little is said in *Topchords* about the current lives of the stars. It is rather the fantasy of having "chance," of having "FAKTOR X" suddenly occur in the *remaja* so that he or she will have a biography, or will have one sometime in the future. It is a fantasy of knowing that, later, one will become "someone."

Remaja, unlike "adolescent," is not a family term. It comes as a result of the depoliticization of youth in the New Order. In that sense it replaces the Indonesian term *pemuda* ("youth"), a term whose sense always includes political activity of the sort that the Suharto regime has made difficult.[34] It is tempting to make *remaja* the equivalent of adolescent. However my own observations in Solo show that the familial dimensions of such a role are not great. A *remaja* behaves in the same way as children of a generation or two before him in regard to his siblings. Nor is it clear that relations with parents have changed, at least in regard to the notion of *remaja*. There is very little, for instance, in popular music or in *remaja* talk about parents.

It is this isolation of the status *remaja* from familial roles that helps to allow for an accommodation between Javanese and Indonesian notions of hierarchy. Javanese tries to accommodate Indonesian and vice versa, but in their ultimate justifications, they are at odds with one another. When, however, one can be a *remaja* and not have it affect one's behavior as a "Javanese" within the family, one is free to make accommodations outside the family. Thus *remaja* is a notion that pertains between *remaja*, and only to a small degree affects the relations of *remaja* to adults or small children.

Remaja may be relatively free of conflict with their parents. Nonetheless the strong impulsive life associated with adolescence is found also in *remaja* music. That it does not lead to conflict may be because although the music itself is the type to suggest to Indonesians *goyang* or "hip-swinging," the lyrics are different.[35] Rhoma Irama, for instance, sings mainly about religion ("Mankind has forgotten its Creator" goes "Nafsu Serakah" ["Greed"]). But most popular songs are love songs infused with pathos:

"When will you come back? I don't know how to contain my loneliness."

("Kapankah" ["When"] by Usbros).

"The seasons pass, hot, cold and rain . . . [but she] waits for the season of love with him, none other than him."

("Musim Cinta" ["Love Season"] by Dewi Puspa).

"Lonely and by myself, no life-long friend."
("Rindu dalam kesunyian" ["Lonely and Empty"] by
Hetty Koes Endang).

"Why so sad? There's no reason. There's no use in being
so sad, these days will pass. Sometime you'll understand the meaning of love. Later a time will come, you
will come back."
("Untukmu" ["For You"] by Lenny Bahar.)

Such pathos mimics strong feelings pent up. Thus Hetty
Koes Endang sings of having "no life-long friend"; she
"suffers," and "my lonely heart stores up your love." The
pathos is the source of reserve.

This reasoning leads us to examine the attitude of *Topchords* readers towards the fashions they want. They use
a strange word, *panasaran*, which in ordinary Indonesian
speech means "frustrated," "embittered," "irritated," or
sometimes "fed up." Thus one reader says, "Recently I
was *panasaran* by your models, which always appear (*nongol*) in the centerfold of your magazine to promote *Topchords* products, especially Fashions." He (or she) goes on
to ask for their address.[36] When he says he is *panasaran*,
he means he wants badly to know the models. In *remaja*
slang, *panasaran* retains the meaning "frustrated" in the
sense that a certain desire has not yet found its fulfillment. This, for instance, is the traditional usage in the
phrase *mati panasaran*, "to die frustrated," said of someone who wants something badly but who dies before he
or she gets it and whose soul consequently roams the earth
after death trying to fulfill that desire. But the sense of
embitterment is lost in *remaja* usage. What is retained is a
sense of desire that will at some time or other find its way
to its object.

It is not only the word *panasaran* that takes on this new
sense; so do its synonyms, such as *gemes*, which accord-

ing to Anderson in its former usage meant "'angry' but ordinarily refers to an irresistable desire to touch something adorable—this touching taking the form of an often painful pinch."[37] One letter writer says, "We are more and more *gemes* to see your increasingly sweet face [a traditional rhetorical figure] . . . which was recently embellished by your fashions which have so many admirers."[38] He goes on to ask how he can become an agent for them. By *gemes* the writer means he feels he lacks something; he cannot be called disappointed since he has not accepted his lack. Rather he feels desire stored up within him. A similar word is *keqi* or *keki* ("upset," "angry"), which is used by the following writer as a synonym for *panasaran*:

> Each time I open the *Topchords* centerfold I am sure to meet new designs which really attract the tastes of young people these days. They penetrate me and make me upset [*keqi*] about them, even to the point of being *panasaran*.[39]

The reader expects to meet "new designs" that he will want. His expectation precedes whatever design he will later see. He wants an indeterminant something first. Then, meeting it, he feels a comfortable surprise as though he has come across something that he had not known he was looking for in any precise way. He is then in a position similar to the guitar player who, trying to read the *Topchords* diagrams, "bumps into" "strange" chords by accident. But these strange chords are the ones he is supposed to play. Similarly the reader who is *panasaran* has found the design he did not know he had been hunting for. At that moment he sees himself dressed in *remaja* fashion, a *remaja* in the eyes of *Topchords*.

Looking back on the traditional Javanese notion of the image, one sees that it functions differently for *remaja* than for other Javanese. It is no longer a question of a facade behind which one can find the realm of the *anéh*. But in both cases imagery functions to promote reserve. In the case of older people, it is an aid to notions of respect because it recalls the foundation of respect in fear; it thus promotes a sense of an unspoken reserve. For *remaja* it is by identification with fashion imagery that reserve is generated. The sense of *panasaran* comes from "accidentally" coming across something and wanting it. It is a form of the "chance" that *Topchords* says is the determining factor in musicians' careers. Popular music itself, in the sense that a fan "comes across" it and wants it, is comparable. It raises a sense of potential unreleased energy.

In that sense it marks "FACTOR x." But it differs in that *remaja* as yet have no biography. Fashion and music for them is the potential for biography. Experiencing *panasaran* is practicing for chance, as it were. It proves "it" will happen to you. As potential for biography, fashion and music have to be seen in the context of school. It is the Indonesian public schools that make students feel they are in a privileged relation to the future. But, like most students perhaps, the relation between that education and life outside school is murky. In the absence of the political life of their predecessors, students, liking music and fashion, can find the sign of their own biography in them. It is for this reason that *remaja* are the first element of Solo's population to be struck by a Western notion of fashion.

The isolation of the status *remaja* from other statuses held by the same person affects its cultural attributes. It means there is very little consolidation of fashion, for instance. Ben Anderson has pointed out that *Topchords* fashions are never ensembles.[40] Anything goes with anything else in the same way that the locales in which they are worn do not combine with fashionable clothes to create a single psychological effect. There is not much need to try to integrate clothes and music with the rest of one's life. At the same time, the notion of "career" may be the means for generating a notion of biography, but there is not yet full-scale acceptance of the idea. Thus popular music does not draw on memories any more than *remaja* fashion does. The music usually has a sentimental quality. But if one follows the reference of the tunes, it leads not to earlier Indonesian music, but to unknown outside influences. It is like memory that ends in blankness. In the same way, Indonesian popular music is for the most part sung by adults for teenagers. It is not likely that these teenagers have had the experiences of love and loss that the songs center around. It is more likely that teenagers would like to have had such experiences. It is as though they would like to have had a past to go with the biography they hope for. This results in an indeterminateness of notions such as *panasaran*. They point to reserve in the way that I indicated, but they are considerably less precise than comparable notions in traditional Java. One sees as well the fluidity of market and money as clothes and music come and go. *Remaja* seem barely able to consolidate this randomness.

Given these qualifications, I would like to stress how different *remaja* notions are from traditional ones. The degree of difference is seen by comparison with *karawitan*, Javanese traditional music. *Karawitan* is mainly ritual music. It does not much matter whether anyone listens or not. No one hearing it has to give any sign that they are affected by it. The music *remaja* listen to, by contrast, seems to pass through them; it matters to them that it does so. This accounts for the popularity of the guitar, which actualizes the melodies that wander through their minds. For all the indeterminateness, *remaja* notions of person, music, and fashion make it clear that *remaja* have the fantasy of an integrated self, distinct from its environment and affected by it.

A decided change in the conception of language comes with the notion of *remaja* and their "expressiveness." This change can be seen by comparison with traditional Indonesian literatures, Javanese or others. In traditional thought, speaking well is conflated with acting well. To speak very well is to imagine an entire hierarchy, a state with a king and nobles. The fantasy of the state and the conception of reserve in language are linked. To speak properly is to hold something back; to pay respect is to be reserved; respect is the basis of hierarchy; hierarchy is imaged in the notion of the state. Javanese is probably the regional language in which this paradigm is most explicit, but it is not lacking in Malay or Acehnese, to name the other Indonesian languages with which I am familiar.

With the rise of popular music the connection between speaking well, acting well, and a totalized hierarchy is broken. In its place there is one's "own" language, the language of "expression." Politics are not entirely missing from popular songs. There are songs about the environment, for instance, or songs that sympathize with peasants and try to imagine their lives. In traditional literature, such attempts at imagining the lives of another would be out of place. Imaginings of this sort reflect the sense that one might be able to change places with someone of radically different status and that the status itself is something created by effort and by "expression."

One sees the hierarchical difference in the distinction of "habit" and "taste." Javanese lacks a word for "habit" that does not include the sense that the content of the habitual is part of tradition. The reason that Javanese speakers insist that every act they habitually perform has been passed down to them, even when such acts are by no means standardized, is that the alternative would be to think that their "habits" are their own products. Such personal habits would be their own fictions, the gestural equivalent of *Ngoko*, and thus incapable of being positively reflected back to them; they prefer believing that their habits show that they know how to defer, no matter how eccentric the actual practice.

Musically, the traditional equivalent is forms about which one is not expected to have an opinion. Traditional Javanese music (*karawitan*) is mainly ritual music. One is not supposed to like it or dislike it. But popular music depends entirely on taste (*selera*), a notion new to Java. "Taste" is mainly talked about in *Topchords* by the editors and the stars and relatively rarely by the fans in the letter column. *Panasaran*, reflecting surprise, is more often used than a notion such as "taste," which implies thoughtfulness and considered judgment. But the idea that something is "meant" for one or not remains in both cases.

Notions of "taste," of *panasaran*, and of "habit" come with the change of language that is marked by popular music. Underlying them is the conception of accession to language seen in the classroom, seen in learning to read chord diagrams, and seen again in being affected by fashion. These new notions require new circuits of exchange. The creation of a circuit of fans and stars shows that one has not wasted one's efforts by sending out signals that were never receivable. The assumptions about language seen in *remaja* songs and fashion require that the circuit not be broken by, for instance, a relapse in which, although one is still being seen by others, one feels one's words do not reach anyone, that one is blundering wildly.

CHAPTER NINE

Money Comes Into View:
Students, Their Fashions, and Chinese

ON WEDNESDAY, November 19, 1980, as students from the
School for Sports Teachers in Solo were returning home,
according to the newspaper *Suara Merdeka*, one of them,
riding a bike, ran into a Chinese youth.[1] There was a fight
in which the Chinese, helped by a friend, struck the student with a rock. The next morning students from the
school involved began hunting down the Chinese youth.
Not finding him, they stoned Chinese shops and homes
on the street where the incident had taken place. This was
the beginning of riots that spread throughout Solo, ending only the following Monday in the city but continuing
after that in several places in Central Java. In Solo two
students were killed by government forces. One Chinese
was said to have died of a heart attack when a gang of
youths burst into his home. In other places casualties were
greater, with deaths occurring in the port city of Semarang.

Police stopped the demonstrators on Thursday, November 20. Two university students later confessed that
they had prompted the School for Sports Teachers students to continue their anti-Chinese activities despite their
promise to the police not to do so. They admitted planning further demonstrations involving students from Surakarta's other high schools. Students were to mass on the
street where Chinese dealt in gold. They confessed they
also planned to distribute pamphlets, though no one in
my experience ever saw examples of these.[2]

Events surpassed these plans.[3] On Friday, November
21, more Chinese stores and homes were pelted with

stones, though in the same vicinity as the earlier incidents. Police broke up these demonstrations more than
once. Toward midnight, however, a student who had been
wounded by police died. Major rioting occurred on Saturday and Sunday. Youths lined the streets in the areas
of the Chinese shops. One youth was shot, whether by
police or by army troops is unclear. His body, carried
through the main street in the open back of a police pickup
truck, was visible to the youths lining these thorough-
fares. Truckloads of paratroop elite from nearby Kartasura
also cruised the main streets. (Shops were open Saturday
morning but had their windows shuttered on orders of
the police, who had told merchants on Friday to expect
trouble for the next few days.)

Though the streets were filled with later-to-be-demon-
strators on Saturday morning, there was little activity until the afternoon. For the most part, youths stood around,
often with motorbikes parked on the curbs, apparently
waiting. They tended not to move about, but to stay in
one place. They struck me at the time as waiting, but
without tension, as though something might happen, but
then again it might not. Either way it seemed all right to
them. They were in no hurry and displayed no particular
excitement. They did not exhaust what there was to see
and then move on, as though they were seeking out the
places where something was happening or about to happen. A newspaper report put it as follows:

> authorities continued to exercise surveillance and to di-
> rect groups who still often gathered in various places,
> such as happened Thursday night when many of them
> who were sitting aimlessly on vehicles [meaning motor-
> bikes] or on the railing of the Pasar Gede bridge. When
> asked by officials they answered they just wanted to
> look.[4]

An American with long experience in Solo who travelled
one such road wrote, "I had the eerie experience of
watching the 30 kilometers stretch between Klaten [be-

tween Solo and Jogjakarta] literally filled with people sitting, standing, staring as if watching a parade that wasn't there."[5] Youths appeared to be looking but, since they tended to stay in one place and since the shops were shuttered, their looking appeared to me to be without object.

Saturday afternoon, youths began stoning most business areas and continued to do so until rain brought them to a stop later that evening. Early Sunday morning I rode for three hours through the main streets without once seeing an unshuttered pane of glass on a Chinese residence or store that was unbroken.

One feature of this riot was its specific trajectory. First was the period of waiting and looking, which lasted for several hours on Saturday morning. This was followed by the breaking of glass, unaccompanied by much other damage. Of course glass is particularly vulnerable, but there were other possible targets, particularly since rioters often had hours before being bothered by government forces. In one case a metal sign was bent out of shape. In another, students broke through the wooden shutters of a Chinese shop across from the place where they had rented cars for the funeral of the first of their fellows to be killed. But only two other such incidents are known to me.

Only after they shattered all exposed glass did the rioters move on to other activities. On Sunday afternoon demonstrators broke into shops, dragged the inventories onto the street, and burned them. They also burned what they took to be Chinese-owned automobiles. On Sunday afternoon one could look in any direction and see columns of smoke. Police and army were active. One frequently heard shots. As troops arrived, however, youths scattered down the alleyways on motorbikes to reform in other places.

It was my impression on Sunday afternoon that rioting was bound to continue many more days, since demonstrators were so easily able to elude troops. However, by Monday morning the riot was over. By that time the main streets were nearly deserted. One saw only a few pedestrians and occasional army trucks, packed with troops firing warning shots or with prisoners.

Who were these demonstrators? That they included high-school students is indisputable, attested to as it is by the "confessions" and by the numerous students I spoke with then and later. On Saturday morning large numbers of students reported to school and then left to take to the streets. Youths tended to demonstrate in small groups from the same school. There were also many who were unidentifiable. These were youths who did not wear school uniforms, often because they were afraid of being identified, and sometimes because they were not students. The report of the Director General of the Ministry of the Interior began to list those arrested, but gave up after naming only 12.[6] Five of these were students, seven others were listed as "laborer" or "trader." They ranged in age from 14 to 22 with one other being listed as 30. My impression, impossible to verify, is that the bulk were students. For one thing, workers in Surakartan factories often are villagers who return home when not working. The unemployed from Solo who might have participated are likely to have had high-school education and to think of themselves, therefore, more as "students" or ex-students than by profession. Furthermore, the tendency of people I spoke with was to call the demonstrators "high-school students" (*pelajar*).

The riot had some odd features. For one, it was unaccompanied by slogans. No one painted signs on the houses or stores and, as I have mentioned, no printed material appeared in the experience of anyone I spoke with. Furthermore the stoning and burning was done in an unhurried, rather deliberate manner, similar to the way in which the thief I saw beaten was struck. There was calmness; one seldom heard shouts or verbal abuse. This deliberate character contrasts with the disavowal of any major aims other than expressing anti-Chinese feelings. Speaking with demonstrators at the time one could easily enough elicit anti-Chinese sentiments. These focused on the wealth of Chinese. The repeated charge was that Chinese refuse to assimilate to Indonesian ways, that it is not their country and yet they are wealthy whereas "we" are poor. The initial cause of the conflict, the fight between Chinese and Javanese students, was lost sight of after the first day.

Even later, demonstrators were unclear about their aims. Another American, friendly with three students in the compound in which she lived, at my request took down this interview, conducted in Indonesian, three weeks after the incident:

Questioner: "So, what were you after in the demonstrations?"

Student A: "In fact we really had no aims [tudjuan]." (Other two agree heartily.)

Student B: "It was just adolescent [remaja] business."

Student C: "It was only a question of emosi [from the English 'emotion,' meaning an outburst of strong feeling]."

The youths who came to the demonstrations did so because they heard there was going to be action taken against Chinese. Yet they could not seem to say what, exactly, they were expecting. It is not that the students whom I or others knew well wanted to deny their participation or were ashamed of it. It is rather that their actions to them had no precise goals, though their sentiments about Chinese were clear enough. Their attitude while they waited on the street for hours on end was one of "just looking," not in the sense of excusing themselves from the action, but in the sense of passively waiting for something to happen, something like the "just looking" of Javanese window shoppers. When they did act, their actions collectively took on form—first the breaking of windows, then the burning of goods—but this was unclear enough to them that they could not verbalize it, despite the general articulateness of many.

The riot was instigated by a traffic accident. We have seen that Solo's traffic regulations are not in the idiom of public rights but of hierarchical assumptions. It follows that the idiom of accidents is also hierarchical. There are, indeed, a great many accidents in Solo. On May 7, 1981, a school bus ran the red light at a railroad crossing. The ensuing accident resulted in 31 deaths. The crossing had been the site of several accidents. It was said that the spirits of previous victims waited there to claim more victims. Such stories are told after accidents occur. They do not do much to make the accidents explicable, however. The victim of a spirit, unlike the victim of God, is devoid of the comfort of being the instrument of a higher purpose.

The railroad crossing is not the only place that is said to be haunted. All along Solo's main streets there are well-known haunted spots. These sites are unavoidable; to pass through the city one must travel by them. The logic of this thinking seems to be that of the mountain picture. In the picture, well-being occurs in the presence of potential fright (*wedi*). The possibility of the emergence of a hidden presence is thought to frighten people into behaving acceptably. On the streets, spirits threaten accidents. In the context of Solo's chaotic traffic, such stories reassure, guaranteeing that people on the street will defer as they ought.

When accidents do occur, they generate a good deal of excitement. The story of the railroad accident reached my neighborhood ten kilometers away by word of mouth within an hour of its occurrence. It spread to at least several other distant parts of town in an equally short time. The urge to tell these stories is understandable; the accidents are expected in the sense that they confirm Solonese fears not of accidents themselves, but of the unexpected emergence of spirits into the world of hierarchy.

Early stories are about the accident; later stories concern the spirits. In the case of the bus accident, the tone of the stories was usually not grief at the death of so many children, but a quiet excitement, almost anticipation or pleasure. Like most spirit stories, they confirmed that the world has a certain order to it; "some people may not believe it, but that is the way it is," was the attitude. Hierarchy means that the ranked elements are kept in place. Accidents would seem to refute this. But by invoking spirits, stories of accidents in Solo confirm that the forces that promote order on most occasions are still present.

The accident that triggered the November riots brought to mind, not spirits, but "Chinese." Who are "Chinese" that all Chinese, not just the boys involved, should become the targets of the rioters? Anti-Chinese rioting in Indonesia is not new. It would be precipitous, however, to see all anti-Chinese sentiment as having the same source. Solo itself has been relatively free of anti-Sinitic violence. The last major incident occurred in 1910. The historian Shiraishi Takashi has shown that the events of 1910 involved Javanese competitors of Chinese batik merchants.[7] Javanese also complained that Chinese had boasted that soon ships from China would come to conquer Java, and therefore they wanted the Javanese to address them as "tuan." The boast about ships was an insult from the Javanese point of view, an arrogant refusal to accept the social order. However, in their massive survey of the batik industry done in the 1920s, de Kat Angelino and his colleagues noted that Solo was relatively free of the disruptions that marked the industry in the north coast of Java.[8] They attributed this to the ability of the long-settled Chinese community to adapt themselves to Javanese ways. Workers may not have been much better off, but they were not as often subjected to what Javanese considered insulting behavior. The historian James Rush has pointed out that the Javanese hinterland was monetized by the

Chinese.[9] This, however, did not lead to anti-Sinitic violence, apparently because Javanese and Chinese had an interest in suppressing it to continue the profitable opium trade in which both were engaged.

The events of 1980 in Solo were attributed to student activists. Students are perhaps the group who have least to do with Chinese. The Chinese are not allowed into the Surakarta public schools; Javanese students therefore never see them as fellow students. Students are ordinarily neither employees nor employers of Chinese. At most they see them in their neighborhoods. To the degree that neighborhoods had the close solidarity described in Chapter Two, Chinese were protected. The same youths who protected the Chinese in their own neighborhoods, however, often went out to stone Chinese residences and businesses on the main streets and in areas without effective local organization. Chinese and Javanese youths thus were free of nearly any significant relationship of any sort.

It has been often said that anti-Chinese violence in Indonesia occurs during periods of political suppression. The argument runs that anti-Chinese sentiment can be stirred up and used to show the weakness or inability of authorities to keep order. It is plausible to me that elements active on the national political scene took advantage of the incident in Solo. The chief of national intelligence, Admiral Sudomo, himself suggested as much. That it was university students who called the meeting to plan further demonstrations is itself suspicious. The university was not in session at the time except for one department, and for that reason youths often said that few university students took part in the demonstrations. It was as a result of the planning meeting that the heads of the student councils were notified to inform students in their schools to demonstrate. Without this coordinating effort, it is quite possible the events of Saturday and Sunday, the days of widespread window-smashing and burning, would not have occurred. That the demonstrations were not entirely spontaneous does not, however, explain why thousands of youths (the precise number is not known) responded to the call to demonstrate and did so on such short notice.

The accident that instigated the riots entailed no stories of spirits. It is remarkable that though the newspapers and radio reported that a Javanese student on a bike had run into a Chinese youth, the many rioters who told me the story all reversed it. According to them it was a Chinese on a motorbike who collided with a local student. Several times I was told that the Javanese student had been polite and tried to act civilly. The Chinese youth, however, was a recognized tough and responded violently. "Typical Chinese arrogance (*angkuh*)," said one person. Had the story not been turned around, had the person on the motorbike, the one responsible for the accident, been Javanese, it seems likely to me that ghost stories might have followed. The event would have been in the idiom of hierarchy disrupted, the revelation of what keeps hierarchy intact and its consequent restitution. Or quite possibly no stories of spirits, or of any kind, would need to be told, because for a Javanese to hit a Chinese would not upset the proper order of things. But when the story was reversed, social order was threatened, and yet spirits were not invoked to show that fundamentally there was no reason to be anxious.

As it was, the charge against the Chinese was that he was the aggressor and that his aggression was typical, the sort of behavior one could expect from Chinese. They refuse to assimilate, the tale continues; they follow their own ways; consequently, it is implied, one can expect them to be disruptive. These stories reflect a strange charge against Chinese. They are said not to be able to speak *Kromo*. This is not so in the cases I know about. The Chinese I know, shopkeepers, manufacturers, and even laborers, spoke adequate *Kromo*; though many were diffident about it, this is also true of Javanese themselves. Even in the case of a

Chinese who is a high-ranking official of the palace, adept at the language of the court, and in the face of experience in speaking with him, there were Javanese who refused to admit that he could speak High Javanese.[10]

When I inquired I found out that there had been a previous incident of fighting between Chinese and students, but on a small scale. It was not an incident known to all students; nor, in the minds of those who did know about it, did it amount to a history of feud or even rivalry. Unlike the grievances of Javanese laborers against their Chinese bosses, then, this incident could not be said to sum up resentments based in experience.

The reversal not only accused Chinese of disrupting order, it also made Chinese a sign of money. Not merely was there an accident, but in the reversed version the aggressor was rich (he was riding a motorbike), whereas the Javanese was poor (he was on foot). (In reality, the Chinese was on foot because he was poor.) Making the Chinese youth the aggressor in the accident and making him wealthy established a connection between the inability to control oneself, desire, and money. The connection is best seen by turning back to the notion of *pamrih*. Anderson says that "only in the light of the concept of *pamrih* can the attitude of many Javanese toward the accumulation of wealth properly be understood. Personal acquisitiveness, like sexual indulgence and political ambition, is one of the most obvious types of personal indulgence or *pamrih*. . . . Money in itself should never be the object of active pursuit. Wealth should flow to the holder of Power."[11] Because the Chinese youth lacked restraint, he was ruled by self-interest. Lacking detachment (*iklas*), he was associated with money.

I never heard the word *pamrih* in relation to Chinese themselves, no doubt because it is a word that was traditionally applied to warriors and figures of state and was considered too exalted a term for them. The recourse to money as the explanation for the behavior of Chinese, however, implies the notion. To the degree that such an assumption actually was in the minds of the rioters, the accident was kept within the bounds of hierarchical thinking. There need be no recourse to stories of spirits when, by invoking money, one could explain the accident within standard Javanese terms.

The accusation made against Chinese in general about their wealth is not that they made it by exploiting other Indonesians, but that they do not deserve it; it belongs to "the Nation." It is often said by those old enough to have the revolution within their experience that the Chinese betrayed the nation. Older people in Solo, for instance, often told me how, when the Republican forces established themselves in Jogjakarta, nearly all the Chinese fled the city, returning only when the Dutch retook it. People who tell this story are bitter. For them, Chinese cannot be trusted. Rather than help the nation when it most needed it, they deserted it. It does not mollify these people that some Chinese were active participants in the revolution. Our purpose is not to establish the historical facts, however, but to explicate what Javanese have made of them.

Javanese bitterness indicates that they had hoped for something different. The story implies that they had relied on Chinese to act otherwise. Their explanation for Chinese actions is money. They, the Chinese, acted out of narrow self-interest. That so many years later many Javanese are still so bitter reflects their sense of betrayal, rather as if they had, in talking with Chinese at the time, assumed a certain identity with them, only to find out that all the time Chinese were thinking in different terms. They tell the story as one of deception, as though never before that time would they have expected Chinese to act in ways governed by calculation.

Actions against Chinese after independence continue this thinking. During the Sukarno period, Chinese language schools were greatly reduced in number. The first two years of the New Order were marked by heavy anti-Chinese activity. For instance, Chinese language usage was further restricted. In particular, Chinese signs were banned, and Chinese language schools were entirely eliminated.[12] Anti-Chinese activity has to be put in the perspective of national politics, including divisions within the Chinese community itself and the role of the Indonesian Communist party and the army in acting for and against the Chinese. That anti-Chinese activity has wide popular support, however, is not merely a function of such politics. Action against the Chinese language, in particular, reflected a view of Chinese as incomprehensible and for that reason potentially dangerous. Regional languages are also mutually incomprehensible, yet there has never been a move to ban them, nor have their speakers ever been accused of being incomprehensible. The danger seen in Chinese is precisely that it is not a regional language. That it does not have an established place with respect to the national language. A place that might be viewed in the operations of the classroom, for instance, where it would be clear that Chinese could be reserved in favor of Indonesian.

The mythologized history of Chinese during the revolution is certainly one reason why Chinese languages have never been considered the equivalent of regional languages. But to be understood, this mythology has to include the equation of Chinese and money. The story of betrayal says that Chinese seemed to be like us, to be comprehensible, as we Indonesians are to each other. We may speak different regional languages, but as citizens we speak Indonesian. Chinese, too, speak Indonesian. But amongst each other they speak a language that is at odds with Indonesian, one they use in calculating personal advantage. The banning of indecipherable Chinese characters, visible to most Indonesians as shop signs, can be taken as the point where Chinese and money were most explicitly equated. The banning of Chinese characters can be seen as a means to curb the calculation of monetary interest that resulted in presumed Chinese wealth. It was a way of saying that outside of ordinary discourse there is another, secret discourse whose name is money. ("*Pamrih*," says Anderson, "is best translated as 'concealed personal motive.'"[13]) This is the language of deception, betrayal, and greed. "Chinese" at this point came to designate those incapable of social behavior because their language was incapable of being suppressed or reserved.

The equation of Chinese and money, however, can be made without accusations of the sort summed up by *pamrih*. The position of Chinese within Javanese neighborhoods, protected by their Javanese neighbors, illustrates the point. I have shown in Chapter Three that when Chinese are thought to follow Javanese customs it is taken as a sign of the superiority of Javanese ways rather than the conversion of Chinese into Javanese identity. Acceptance of Chinese in neighborhoods implies that the Chinese are capable of deference. Since they are charged with being unable to speak High Javanese and thus being incapable of deference in other contexts, one might ask why within the neighborhood things are different. One remembers that in the neighborhoods, one's "natural" language, Low Javanese in the the case of Javanese speakers, is made analogous to High Javanese by showing that there is a certain reserve in speaking it. The incomprehensibility of Chinese languages, as we have seen, is conflated with the mystery of money and calculation. "Money" is thus the "natural" language of Chinese. In the neighborhood, however, the Chinese are allowed to speak money in wholly acceptable fashion. They are the largest givers whenever there is a collection for any purpose. They thus demonstrate the control of their own language.

The complaint that remains about some of them is that they do not sufficiently socialize with their neighbors. The complaint assumes that they are capable of doing so. One must contrast this with the Javanese refusal to allow Chinese to enroll in Surakarta's public schools. In that context they are seen as rivals—a charge we will take up later. But the refusal also reflects the inability to consider Chinese itself as a "natural" language capable of being reserved. The public schools do not offer the same scope for the demonstration that the "natural" language of Chinese is, actually, reserved. In that context the charge of the students that Chinese are "arrogant" arises again.

The burning of goods with its implication of the disavowal of *pamrih* (others may steal, others may seek wealth; we display our lack of interest in it) ended the riot. One can describe this ending in hierarchical terms. Yet for several reasons the disavowal indicates that the riot exceeded hierarchical concepts. Thieves are beaten, Chinese shops are stoned. There is a similarity. But those who beat thieves had clearly defined aims: they intended to "teach a lesson." The stories of the origin of the riot included the attempt of Javanese students to come to terms with Chinese in a polite way. In these accounts, Javanese attempts at good manners were met with violence. The lesson of the riots was that Chinese should respect Javanese usages: they should not be "arrogant." But this initial aim was, by the admission of many rioters, lost sight of once the rioting began. The statement of those I spoke with that they had no aims makes their actions, at least after a certain point, different from the actions of those who beat thieves.

The position of Chinese within the community after the riot was precisely as it was before. Indeed, just after the riot, the demonstrators of the days before spoke with Chinese in the same polite way that they had before the riot began. The position of thieves after being beaten is made clear to them (if they are still alive) and to others. But the status of Chinese remained as before. In the case of thieves and those who beat them one can speak of mastery, by which I mean the consolidation of a position of superiority. In the case of Chinese there was no demonstration of mastery. What was demonstrated was students' repudiation of their own desire to own what Chinese possessed. The hierarchical meaning of the position of Chinese was not altered, nor was it even at issue. Student actions instead made an issue of their own moral status. They destroyed Chinese wealth not to shame Chinese, but to show that they were unlike them.

The possibility of being like Chinese is seen in the exclusion of Chinese from the Surakartan public schools. Surakartans I spoke with were curiously devoid of reasons for not admitting Chinese. The usual statement was, "It has always been like that." I had expected people to invoke the superior rights of indigenous Indonesians on the basis of the stories of revolution cited above. But I did not hear such reasoning. To keep Chinese out of the schools is to admit that Chinese and Javanese are in competition for the same thing. The "same thing" presumably is whatever school leads to: in the first place, jobs, particularly government jobs. But since the likelihood of Chinese becoming civil servants is extremely low, it is not necessary to keep them out of the schools for this reason. Nor do Javanese by and large want the jobs Chinese presently hold in the distributive sector. Javanese complain about Chinese wealth, but that is different from feeling that they would themselves like to become merchants. Even Javanese merchants often see schooling primarily as a way for their children to avoid becoming merchants themselves. Exclusion from public schools is more likely linked to the question of language we have already mentioned— to the inability of Chinese to adequately defer; to the fear that the Chinese act in terms of monetary calculation that cannot be adequately suppressed. To the degree that Chinese are considered rivals, it is not out of the likelihood that they will take the rightful place of Javanese.

Instead, keeping Chinese out of the public schools is a tacit admission that Javanese fear that Chinese will corrupt them into being like them. The story of the attempt to deal politely with Chinese and being rebuffed is a story of the failure of polite language. This repeats the scenario of *latah* as described in Chapter One. When people are unable to speak High Javanese, shock results in compulsion. We saw mimicry as a partially successful solution, when recourse to High Javanese was not possible. In the story of the origin of the riot, the Chinese youth replaced polite speech with blows. The Javanese youth responded in kind. When pressed, a few students after the riot spoke of *dendam*, "revenge." *Dendam* would again keep the riots within the boundaries of hierarchical thinking. But only a few students mentioned it, and only later. None spoke of *dendam* to me during the riots. Indeed, many disavowed it, repeating again that the riots had "no aims." The deliberate quality of the stoning of Chinese windows is a way of repeating something, mimicking it, in a form that makes it one's own, and thus is a way of ameliorating, if not entirely avoiding, the compulsion to repeat exactly. That Javanese responded in kind, violently, already suggests *latah*. Without the deliberate quality of their rock-hurling, Javanese students could have been accused of being exactly like Chinese (as they saw them): of acting entirely without self-restraint.[14]

The burning of Chinese goods was a disavowal. If it was a message, it was one rioters sent not to the Chinese but to themselves. The need to do so I believe follows from the lack of signification of the stoning. Had the stoning been a message to Chinese in the way that beating a thief is a message, there may have been no need for the subsequent disavowal. The rioters' repudiation of any interest in Chinese goods for themselves could have been achieved simply by ending the riot with the stoning. No goods would have been taken and hence no need aroused to disclaim an interest in them. Major looting occurred only late in the riot; it was not as if "students" had to distinguish themselves from "delinquent gangs" (*gali-gali*). Rather, the display of lack of *pamrih* was clearly intended to distinguish the students from Chinese. One heard little in the way of disavowal of the *gali-gali*, which would have indicated an interest in distinguishing them from *remaja*. The beating of thieves indicates who is a thief and who is a guardian of morality. This distinction is firmly consolidated when, as blows become language, it is thought that the thief has learned his lesson. When blows are mere violence and that violence resembles Chinese violence, something more is needed to differentiate the students from Chinese.

If one can believe those who confessed to instigating the riot, the original plan was only to demonstrate. In light of this it is necessary to ask again how, precisely, the riot began. The plan was for students to congregate in front of the Chinese-owned gold shops. In fact, students lined the streets wherever there were Chinese stores—not "Chinese" as in those who lived in their homes apart from shops or other work places, but "Chinese" as it was equated with stores. Wealth formed the setting of the riot— not wealth as meaning "gold" or whatever valuables were privately owned by the Chinese, but wealth in the form of commodities, the contents of the stores. The stoning of the shops was directed at the commodities behind the glass.

To see why the riot took this shape, one has to turn back to the difference between students and others. Students' relation to commodities is different from that of their elders. The difference is summed up by the difference between buying batik for traditional dress and buying an item of fashionable teenage wear such as, for instance, a T-shirt. Buyers of batik seem to have the feeling that the design of the cloth hides something. We have seen how Javanese speak of batik as though between the two identical designs on either side of the cloth there is "something else" or "someplace else," thus following the same logic as the geography of the spirits. To sense this realm and yet buy the cloth for "oneself" may be to identify oneself with whatever the cloth reserves. Traditionally patterns announced rank. Today, they announce the "alusness" or refinement of the buyer, the same quality that appears in the speaker of High Javanese. The "I" that buys the cloth is the reserved "I," analogous to the reserved "I" who speaks High Javanese.

Such batik is not imbued with the personality of the speaker. The visible cloth announces designs that are limited in number and generally recognized by Solonese. Because of their uniformity and because they are not tailored to the shape of the body, they can be borrowed and worn by others.

The "I" who sees himself as the owner of a particular T-shirt thinks differently. The T-shirt, its color, its trim, and so on, are thought to be suitable for him. Whatever it is that he sees as appropriate to himself is clearly displayed to others. This constitutes its "newness" and marks the wearer as involved in the contemporary scene. The display of newness in teenage fashion that is thought suited to its potential wearer makes such clothing less interchangeable than batik. The person of the wearer is intertwined with the garment, and thus it is most appropriately worn only by its owner.

For *remaja*, newness comes accidentally and takes the form of commodities. The contemporaneity of commodities confirms what students learn in school: that their education guarantees them a special access to the future, that they are the figures in whom the future will be embodied. When, however, through the working out of the events of the accident, commodities became identified with Chinese, the identification of *remaja* and commodities, already established, had to be disavowed. This is why rioting on a city-wide scale began with the gathering of *remaja* at Chinese shops and why their first action was against the glass, behind which sat commodities.

We can sum up the incidents of November 1980 in the following way. A Javanese student on a motorbike ran into a Chinese youth. At that point, the usual explanation for inexplicable traffic accidents, the intervention of spirits, was not invoked—no doubt because there was an equivalent in the connotations of "Chinese." The story was reversed: the Chinese became the rider of the motorbike and the aggressor. The Javanese youth's attempt to restore good relations through polite behavior failed. The Chineseness of the aggressor alone could account for the accident since "Chinese" could easily be equated with lack of proper behavior and speech, and with obsession with money. Making this identification, however, endangered *remaja* identification of their potential selves, their future, with commodities (a connection doubled by the involvement of "chance" both to instigate biography and to account for traffic accidents). It then became necessary to break the identification. The breaking of the identification explains the peculiar trajectory of the riots: first glass was broken, then goods were burned, then the riots ceased.

"It was just *remaja* business"; there was "no aim" to the riots. "No aim" means that there were no certain goals nor anything in particular that was to be conveyed to Chinese, which is understandable if the purpose was to break an identification between *remaja* and Chinese. This brings us back to the points where the identification was established: first when, after not being able to speak to each other, Chinese and Javanese involved in the accident fought, and second when, after students had spread themselves in front of Chinese shops and waited there the greater part of the morning, doing nothing much more than staring at shuttered shopfronts, the stoning began. The first incident is the failure of linguistic conventions that ordinarily pertain in Solo between Chinese and Javanese. The next invokes the imagery of commodities in the form they take in *remaja* fashions. It comes at the point where ordinarily *remaja* would have looked for "FAKTOR x," for "chance," to show them their own selves in the form of certain commodities. But in place of the benevolent "FAKTOR x" stood the shocking aggression of the story of the accident. It is at these points that violence without aim broke out.

We have said about the first incident that the violence of the *remaja* was a compelled imitation of the violence of Chinese. In the second incident, Chinese were hidden behind their shuttered windows and bolted doors. At that point it was not the violence of Chinese that instigated the *remaja* violence. It is rather that the identification established in the story of the incident led *remaja* to see themselves in the form of the commodities they ordinarily desired, to see themselves as wanting money or commodities just as they claim Chinese do. The "aimless" violence of the riots may have had the effect of breaking the identification of *remaja* and Chinese. Before it achieved that, however, it was an imitation of what *remaja* feared in Chinese and, thinking themselves to be like them, saw in themselves. It was the sort of *latah*-like behavior that is produced not by actual imitation of a model, but by the administration of a shock. It sets off the type of wild gesticulation that comes with such other aimless gestures as trying to learn to read guitar chords. It converts the desire for commodities into squandering.

To see oneself in the form of commodities is to feel oneself to be on view. It is to be seen by an "other" who is the same as oneself, at the point where the original self and its double cannot be distinguished. Disavowal begins by calling the other who sees oneself "Chinese" and equating that term with the people in their sealed shops. Just as the equation *Chinese = commodities* works to forge an identification of *remaja* and Chinese, it works also, later, to break it.

The accident occurred between two people, each, of course, with a name. But when the story was reversed so that the Chinese youth became the aggressor, it was told not as the story of particular persons but as the story of high-school students and Chinese. The establishment of these catagories alone, however, cannot account for the scale of involvement. To see why so many *remaja* should have turned out in such a short period, we need to return to the situation of *remaja* and to the story. On the one hand, we have a group who believes in benevolent accident in the form of school learning and commodities. On the other, the accident in the story was made into the administration of an unanticipated shock. Not ghosts but Chinese, who should be kept in place, are the source of this shock. In making the accident explicable by identification of Chinese and money, the story also turns the source of benevolent accident—commodities that one merely meets up with on the street—into a source of unanticipated disruption.

One can make the comparison with gambling. Javanese gambling has the strange feature that the same number can win for one person and lose for another. Winning numbers originate "someplace else"; a place connected with spirits. These numbers can turn up for someone else if one has not appropriated them properly. Commodities seen traditionally, as images, make the same acknowledgment of a "someplace else" and offer also the possibility of making them one's own. That such commodities can also turn up for others, that one's "own" batik might end up being owned by another person never becomes a problem. On the contrary; it confirms the existence of an "elsewhere" from which commodities issue and a system by which all possibilities are realized.

The benevolent accident by which *remaja* come across suitable fashions is only the confirmation of their experience in school. It tells them that they really do have a privileged access to the future; they are the figures in whom Indonesian history will be enacted. They will have careers. Fashion corroborates their sense of their education; what turns up in the world is for them; whatever turns up always has a destination. Chinese, from whom they buy their fashions, are merely agents of (good) fortune, figures who aid in the domestication of money.

In the period of the riots, however, after the story of the accident spread, Chinese were no longer merely the means by which fashions intended for students reached them; they were instead the source of commodities students could not truly appropriate. Commodities were then no longer what was meant for students, but instead were "money." The difference between money exchange and deferential exchange meant that what one owned was not truly one's own. It was not assimilable to the self that has its future laid out for it by the administration of knowledge. The school's monopoly of shock was challenged, and with it, students' futures. In this situation, mastery was out of the question. Disavowal was the only possible solution. In the context of the traffic accident, Chinese did not threaten students with their economic or political power; they threatened by becoming a site from which Javanese students saw themselves assaulted and their future dispersed. This is how the story of the accident elicited massive reaction.

The possibility of the desirable coming from sources that one cannot anticipate, the possibility of the desirable being inappropriable, is the possibility of *remaja* being owned by commodities rather than owning them. It is the possibility of *remaja* seeing themselves to be like Chinese because they wore what the Chinese sold rather than having their clothes express themselves. This, I believe, is the essence of the charge that Chinese had unjustifiable wealth. When, in gambling, one's number turns up for someone else, it is because he deserved it; he had a system that was right for him, and thus the winnings rightfully belong to him. The possibility of one buyer seeing something in a cloth that the other misses is comparable. But the wealth of Chinese is different. They were charged with not deserving their wealth, with holding it inappropriately, which means

possessing it without going through the process of obeis-
ance to the values of respect that the buyer of batik or the
winner of a lottery go through, and without submission
to the process of national education. Chinese wealth comes
through unrestrained urgency. It is not rightfully theirs at
all. It is rightfully "the nation's," which means that no
rightful claimant has appeared from among the nation's
citizens. It is actually unowned. This wealth is thus an
unrealized possibility, like a winning number that at-
taches itself to no winner, a truly lost bet: unredeemed
even later by someone unknown. In the view of students,
the wealth of Chinese is the possibility of money circulat-
ing without ever coming to rest.

PART FOUR

Language against Hierarchy:
The Failure of Translation

CHAPTER TEN

Images, Odors, Javanese Death

LANGUAGE CAN work against hierarchy in various ways. In this section, I describe three instances where hierarchy threatens to come undone as translation fails. The first concerns Javanese treatment of death. I describe a society without mourning but with an equivalent in the operations of deference. We saw in Chapter One that respect did not generate a notion of privacy in the Western sense, but nonetheless it created a space for the speaker removed from deferential exchange. So, too, Javanese treatment of death does not result in a privileged personal past, but nonetheless it establishes a sense of loss. But the linguistic operations that structure notions of death can break down, and the notion of "loss" itself can vanish.

A person is dead when he has been given up for dead by those closest to him. In Solo, as in other parts of Java, the time between biological and cultural death is short: sometimes even minutes. I was present when a man in his fifties was brought the news of his mother's death. He shed one tear and after that was able to act as he would on ordinary occasions. One seldom sees expressions of grief or mourning.[1] It is common at funerals to be greeted, for instance, by a widower who shows no sign of bereavement, though his wife may have died less than a day before. Clifford Geertz has described the atmosphere at funerals:

> The mood of a Javanese funeral is not one of hysterical bereavement, unrestrained sobbing, or even of formalized cries of grief for the deceased's departure. Rather, it is a calm, undemonstrative, almost languid letting go.

Tears are not approved of and certainly not encouraged; the effort is to get the job done, not to linger over
the pleasure of grief. . . . The funeral and postfuneral
ritual is said to produce a feeling of iklas, a kind of willed
affectlessness, a detached and static state of "not car-
ing."[2]

Even the family members closest to the deceased often,
perhaps usually, are *iklas*, "detached," within minutes after
a death.[3] How is this achieved and how is it maintained?
I will focus on two bits of paraphernalia to find an answer: photographs and incense.

The funeral ceremony has been described by others;
briefly, it consists of oratory, thanking the guests for their
attendance, and eulogies of the deceased in the highest
possible Javanese.[4] There are minor differences between
ceremonies depending on the religion of the deceased. But
a Christian funeral, a Muslim funeral, or the funeral of a
nominally Muslim person are in general outline the same.
After the oratory and prayers, the body is transported to
the cemetery. There are further ceremonies three, seven,
forty, a hundred, and a thousand days after the death, as
well as ceremonies at the erection of the gravestone and
on the first and sometimes second anniversaries of the
death. On those occasions people pray that the soul of the
deceased be accepted by God.

For the ordinary guest at the ceremonies, most time is
spent waiting for the oratory to begin. There is quiet chat-
ting but no special mood of piety. People talk about anything at all, not avoiding mention of the deceased and not
changing their tone when they do so. The coffin is usually
draped in white ruffled cloth and ornamented with flow-
ers. An announcement that it is about to be brought out
of the house is made over the loudspeaker; often the announcement includes an invitation to those who wish to
take photos to come to the front.

The tone that is appropriate to everyday life is also appropriate at a funeral. Smiles are not out of place. Anyone who showed a special sense of the occasion would, in fact, be thought to be acting not quite properly. Such a person would be thought unable to control himself or herself, in which case it would be better if they were not to come. As I have said, there is no attempt to avoid mentioning the deceased as one chats. There is, however, very little in the way of sentiments regretting the death. One's death is thought to be in the hands of God; acceptance of this fact is part of being *iklas*, detached. Possibly for the same reason there are few of the usual questions people in the West ask at a death, questions that betray the fear that they too could die: what did the deceased die of (frequently no one seems to know), and how old was he.

People give various reasons for their ability to become *iklas*. Ordinarily they say that it is God's will that the person died. "What comes from God must return to God and therefore one must be *iklas*," said one person. (This answer in my experience is the same for all Solonese, regardless of their religion.) They also say that the deceased is not really gone, he or she is only somewhere else; that, if the spirit (*roh*) were to see you upset, it would be upset. What one wants is to remove the spirit, to send it on its way rather than to keep it in memory.[5] Indeed, it is a mistake to speak of mourning in a Javanese funeral if this means working through memories of the deceased in order to put them to rest. The point of being *iklas* is that one is not affected by such memories, that this absence of affect is almost instantly attained and that it is in everybody's interest: the deceased, the deceased's close relatives, and those with whom the latter have social intercourse. There is an immediate idealization of the deceased, as though one has only certain limited memories of the person, and these are not burdened with the added thought that he or she is no longer here. The funeral orator often, for instance, gives the biography of the deceased. But there is no attempt in doing so to show his or her commonality with those who are left behind. For example, at the very large funeral of one woman who had been active in many organizations, the offices she held were enumerated, but there was no attempt to give the details of what she did in such a way that one would have felt her energy and realized one's loss. It was rather as if one were supposed to equate her with the titles she held.

Photographs serve the same function. Many families have albums of photographs of relatives' funerals, which include pictures not merely of the crowd and the speakers at the ceremony, but also of the corpse and of the coffin after it had been lowered into the grave. Ordinarily photographs of people we know stimulate recall: being taken at a particular moment in time, they seem to capture the person as he was when the picture was taken. Looking at the picture, one has the impression that, just before and just after it was taken, things were different, and we draw on our memories to fill out what we see. A photograph of a corpse, however, has a different effect. A body devoid of life remains as it is. Rather than being unique to the moment in which the picture was taken, the same condition of the body continues after the picture was taken. There seems to be nothing outside the picture, nothing more to the corpse than what is visible. The effect is one of immunity to changes of time. When that is the case, the person is no longer the person as experienced and held in memory but the person as "dead," that is, fixed. Javanese funeral photography thus operates against memory; it is the person as image, and not the person connected with memories of him, that survives.

When death arrives, it brings with it a view of the person that is intended to replace thoughts of him or her alive. The ornate quality of the eulogies is appropriate here. It was, in fact, during one such eulogy that my neighbor remarked to me on the extraordinary *alus* or refined quality of the speaker's language: "He has spoken a long time and said almost nothing" was his admiring comment. The stereotyped quality of the photographs of funerals are analogous to this High Javanese oratory. The stereotyping indicates that it is the static quality of the image that is desired, not the unique moment of a particular funeral. Death brings with it a degree of respect and an idealization of the deceased that he or she was unlikely to have gotten by birth or achievement.

Solonese say that they fear "the dead." Graveyards, indeed, are generally thought to be haunted. It is remarkable, then, that a new corpse is not an object to be feared. The corpse is generally laid out in the main room of the house. The youths of the neighborhood sit up with it through the night. People come to view it sometimes, but this is not an obligation. There is none of the feeling of solemnity in its presence that there is in the West and none of the feeling that one is paying one's last respects to someone one knew. This is because the corpse acts as a sign of death rather than as a reminder of the person as he was in life.

The fear that can arise when for some reason a funeral's progress has been interrupted has been excellently described by Clifford Geertz. In his account, a corpse became rigid, making it necessary to cut off the clothes with a knife, "an unusual procedure which deeply disturbed everyone. . . ."[6] In the view we are proposing here, the cutting-off of the clothes would be disturbing not only because of the novelty of the procedure, but also because it emphasized the changing state of the corpse, which became a thing in its own right, not an image of death. Indeed, in Geertz's description the increasing nervousness corresponds to a sense of time out of control; the inability to proceed with the funeral is contrasted with the progressive change of state of the corpse, as though decay would not have occurred had the funeral taken its course. It is the fixity of the impression that is challenged by decay. Geertz's account allows us to see that, before photographs became common in Java, the corpse itself, in its

presumed unchangingness, furnished the image sup-
plied, or perhaps merely supplemented, by photographs
today.[7]

Yet we still do not know how that sign achieves its special place; how it is that, seeing the corpse, people do not
grieve. The almost instant detachment Solonese achieve,
however, becomes understandable through that part of the
funeral ceremony known as *trobosan*. Just after the coffin
is taken out of the house, borne on the shoulders of pall-
bearers, it is held up for a moment. Younger relatives,
usually children and young adults, circle in and out under
the coffin. The word for this practice, *trobosan*, means "to
penetrate" or "cut through." One man explained to me
that it means "to cut holes" in the space beneath the coffin (Javanese has a word for defined space—*longan* or *ko-
longan*—referring not to the boundaries of the enclosure
but to the space itself). By so doing, one positions oneself
for blessings (*pangestu*) from the dead. This is considered
a transitional moment for these younger people. It is the
one moment at a funeral when one can expect to see grief
expressed, though it only sometimes materializes. Partly
this is allowed to persons who are not fully mature, not,
that is, fully in possession of themselves and not—the same
thing in Javanese thought—full masters of Javanese language. For them it is considered a leave-taking: "the final
goodbye," one man told me. But also, at that moment the
deceased person is defined as "dead," by virtue of which
he can control blessings. To treat him as belonging to the
realm of death means to receive blessings in return. Passing out of life, he becomes fixed in the mind as "dead"
and simultaneously the source of all that is good in life.

Pangestu, "blessings," that which he facilitates, refer to
everything desirable that one might get in the course of
one's life: a family of one's own, money, good marks on
an examination, and so on. People seek *pangestu* in graveyards, going on Thursday nights to graves reputed to be
the abode of powerful spirits and at least annually to the

graves of ancestors. In this sense *pangestu* means not merely blessings but, when one seeks them, wishes. The deceased becomes the focus for wishfulness. The replacement of the memory of the person alive by the image or idea of him dead is fostered by the possibility of good things for oneself when the transfer is made. It is as though each resurgent memory of any deceased person would lead not to dismay at the loss but to confidence in oneself, so long as one could be sure the person really was "dead."

We can deepen our understanding of the role of imagery in Javanese ways of establishing "death" by comparison. Javanese do not grieve in the sense that Freud described in "Mourning and Melancholia." Freud thought of grieving as a form of "reality testing" that "shows that the loved one no longer exists." It "requires that all the libido shall be withdrawn from its attachment to this object. . . . Each single one of these memories and hopes which bound the libido to the object is brought up and hypercathected, and the detachment of the libido from it is accomplished."[8] Freud does not elaborate on the process. The relinquishing of the deceased in the memory of the bereaved is a question of thinking memories once again. Freud does not say that the second revises the first. It seems to be an identical account of the event remembered, the image of the first. By remembering a second time, it is possible to attach oneself to (hypercathect) the second memory and relinquish the first. The second account establishes the memory qua memory or image, set apart therefore from any association with the content of other thoughts.

This recourse to imagery establishes the person as image, not reality, therefore as "dead." The assumption of this reality testing is that the second remembering, the imaging of the first memory, is an encapsulation. Remembered the second time, the original memory is inscribed in an image that, after comparison, is set off from one's "hopes." Imagery becomes a form of mechanical memory, memory set off from the rest of one's thoughts. Javanese practice differs on the first count, but not the second. The encapsulation of the memory of the dead person, the removal of the person from one's hopes, plans, and memories, seems to happen without reality testing.

What Freud called the work of mourning takes a long time, and he could not explain why. Part of the answer is that Westerners who grieve do not want to give up the deceased for dead. Javanese feel the same way, but they are aided by thoughts of blessings, by the different status of the "dead" in their thought. Still, this does not fully account for the absence of the work of mourning. There are two contradictory wishes: for the person to be alive, and for him to be "dead." The early resolution in favor of one over the other needs more explication.

Another reason for the absence of the work of mourning has to do with the role that imagery of the "dead" plays in Javanese society. The corpse itself is a model of appropriate facial expression. The Western humanist notion of expression of character in facial expression involves thinking that disparate features are held together by a conscious, experiencing mind. The life in someone's face depends on the degree of tension and flexibility in the features, as though they could move, but could also move out of control.[9] In Java, the ideal face is round and rather fleshy.[10] Roundness and fleshiness bring with them a good deal of inanimate space between the features. The result is neither tension nor relaxation, but an expression that seems not to try to impress. It is marked by the tensionlessness that one finds also in the faces of corpses. If one examines the photo albums of funerals, one finds pictures of family and neighbors gathered around the open coffin. In such photographs the similarity of the corpse's expression to those of the spectators is evident.[11]

The expression, however, is the same one Solonese put on whenever they expect their photographs to be taken. The similarity of facial expression thus might be due to imitation, or it might be coincidence. If it is imitation, it would proceed from the guilt felt at death, from the feeling that one should be more like the deceased.

Posing for one's picture, presenting one's best face, one pretends to a certain perfection whose model is the person freed from speech. What is imagined is not silence, which might, perhaps, be the place where speech would originate. It is, rather, freedom from the pressure that would dislocate one from one's social position. The attractiveness of the corpse is precisely that he or she cannot speak. Deceased persons are freed from the pressures that result in slips of good speech, marring perfect behavior. By looking like a corpse one puts oneself in its place. It is the corpse who is the most honored person in Solonese society, partly because the corpse is without the impulses that disrupt behavior; he thus fulfills a Javanese ideal. His position is indisputable and can be marred only by unwanted memories of him still alive.[12] To those without knowledge of the Javanese language such a proposition may seem bizarre. However, in the context of Javanese speech levels it is reasonable.

The corpse, of course, cannot speak at all, in either High or Low Javanese. It nevertheless becomes an image of proper speech because it refers to a realm of potential disruption that exists apart from it. The corpse is "dead," which in Javanese usage means that the *roh*, or soul or spirit, is separated from it. It is usually through the mediation of the *roh* that blessings are said to return to the living. There is also a gamut of spirits called by various names such as *jim*.[13] Though they are seldom identified with named persons, they are described as the energies of people continuing after their deaths. Under ordinary conditions these spirits are invisible. Since they are invisible, the corpse cannot be identified with them. The corpse is simply their visible sign. That the corpse is so highly honored is in part because the terms of this separation allow the disruption of the spirits to be conflated with the disruptions of Low Javanese. Unlike the person who carries the source of disruption within himself, the corpse is separated from it. The tensionless expression of the corpse is taken as the mark of someone no longer disturbed by the potential outbursts that prevent a living person from behaving (that is, speaking) as he or she should. The corpse thus looks the way one who is a perfect master of High Javanese should look.

One can try to look like the corpse, to take on the configuration of his or her facial features, which means to borrow that expression as an indication of something else, of the inability to be socially inept. The lack of expressiveness in corpses' faces, as is also the case in *Kromo* usage, does not, ideally, result from a struggle against expression. Rather it is entirely sign: it should not reflect interiority, but what has been taken on properly, what does not originate in oneself and, precisely for that reason, is "proper." Thus, to imitate the dead does not imply an agent, an imitator, identical to the Low Javanese speaker, who controls the imitation. What would be the agent is simply left behind. Furthermore, it is perfectly safe to look like the "dead" because the "dead" themselves cannot be equated with their attributes. "They," too, are somewhere else. In taking on the aspects of the corpse, therefore, one is not exactly in the position of the "dead," who, in their active form, are separated from anything visible.[14]

Javanese believe one's death is predetermined and one cannot know the time of its occurrence. "Death" is thus removed from experience. It is not the natural end of biological development, thought to coincide with an arc of experience, but merely that which ends biological existence at any stage. It is, in this conception, another form of accident. But when one can accede to the signs of "death," it is reintroduced into social life as a regular feature. Conflated with proper social form, it becomes the basis for the social order itself. The disjunctive quality of speech levels, the quick changes in tone as a speaker moves from one to the other and then back again, are wholly congruent with another kind of integration, one in which "life" and "death" alternate.[15]

One pays respect to those who are most capable of themselves mastering High Javanese, those who, ideally, look as though they are not bothered by an unwanted intrusion of Low Javanese. The exaction required by hierarchy is that one should not speak one's "own" language when one addresses a superior but should substitute for it High Javanese. In speaking High Javanese, one is thus separating out one's own thoughts in favor of a certain image. If, following a death, Javanese more quickly resort to imagery to establish a line between life and death than Westerners, it is because they have already done so before the death occurred.

It is not a system that always works, however. By June 1981, all of the corpses in the municipal cemeteries of Solo had to be moved outside the city limits, the land being reappropriated for other uses. Generally this meant holding a *selamatan*, a ritual feast, to appease the spirits before the transfer of the bodies. Families began to move their deceased relatives in February 1981. Rather than producing tension, the process went on like a quiet picnic; those in the neighborhood would come by to watch as the bones were dug up and laid in new caskets. One could see, for instance, a man arranging the bones of his father, with no apparent intensity of feeling.

The exception, however, was when the flesh of the corpse had not completely decayed. Laborers were ordinarily paid Rp 1,000 or Rp 1,200 for moving the body. This was a wage only slightly above the usual rate for daily labor in Solo. If, however, an odor was still emanating from the corpse, the wage climbed to Rp 25,000. This meant about $40.00 for a day's work, an unheard-of sum for a laborer. The reason was, to Solonese, obvious. If one smelled the corpse, one could oneself die. The contagion of death that no one seems to feel in a Javanese funeral became evident in these incidents.

Indeed, the smell of a corpse is said to be over-whelming. "If the body of a mouse stinks, how much more so the body of a man. It is unbearable [*ora tahan*]," one man told me when I asked why laborers were paid so much to move rotting corpses. No matter how strong and unpleasant the stench might be, there is no obvious reason to think that it will kill you; this, nonetheless, was the opinion of all the numerous people I asked about this matter.

Death is contagious for Surakartans when the corpse is smelled, when the odor of the corpse indicates its decay. When the corpse is thought to have changed states, it can no longer be thought of as an unchanging image, as portrayed in the funeral photograph. The corpse is then like a living person in a photograph: before and after one sees it, it was and will be different. If it can change state, one has to think about it as one thinks about a person in an ordinary photograph: what, exactly, happened before one saw it, and what will (or, in the case of photographs, did) happen next.

Once one begins to wonder about the corpse, he or she becomes connected to the rest of one's thoughts, functioning in them as a live person would. The single thought that one should be attached to him, that he belongs to the realm of the dead and is a potential source of *pangestu*, blessings, or, minimally, that he is at least appeasable as Javanese spirits are, is put aside. There is no limit to what one could think about him after that. There is no way to separate him from any thought one might have. The difference between life and death, between oneself here on one side and the corpse on the other, has been obscured. If there is no decisive difference between the living and the dead, death is already contagious. One could die smelling a corpse.

Nonetheless, since I have claimed that Javanese identify with corpses, this would not necessarily be undesirable.

What makes it so is that the identification cannot be with the corpse as it exists in High Javanese usage, as an image. This is in part due to the nature of odor. Smell is not easily mastered. One can refuse to touch or taste something more easily than one can block a smell, for instance. Moreover, odor has a closer connection to experience than sight or sound. What we recognize through sight or sound we might have seen in a picture, or heard on a recording, or have had told to us. Odors, however, are not reproducible; there is no equivalent that can be printed, and odors are generally thought to be indescribable. The capacity to recognize a smell seems to depend on having smelled something like it before, rather than having learned about it some other way.

When one recognizes the smell of the corpse, it is unlikely that one does so on the basis of what one has been told of the way corpses smell. The particular odor is as difficult to describe as any. One can know that the smell of the corpse emanates from it, and recognize it in that way. But if that were all that were involved, it would not evoke terror as it does. The terror is, in the first place, the result of not being able to appeal to idealized notions, of not being able to compare what one smells with what one "knows" and so lock the odor in place.

It is a problem that is particularly acute for the Javanese. Their archaizing of experience, for instance, depends on equating it with a previous ideal. Smell only weakly possesses such an ideal. Yet its recognition appeals to idealized memory. Javanese cannot be sure how they recognize odor. Such recognition is thus potentially uncanny.

Even when it is short of the uncanny, however, it still is not a desirable identification with the "dead." The "dead" are those who are immune to the irruption of their "own" thoughts or their "own" language; one owes them the equivalent behavior. Seeing the corpse, the viewer should be able to suppress his own thoughts, in turn, as he recognizes it in terms of the High Javanese language it deserves. But odor prevents such recourse. It has no High Javanese equivalent because, as we have seen, it is not amenable to becoming a recognized sign. Odor appeals, then, to one's experience, to what one has learned without being taught. It sets aside whatever one has been taught, and opens the possibility of filling one's mind with unrecognizable thoughts. The odor of the corpse thus inaugurates the process that it would be the role of the idealized corpse, or the corpse as image, to stop.

This must be put into the context of language and hierarchy. We have seen that when one speaks *Kromo*, High Javanese, one keeps one's "natural" speech, Low Javanese, to oneself. One does not say what immediately comes to mind. *Ngoko*, Low Javanese, thus comes to stand for what one reserves to oneself, apart from hierarchy. The self that goes out of existence when one dies is the speaker of Low Javanese. The speaker of High Javanese is, ideally, equated with the "dead" even before his biological death. It is *Ngoko*, Low Javanese, which, kept out of speech, keeps one on this side of a line between "life" and "death." It is this self that is the object, for instance, of the blessings that cross that line from the "dead" to the "living." After "death," the loss of the reserved self is inscribed in idealized memory. But the stimulation of odor threatens a limitless expression without subsequent idealization. It is the evacuation of this self without recuperation that Javanese refer to when they say that, smelling the corpse, "one could die."

Most Javanese deny being afraid of "death." If we judge by those who prepare themselves by becoming like the corpse or by identification with corpses in everyday life, we can understand the basis for their statement. Within quotation marks, "death" means being an image oneself and being devoid of the impulses that disrupt proper speech and behavior. The death that is thought to come with odor, however, is devoid of imagery and leaves disruptive impulses problematic in status. Hence the implicit acknowledgment of fear in the statement, "It could kill you."

Spirits frequently disrupt Javanese life. But spirits, by their identity as spirits, invisible beings, can be dealt with. Before the corpses were uncovered, many of their living relatives consulted soothsayers to determine if the spirits of the dead were still present in or near the graves. The purpose of the ritual feasts was, indeed, to appease these spirits wherever they might be.

The uncovered bones of the dead were themselves an assurance that the active "dead," in the form of ghosts or spirits, were somewhere else. The very invisibility of these spirits was a guarantee that they need not be equated with the visible remains of the dead. This made it safe to pay respect to the dead. It was, for instance, a gesture of respect to arrange the bones of an ancestor as they were uncovered. With this action, the bones were not put into a mental series beginning with the bones, perhaps running through the bones as corpse at the time of death, and continuing with the person as he was in life. Their reference was unlike that of the decaying corpses, which set off thoughts that the sight of the corpse should have suppressed, and charged the decaying corpse with danger. The visible corpse, the corpse as image, ensured that danger was elsewhere—or at least should have.

Were the decaying corpses said to be infested with spirits, they could have been dealt with. On the face of it, it is surprising that no one resorted to such an explanation; it is the common recourse in Java. But once the corpse was charged with danger, it did not refer to a place somewhere else that could become the scene in which fears were embodied. It could not act as the sign that made displacement possible—displacement of the fear of disruptive speech into an invisible, removed realm of spirits. The corpse devoid of this reference should have been just a dead body. Were it thought of that way, it would have been possible to speak of odor as the route of contaminating disease. Although Javanese are capable of such an explanation, no one thought of smell in this way.

The corpse, charged with danger, functioned to stimulate a displacement without ever achieving it. Because it was the remnant of a once-living person, it should have indicated "death" or taken on a new meaning. But it was devoid of life and yet without the capacity to refer to death in any sense. Within the framework of Javanese hierarchical use of language, it should have evoked the proper restraint in those who viewed it. But without a notion of "dead" to which to appeal, without, that is, the corpse as image, it had the opposite effect.

The question is the operation of displacement in Javanese speech and in Javanese "death." Low Javanese is replaced with High Javanese; disruptive impulses are replaced with the image of serenity. Replacement obscures what it has replaced. Slips, disruptive impulses, are not entirely effaced. They reappear as the fear of the inability to speak High Javanese and as the spirits. One can speak of displacement into the future in one case, into a removed realm of spiritual geography in the other. Such displacements give substantiveness; they picture or figure what it is that one has put out of mind, but in a disguised form. They bring it back to mind in a way that distances it. They thus obscure and replace what has been obscured in another form somewhere else.

The fear of decaying corpses is the failure of this process. It says that something has been obscured but that there is no replacement. The content of memories that return in this situation is not problematic. Those who disinterred the corpses, for instance, were unlikely to have known the deceased and so could not have been burdened by memories of them. Rather, in the failed recourse to either the located memory of an odor or the image of the respected person, there is no stability of remembering. This is the panic. It is not that there is no memory but that there is too much of it. As though the gravedigger, for instance, has to recall multiple memories because none of them are right. As though he understands only that there is something that he cannot bring to mind. He knows at that point only that he has forgotten something and does not know what it is. This would be the process of obscuring. It is also the failure of respect to block one's thoughts and the concomitant instability of any thought.

People spoke of the odor of the corpse as a way of saying that it assailed them with a barrage that both stimulated and refused sense. Such a barrage would be the stimulus to *latah*, the blurting out of whatever comes to mind. Odor was not so much what people smelled, or even feared they might smell, as an oblique reference to a point where language was upset.

Any odor has the capacity to stimulate memory and thus threaten the role of imagery in keeping memories of the dead apart from other thoughts. To guard against the unexpected stimulation of memory, Javanese use a special incense called *menyan* or *kemenyan*. When Javanese make offerings to the spirits, who, one remembers, are thought to be the remnants of once-living persons, or when they make offerings at graves, they burn incense. Their incense is different from the Chinese variety. Chinese incense has a pleasant aroma. *Menyan*, however, is unpleasant to Javanese unless, as is only occasionally the case, honey is added to it.[16] Incense, *menyan*, is called "food of the spirits." None of the numerous Javanese I asked liked the smell, unless it was of the variety that has honey added. Generally people would say that it made them afraid, since it was intended for *jim* or spirits. What is remarkable, however, is that I could never elicit any associations connected with it.[17] It is an odor that, rather than evoking memory, seems to repress it, as indeed, the fear it stimulates might suggest.

Though it does not appear to be a widely known belief, one teacher of Javanese mysticism told me that *menyan* was designed originally to cover up the smell of the corpse. Its use, however, is not for that purpose today. Though used in funerals, it functions mainly in ceremonies connected with the dead who are already buried and out of sight. It does not suppress the odor of the corpse; it indirectly suppresses memory. By suppressing other smells, it guards against the associations that any odor can stimulate. The odor of *menyan* generates the sense of "death" in its Javanese meaning. One cannot escape the smell and, though it is unpleasant, one does not want to. The meaning "death" replaces any particular memory that would otherwise surface. *Menyan* thus evades the general inability of smell to become a recognized sign.

Again, it does not always work. I have mentioned the two cases where it is least likely to work. Young people, those up through their middle teens whom one might see grieve at the *trobosan*, are one case. They do not yet have full access to imagery, being thought of as immature. The other case is mothers who have lost children. In my experience, it is particularly mothers who have lost older children who are vulnerable to grief. It is not only that they have a full store of memories to contend with, but also that it is harder for them, too, to have recourse to imagery. Imagery implies blessings, and blessings should come from the senior to the junior, other aspects of status being equal. When children die before their mothers, the situation is reversed. Fathers, on the other hand, are more remote from their children and have less to cope with. Despite this caveat, however, it is my experience that most Javanese do not grieve even when they are most vulnerable.

I once visited an upper-class couple whose son had died in a motorbike accident a year earlier. The mother still occasionally was affected by memories of her son. Perhaps for that reason the father, though he kept a photograph of his son in the living room, kept it face down. As we were talking, a group of their son's friends, including his former fiancée, came to call. They talked about the boy, how he would have been a doctor by this time, how he had died, with no signs of grief. Then for my benefit, as I had not known the son, the father picked up his photograph and showed it to us. As the company left, the mother and the fiancée were in tears. Face-up, the photo would have indicated the "death" of the boy, the encapsulation of his memory apart from other thoughts. Unexpectedly revealed as it was, the photograph was not a static image but a sudden reappearance.

To affect his mother and his fiancée as it did, the photograph of the corpse must have awakened memories. It functioned as a souvenir, a reminder of past events and of the boy's absence. The decaying corpse, by contrast, threatened anyone who might chance to smell it, whether they had known the deceased person, and thus had memories of him, or not. The odor of the corpse did not stimulate association with the person as he was when he was alive. It stirred thoughts that could have had nothing to do with the experience of the deceased. It caused not grief but terror.

These examples are unusual. More often there is an immediate division of experience: images on one side, idiosyncratic memories on the other. There is no need for grief or mourning, and little sign in daily life of memories returning to disturb survivors. And there is little of the shock caused by odor. The living are *iklas*. But their detachment can vanish if the image comes to life, or when, with a random whiff, it is no longer an image.

I have described a society without mourning (though not without suffering). In Western conception, the work of mourning transforms memory into loss. The past time of such loss is distinguished from another sort of past, one not experienced and remembered, but learned through the language of others. The difference between these two pasts corresponds to the differences between private and public, interior and exterior.

Javanese seem not to mourn; or when they do, their mourning is not valorized. It receives no approbation; it is merely tolerated if it is unavoidable. The difference between one's "own" past and the public past is not marked. The lack of this distinction is replaced by another form of conceptualizing that underlies many of the actions we have described. For example, the insistence that what we call habit, one's "own" product, is really "tradition," the right way, followed by all proper persons, even when it appears to an observer to be idiosyncratic; or the instant archaizing in which what one has recognized out of experience is thought to be what has always been Javanese.

Javanese do not mourn. That is, they do not create a notion of loss through a transformation of memory. In place of the work of mourning there is accession to High Javanese, seen in funerals to be a form of identification with the idealized "dead." This is an identification that depends on imagery, particularly, today, photographs, to indicate the presence elsewhere of spirits. This "elsewhere" marks "loss" in its Javanese sense, one that does not depend on memory.

Javanese "loss" is thus inscribed in a distinction between two languages and in the translation between them. In the panic caused by the fear of the odor of decaying corpses this distinction did not operate. One could not then speak of "death." The panic set off by the fear of odoriferous corpses marks the breakdown of domesticated language, of translation in particular, and with it the disappearance of "loss" and the resurgence of untranslated material.

CHAPTER ELEVEN

The Durable Jokes of the New Order

ON SEPTEMBER 30, 1965, six Indonesian generals and a lieutenant were abducted and their bodies thrown down a well on the outskirts of Jakarta. This was the presumed coup that resulted in the removal of President Sukarno from power and the establishment of Suharto as president. The killings ensued, instigated by the government in most cases, of at least a half million people accused of being Communists; tens of thousands more were imprisoned.[1] The establishment of Suharto's authority as president, even in Sukarno strongholds such as Surakarta, was rapid and firm. We have already seen how Javanese notions of hierarchy, expanded to include those with national offices, provided a means of accommodation. But it is not clear that statist notions and actions and Javanese ideas are always harmonious. Some ways in which they work with and against each other form the topic of this chapter.

The anniversary of the killing of the generals is celebrated as a national day of commemoration. In 1980, national television broadcast the ceremonies. Practically the whole of the national news on October 2 showed the celebrations, which largely duplicated each other, at various ministries. Employees lined up, usually in a courtyard, and the director or minister read them a speech, inaudible to those watching via television. After the news there was a program filmed at Lubang Buaya, the place where the generals' bodies had been thrown in a well. On that spot there is now a monument with the seven slain figures shown larger than life-size, while above them is an enor-

mous metal statue of the mythical state bird, the garuda.
In front of the monument a dais had been set up. In front
of the dais were military contingents and schoolchildren.

President Suharto and Vice-President Adam Malik arrived. A master sergeant, flourishing a sword, announced
the opening of the ceremony, an announcement that was
confirmed by the president, who said there would be a
moment of silent prayer, "each in his own way, for the
well-being of the nation." The band played appropriate
music and heads bowed. The Panca Sila, the Five Principles of the state, were read from a document carried by a
schoolboy. Another official read the Constitution of 1945.
A proclamation commemorating the day was read, and
the master sergeant pronounced the ceremony closed.

The television program was not yet over, however.
President and Mrs. Suharto and various members of the
delegation were shown to be exchanging the sort of good-
humored, domestically tinted greetings usual on such occasions. As they did so, they casually moved on to look
at the monument and the well itself, which has been en-
cased in marble and what I take to be granite.[2] As they
did so, the voice of the announcer repeated that "indeed,
that day will never be forgotten," and "it can never be
forgotten," and so on.

There are some peculiar features to this ceremony. In
the first place there was no attempt to retell the story of
the killings. Perhaps the events were assumed to be well
enough known not to need repeating. There was no speech
by the President. Such a speech might have retold the
events commemorated, or it might have drawn the lesson
of those events for contemporary Indonesia, or it might
have been the occasion to make an important announcement about some policy or plan. Even the plainest re-
counting could be considered a form of interpretation, since
it would have told us what events seemed like to the person who recounted them. So, too, a policy announcement
might be said to carry forth the values that one found in

the fallen heroes. But all such attempts at interpretation (and therefore at saying where those doing the interpretation stand at a particular moment in time) were refused. In its place came the incantation of sacred texts and formulae, the president's role being confined almost solely to the verification of the opening and closing of the ceremony.

The announcer, as I have said, kept repeating that "these events will never be forgotten," and yet nothing worked to bring them to mind. What one was shown was the memorial and the marble-encased well. The well without its thick marble rind might have stimulated memory. Seeing it, one would have been reminded that it was in this very place that the bodies were deposited. The marble, however, obscured the well. But the marble was there to ensure that the event would not be forgotten by taking it out of human memory and inscribing it in a sign that did not need individual memory to be read.

During the ceremony the President said very little, and what he said was entirely formal. Like the Indonesian schoolteacher, he made his voice into a reflection of established texts as though he spoke only in quotations. He was not Suharto the locus of unique feelings and idiosyncrasies, but Suharto the embodiment of texts, the one whose acknowledgments made the event into a ceremony, something formal and repeatable. When he himself spoke he said only formulae, yet it is not merely because of the obviously formulaic quality of the words he used that we can say this. Anything he might have conceived of saying would be a formula. For instance, were he to use a colloquialism in acknowledging the master sergeant's proclamation that the ceremony was now open, it would likely be interpreted as a sign of his graciousness and unpretentiousness and thus something to be copied in future years. Had he done so, he would not have been original; this is the style of some Javanese princes, for instance. But few of those watching would be familiar with

Javanese court etiquette. Regardless, he seemed situated to turn whatever he said into something already said, to be an instrument of quotation.

Is there anything other than the fact that one knew one was watching a ceremony that could convey the sense of speaking only through quotation? The beginnings of an answer come in looking again at the motives for the ceremony. It is important that the killings "never be forgotten" and be thought to be "unforgettable." The implication of the announcer's comments is that to forget the coup might mean to experience another one. President Suharto's own role in the events of 1965 was not mentioned in the ceremony; doing so would picture him before he became president; it could stimulate thoughts about the possibilities of others rather than himself taking office. Pictured only as president, he survives in the form of his office, not his person, and is comparable to the Constitution and the Five Principles.

It is not as though a (presumed) coup occurred, was put down, and then was forgotten. The ceremonies say that the events of 1965 should be remembered in order that they not recur. Their recurrence might mean, for instance, the displacement of Suharto from office. His contribution is safest if he is not an historic person but himself an inscription comparable to the state's basic documents.

To make oneself into an inscription, saying only things already said, however, raises the question of the origin of one's speech. Who, exactly, is Suharto quoting? Is it possible for him to speak originally and still be thought to be quoting? An inscription on a marble plaque by the opening of the well indicates that it might be. It reads: "The aim of our [*kami*] struggle to maintain the purity of the Five Principles can not be broken merely by throwing us into this well." The generals thus speak after their deaths in the only form open to them: inscription. Their actual voices may not be heard, but their words are represented as though they emerged from the spot in which their corpses were deposited.

To survive as inscription while one is still living might be thought more difficult. But with the resources of the state, President Suharto has attempted that as well. He has, through the agency of his wife, built his tomb while still alive. He is the first Indonesian ruler to do so to my knowledge. If he were to be successful in associating himself with the power of death (the power of the *anéh*), everyone would have to defer. He would be at the apex of the state not merely by virtue of his office—president— but also because he was not there accidentally. It would not be by the accidents of his biography that he became president, as though it were possible that someone else might have taken his place, but by his supernatural power. It would then be inconceivable that anyone else could have held the office.

Mrs. Suharto claims relationship with the third in the line of the Surakarta junior royal line, the Mangkunegaras. The Suharto tomb is on the same mountain with the tombs of the first three Mangkunegaras. Its name as well, Giri Bangun, is a composite of the names of two Mangkunegaran burial sites.[3] The Suharto tomb, however, contrasts in important respects with its neighbors. The Mangkunegaran tombs, with the exception of that of Mangkunegara VI, who is buried in Solo, are on the tops of mountains in the countryside. To get to them one must pass through several archways. The mausoleums are surrounded by walls. The tombs themselves are completely hidden from view by curtains. As is usual with Javanese tombs, the coffin-shaped monument on the surface is not a coffin at all, but only marks the spot beneath which the body is buried. There is thus a definite sequence. If one accompanies a group of Javanese making a pilgrimage to the graves, it is easy to sense the heightened anticipation as they approach the actual grave. When, finally, the mausoleum is opened and they are allowed in, there is uncharacteristic, though still gentle, shoving and pushing to get into the grave's aura. But one can never arrive; there is continuous recession. As one gets nearer the grave, what one seeks is always one more remove away. The architecture of the grave enhances this sense by cutting the pilgrim off from the landscape. Though there are magnificent views from the top of the mountain, the walls of the cemetery prevent one from seeing them. Separated from the views of everyday activity in the farms and forests below, one is still not fully within the ambiance of the dead souls of former rulers.

By contrast, the Suharto mausoleum, set on a promontory of the mountain, is clearly visible. The walls of the mausoleum are intricately carved wood panels set between posts that allow the inside of the mausoleum to be visible from outside. Display and prominence (the Suharto mausoleum, constructed at a cost of $1.5 million, is considerably larger than the Mangkunegaran tombs) thus replace recession and obscurity.

The Suharto tomb is intended to link itself in the series of Mangkunegaran tombs and thus to participate in their sacredness, the tomb of Mangkunegara I in particular being thought to be a repository of sacred power. But its reversal of Javanese tomb architecture reveals that Javanese notions have also been reversed. Sacred tombs in Java are places where spirits are present. The remnants of the dead found there make it possible for visitors to the graves to hope to receive blessings. By a process of prayer and "concentration" or "emptying oneself," the spirits might intervene for the petitioner. It is customary at many tombs to spend the night in their vicinity, waiting to be visited by favorable omens, perhaps in the form of dreams.

The Suharto tomb tries to say what Javanese guru say when they announce that no one is allowed to take pictures of them without permission. Should someone try, the photographs will never come out. The implication is that since the guru derive their power from their association with death, they are, in a sense, not present. The Suharto tomb, however, does not mark Suharto's death, but the place where he will be buried when he dies. It is the sign of his future death, but it is intended to show his relation to death now. It is an attempt at saying, "I am dead." But it is the living who say this and not, as in the quoted words of the generals, the dead. The Suharto tomb is not, therefore, considered to be a repository of sacred power, though it is sometimes visited as one of a series of tombs on the mountain as a matter of respect.

In traditional Javanese notions of power as Anderson has explicated them, power accrues to someone who might, for instance, have isolated himself in the wilderness and through mystical practice caused sacred power to adhere to him.[4] Without effort such a person would gain followers and might become the ruler. In this formulation, power comes first, and the formation of hierarchy naturally follows. It is not surprising, therefore, that, like President Sukarno, President Suharto takes on the signs of power, especially a relationship to death, to consolidate his political position.

When President Suharto can make himself into an instrument of quotation so that whatever he says seems to have an authority greater than his own person, what is at stake is the relation of language to hierarchy. We have to explain what the source of his authority is, especially since it does not seem to be rooted in traditional Javanese notions despite his own unsuccessful efforts to make it so. We will approach this question through the Javanese language.

We have already seen how Javanese is used to assimilate Solo to the national hierarchy. Anyone with a position in the national hierarchy, such as a schoolteacher, is given respect. Javanese has thereby freed itself from the hierarchy of the local courts in which it developed. Suharto, as president, can command the deference of any Indonesian. He can also claim that the state commands a certain monopoly of access to the *anéh*, so that whatever manifestations of the *anéh* occur are within boundaries whose apex is marked by the president. In this view, Javanese and national hierarchies are thus drawn together.

The accommodation of Javanese, however, also includes resistance. There is a freedom of language and hierarchy in present-day Javanese that is the source of this resistance, at least in Solo. One can see this in the peculiar position of *latah*. One remembers that no one in Solo recognizes *latah*; nonetheless the condition that underlies *latah* is present, as the examples in Chapter One indicate. Why is it, then, that *latah* is not known?

In the reports of *latah* there is a recurrent story. A European accidentally discovers that his servant or someone else is *latah*. He becomes interested. It is not long before the original *latah* sufferer returns to him with someone else. Hildred Geertz, in her careful study, reports an event that occurred about a month after she met her first *latah* sufferer, a woman named Mbok Ti: "About a month later, Mbok Ti held a small feast in honor of her son's circumcision, and I attended it. All of the neighbors were there, politely drinking tea and conversing with proper subdued tones. A woman came in and Mbok Ti came up to me and said, 'Here is a real *latah*, just watch. You should study her not me.' "[5]

We have already shown that *latah* and a weak ability to speak High Javanese are related. The acts that make up *latah* are "at base unconscious parodies of the social relationship between inferior and superior," according to Geertz.[6] We have seen earlier how deferral in the context of Javanese is the capacity to reserve something for the deferring self. *Latah* is the incapacity to defer and so the incapacity to act socially. Bringing someone else who is "a real *latah*" is a way for the original person to deny that she is herself a *latah* sufferer.

In this incident and the others like it, the denial is validated in the eyes of the European who writes about it.

Latah was most common during the colonial period, when Europeans would have been at the top of the hierarchy. They not only received deference but, in these incidents, became its arbiter. Through validation in the arbiter's eyes, a person who was *latah* could find herself not "really" *latah* compared to someone else. The person who received deference was thus not only the second person, the person addressed, he or she was also an observer and thus a third person, standing outside the interaction and judging it.

Latah seems to be a category of Javanese thought and not merely a set of actions to the degree that a third person is recognized as the arbiter of correct linguistic behavior. The instance of superior linguistic capacity amongst the people of Solo (and Jogja) and the lack of recognition of *latah* is a way of saying that Javanese as a language contains its own norms accessible to those who speak it properly. It does not need the presence of a third party outside the code. Joseph Errington has described the special language used in the court.[7] One form of that language is used by courtiers between themselves when in the presence of the ruler. The use of this language indicates their inferior position but also, again, their capacity to defer. Errington's examples, however, suggest that courtiers used this language even when not in the ruler's presence. They apparently carried the sense of the ruler's presence within them. The third party did not need to be present.

Ordinary Javanese functions the same way in Solo. The use of *Kromo* wherever possible suggests that the arbiter of correct usage has been made a part of linguistic functioning itself, independent of any person who might be appealed to as a judge of correct usage. Again, it is not Surakartans' own confidence about the language that distinguishes them from other speakers of Javanese. They show a good deal of insecurity. But although there is no one other than themselves to point out their failings, they nonetheless feel themselves always to be in the presence of a judge.

What one might call the "built-in third person" can be seen in the quality of recognition in Solo. We have seen how in *soré*, whatever one sees, provided one can find an element that one knows one has already seen, becomes "custom" (*adat*). One has "custom" and antiquity, as in the neocolonial bank, without standardization. The lack of acknowledgment of an external, judging third party makes this possible. One does not refer one's own recognition to someone else's authority in order to distinguish what one has only seen oneself a second time from what is standardized.

The eccentricity of Solo rests on this. Thus what Westerners would be likely to call "personal habits," the products of individuals, Solonese call "the right way" to do something. Even though actual practice may vary considerably from person to person, people think they are putting "custom" into operation. It is not a question, then, of an internal authority mirroring an external authority. Rather, the internal authority suffices of itself.

With such a notion, Surakartans can make practically any artifact part of a hierarchical culture. But at the same time they evade the monopoly of criteria claimed by the state. One sees the difference when looking at New Order artifacts. These include ornately carved furniture, often in styles named after Javanese motifs; grandfather clocks; intricately patterned china and glassware; and expensive batik. Some of this is a quotation of Javanese styles, others summon up the style of the Dutch of an indeterminate previous era. They contrast with the "fashions" of Solo by their standardization. Surakartans thus evade the uniformity that a notion of an external third party would impose on them.

We have called High Javanese a second language, the language of someone else other than the speaker. But we have to revise that formulation now. If it is the language of the other, that other is not the second person. It is the internal third party who judges correct usage and who is not identifiable in the world of actual speakers. Javanese is thus a language that belongs to no one identifiable in the sociological world.

The difference between quotation on this basis and quotation in New Order politics is the referral of the latter to an external authority. From a New Order perspective, it may not matter that President Suharto cannot fully equate himself with the dead. Position in the hierarchy itself becomes the arbiter, the third person. And the purpose of such ceremonies as the commemoration of the events that resulted in the establishment of the New Order is to present its quotations and to show them legitimated not by the audience's recognition but by their reference to the President.

The commemoration ceremony seems to inculcate boredom. This would be its motive force in Javanese. But boredom here does not result in people feeling that they have seen the ceremony before and that therefore it is valid. The monument is not widely visited. It has not become a source of sacred power as have the graves of some of the Mangkunegaran princes. It is the tying of quotation to hierarchy that seems to be what is attempted in this ceremony and in the many others that are a feature of life in the New Order. President Suharto becomes an inscription, a quotation of himself, not by having others believe he has a special relation to death, but merely by displaying himself as the authority who decides what it is and is not possible to say in the ceremony, the definer of what has been said and can be repeated.

Solonese maintain the arbiter of correct behavior within language, detached from any particular hierarchy. This means that, at the least, they can wait out any particular regime. And at the most it means that a display of judgment independent of constituted authority could corrode

288 — Chapter Eleven

that authority. There is, in fact, at least one place where this occurs. I refer to certain jokes in Sri Mulat. There are some jokes that are frequently repeated and are always laughed at, for instance, the sight of the boss losing control of himself or the appearance of the man from Jakarta with his exaggerated Jakarta dialect. There is little witty about these scenes; one hesitates even to call them jokes. Yet they invariably provoke laughter. These are stereotypes or quotations: stereotypes in the sense that particular sorts of individuals form the object of the jokes, quotations in the sense that the same joke is repeated from performance to performance. It is thus a matter of asking how a joke can always be funny.

In life outside the theater, the proper response to such scenes would be to ignore them if one were an onlooker; one should act as though one had not seen them. However, in the theater, everyone knows that the scenes are witnessed and that they themselves have been seen witnessing them. That, as I will explain, is the source of the humor.

There is a rough parallel to this sort of behavior that was told to me by the historian Anthony Day. Day had considerable experience playing in Javanese orchestras. Such orchestras are nearly always involved in quiet scandals. The female singer in particular is often engaged in intrigue with orchestra members. Her flirtations are likely to involve the whole of the orchestra. She sits at the front of the orchestra (called the *gamelan*) and might throw glances at some favorite. Behind her sits her husband, who sees what she is up to. And around them both sit the rest of the musicians, who note everything that is going on. In this case, however, the mere seeing of what is happening is not the source of the interest. The interest is in the gossip that ensues afterwards, which centers on the husband's ability to ignore: "The husband was upset," "he got over it" are typical remarks.

In most situations where "everyone" knows something

there may be gossip. What is different here is that the husband too knows. I found myself in a similar situation in the neighborhood orchestra that played the type of music called *keroncong*. The organizer of the orchestra was eager to have me come to their weekly rehearsals. When I went, he was equally eager to point out the attractive qualities of one of the female singers who, indeed, began to flirt with me. Afterwards the organizer of the orchestra was careful to tell me that the woman's husband was a police lieutenant and played guitar in the orchestra. This did not prevent him from continuing to urge me to attend the rehearsals and, none too subtly, to invite me to pay calls on the singer. In this case, my reactions as well as the husband's were the topic of gossip. Unless I was aware that I was watched by the husband and the other musicians, however, the game lost some of its point.

The gossip was interesting, I believe, not because of its content, but because of its setting. The arrangement of the orchestra made it possible for its members not to see what was happening. The subject of their interest was not the flirtatious singer or the object of her favors so much as the reaction of the persons who would have the hardest time in ignoring such outrageous behavior, the husband or the naive visitor. They, in turn, in the small compass of the orchestra, could not but be aware that they were on display.

At stake in these episodes is control of the reactions of the husband. He observes that others see what he sees, he knows that he is himself on view, and he sees that others know what turn his thoughts must be taking; given all this, what matters is whether he will give some sign of being upset. There are not two different views of the situation; each party, the spectators and the husband, think the actions of the wife to be scandalous. The question is whether the husband will nonetheless show himself to be invulnerable to what he sees, whether he will show that a part of himself still remains in control. If he should become upset, it is not simply that he loses control of himself. It is also that he identifies himself with the view of the spectators. He reacts, then, in terms that they have set. In doing this, he gives up that part of himself that exercises control and acts only in terms he shares with the audience.

Without a sociological notion of audience, the spectators in Sri Mulat are like the *gamelan* players. There is no convention that says that they are invisible or hidden, that only the action on stage is on display. They too are aware of being seen and of being able to see their spectators.

In Sri Mulat it is not flirtation that is the object of attention; it is stereotypes and quotations. In Sri Mulat as in much of Indonesian traditional literature, quotation takes the form of mimicry. Quotation and stereotype coincide when it is not the manifestation of the voice engaged in a particular tonality, but the shared attitude about what the voice sounds like that is aimed at. The assumption is that voices are invariable, that they always speak in the same way. The skill in quotation of this sort is in presenting the stereotype precisely as it is generally understood to be.

Quotation of this type thus always reaches to something one knows to be known. It strives not only to make recognizable and to say what someone has already said, but to pick those aspects of voice with which everyone is familiar. This ensures that everyone recognizes that the voice is known to others as well as to themselves.

One remembers that the audience is not a collective entity in Sri Mulat. It is a collection of individuals who have particular notions of the operation of conventional language that pertains between themselves and the actors. They talk to the actors, and they watch as they would watch outside the theater. But the circuit of communication between actors and members of the audience breaks down when they laugh. Rather than restrain themselves, as they would ordinarily be expected to do, they discharge their feelings. Their laughter can be seen as a lack of response—a breakdown of the conventions of ordinary speech. Their laughter is the discharge that comes when response is not possible. A certain moment portrayed on-stage should produce a checking of spontaneous behavior—and it would in ordinary life, if all that was involved was the behavior portrayed. But instead laughter ensues.

What provokes this discharge is someone, such as the man from Jakarta, who could be seen outside the theater as well as on the stage. On the stage, however, and presented with the heightening of his stereotypical features, everyone knows that everyone else knows. Each can see their own ordinarily suppressed reaction in someone else and in seeing that, knows that everyone has noticed. It is not the stereotype that produces the laughter; it is being seen noticing it.

What provokes laughter is seeing that others are seeing, and knowing that one is being seen at the same instant. At that moment the difference between oneself and others that Javanese institutes collapses; one becomes the other who sees, as though the husband whose wife flirts in front of the Javanese orchestra were unable to ignore others' reactions and not only became governed by them, but acted as if he were one of the spectators watching himself.

The laughter that is evoked by stereotypes marks the failure of High Javanese or its substitute, Indonesian, to produce deference. With that comes loss of self and complete identification with the other. This is the total bondage and the compulsion that we initially posited to be prevented by deference. It is the condition for the compulsion that we saw in *latah*. To the extent that the reactions of any spectator are the same as those of the spectator he sees seeing him, it is not different from *latah*.

Under such conditions, to know that one has heard the joke before does not prevent one from laughing at it again. Identity as the other has removed the privilege of one's own memory. The "I" who remembers and who identifies that memory with what everyone knows is dissolved in the identification of itself with the other who notices. Such an "I" is therefore powerless to use its store of memories to respond as, in ordinary life, it would be likely to respond. It may know that it has heard the joke before, but it is powerless to place that memory as also being the memory of the other and thus as being significant.

When the authority of memory is gone and one cannot place what one has seen before, one is vulnerable to the uncanny. As with the smell of corpses, one feels one knows the smell but does not know how one recognizes it. In the case of stereotypes, the familiar becomes strange as déjà vu replaces recognition. It is not surprising then that the comedy of stereotypes is a step toward the appearance of Draculla.

What makes quotation and stereotype candidates for this humor is not that they are inauthentic or unoriginal. The place of High Javanese itself could be said to be that of quotation, of what other people have said, one's original words in a sense being those of Low Javanese. Rather, the stereotypes and quotations of the New Order are unassimilable when they are subjected to theatrical display that disarms Javanese internal authority. Without the particular recognition such authority guarantees, the process of deferral and translation from Low to High Javanese or from Low Javanese to Indonesian cannot go on. It is interesting, particularly given the strong fear of state censorship, that the New Order furnishes so much of Sri Mulat's material.

To its speakers, High Javanese appears as the language of the second person. Given the fear of making a slip and the sense of inadequate control, one understands how the second person is invested with authority, as though the speaker were concealed behind the language that he or she recites rather than originates. The nonfunctioning of High Javanese and its substitute, Indonesian, should therefore be the demystification of authority. To be that, however, would require that spectators confirm their reactions for each other, for each thus to assure the other that it was all right to laugh, that deference and speaking High Javanese really were not the same thing and that everyone knew it. This does not happen. For there to be such confirmation, each spectator would have to appear to the other as distinct from himself. Only then could reactions in their independence confirm each other. It is precisely because this is not the case, because each spectator identifies strongly with the other, that laughter does not confirm anything. And for that reason, the knowledge that High Javanese does not work does not become part of discourse.

Because this knowledge is never confirmed, because it has no certainty, the joke is always fresh. It is laughed at again and again. With the formation of an audience—that is, with the formation of conventionalized reactions in the theater—it might be different.

The stereotyped humor of Sri Mulat is the breakdown of translation. One can look at it as either a forecast of things to come or as an event that never became political. If it is the latter, it gives us a glimpse of a possibility that never occurred.

. . . English, Chinese, Low Javanese, High Javanese, (Dutch), Indonesian . . . : A Note on Communication Within and Between Cultures

WHEN Clifford and Hildred Geertz began their fieldwork in Bali they were, said Clifford Geertz, treated "as though we were not there . . . as nonpersons, specters, invisible men."[1] This changed one day when the Geertzes were watching an illegal cockfight. Raided by the police, they, like their fellow spectators, fled and established an alibi not only for themselves but for the Balinese in whose house they had taken refuge. Geertz tells this story in his piece on Balinese cockfighting, an article concerned mainly with Balinese gambling. In the course of it he establishes a connection between risk and what he says is "that mysterious necessity of anthropological field work, rapport."[2]

The acceptance of the Geertzes in this village did not mean a change of definition of their position. Though they had been ignored up to that point, it turned out that the facts about them were well known. The man in whose house they took refuge from the police produced "an impassioned description of who and what we were, so detailed and so accurate that it was my turn, having barely communicated with a living human being save my landlord and the village chief for more than a week, to be astonished. . . . We were American professors. . . . We were there to study culture; we were going to write a book to tell Americans about Bali."[3] The incident "led to a sudden and unusually complete acceptance into a society extremely difficult for outsiders to penetrate."[4] The Geertzes were not accepted as Balinese. ("Though you are not exactly taken as a Balinese [one has to be born to that], you are at least regarded as a human being rather than a cloud or a gust of wind. The whole complex of your relationship dramatically changes. . . ."[5]) In the aftermath of the incident the Geertzes were taken for what they had stated themselves to be.

Geertz tells this anecdote in the course of an article on Balinese gambling. It was, indeed, the Geertzes' own engagement in risk that led to their change of status. "But above all, everyone was extremely pleased and even more surprised that we had not simply 'pulled out our papers' (they knew about these too) and asserted our Distinguished Visitor status, but had instead demonstrated our solidarity with what were now our covillagers. (What we had actually demonstrated was our cowardice, but there is fellowship in that too.)"[6] It was not a question of who the Geertzes were; that did not change with the gambling raid; they remained "professors who were going to write a book to tell Americans about Bali."[7] Nor does Geertz report that they thereafter acted differently, as though it was some mistake in demeanor that had caused the Balinese to ignore them. No doubt they acted properly by the standards of Balinese etiquette both before and after the raid. One has to ask, then, what there is about risk that seems to open a path of communication.

To answer this question I want to relate an anecdote of my own. One evening I was watching a performance of Sri Mulat with the director from behind the curtain. He asked me if I would go onstage and play the part of a foreigner. He did not tell me what to say; nor were the actors expecting me. As a principle of fieldwork I accept every invitation, or else I would surely have refused this one. I walked on stage, too confused in my fright to remember what the action of the play had been to that point, interrupting whatever was going on. Pak Pandé, the old-

296 - Chapter Twelve

est of the actors, quite naturally asked who I was and where I had come from. I gave him my name and said, in my highest Javanese, that I came from America. "Ah," he said, "you speak Javanese." Again in polite Javanese I denied being able to speak a word of the language, convinced I was relating an unshakable fact. The result, however, was the most intense reaction, unrestrained laughter, that I have received to anything I have uttered. Pak Pandé questioned me about my linguistic ability for a while, and then I exited. The disproportion between what I said and the intensity of the reaction to it struck me then as it still does. It is a sense of disproportion perhaps equivalent to the Geertzes' when villagers believed them to have "demonstrated our solidarity with [them]. (What we had really demonstrated was our cowardice . . .)" In both cases it was a question of intending something, of being taken for having meant something else, the result being an unanticipated flow of "communication."

Speaking of the raid, Geertz said, "On the established anthropological principle, 'When in Rome,' my wife and I decided, only slightly less instantaneously than everyone else, that the thing to do was run too."[8] As in my case, they took their cue from people who belonged there, not knowing what they might be getting into. The risk in my case was not arrest but sowing incomprehension. I could appear on stage, speak, and no one would know what to make of it; I would be talking to myself in front of an audience. My statement that I did not know Javanese was an apology for being somewhere I did not belong. I told the audience that I did not know what I was saying. It was taken, however, as part of the play. I meant "I cannot speak Javanese, I am tongue-tied." They took me as an outsider who paradoxically announces himself as such from inside their language, the equivalent of the boys on the street when a foreigner passes by, as though I were doing their work for them while still remaining a foreigner.

The risk is that one might not get across. But in these cases it is clear that what opens communication is getting something across that one did not intend. When I exited, I was undeservedly applauded. I mention this because it is the only time I remember hearing applause in that theater and because applause denotes appreciation. What the audience appreciated, I believe, is what they appreciate when the Chinese in the neighborhood act like Javanese. They appreciate the triumph of Javanism, which means, we have seen repeatedly, the suppression of what one wants to say in favor of what Javanism says one should say. They appreciated, in other words, precisely the holding back of any particular intention in favor of established forms. I thought I was saying, "I cannot speak Javanese; I can say nothing." They understood that by speaking Javanese at that moment I could not say anything. What they applauded was their victory, my defeat, and my deference to them.

As does anyone who speaks, Javanese gamble that there will be a return, that they will be heard and responded to. To engage in cross-cultural field studies is to make the same bet, but with a category prepared for oneself if one loses. If one wins, the likelihood is that, like the Geertzes, one remains a foreigner in status, but a foreigner that is nonetheless thought to be able to speak, to hear, to understand, and to respond. If one loses, one is a foreigner, but also thought to be outside discourse. What is established by winning is not exhausted by speaking of a change in social position since one remains a foreigner. What is accomplished is, rather, the establishment of oneself as a translatable figure, one who has crossed over the boundary between cultures, able to comprehend within the others' codes, though the crossing usually needs to be accomplished repeatedly.

The ability to speak a culture's language is not necessarily sufficient to bring this about, as the Geertzes' example illustrates. One might speak the language and even be well understood without establishing oneself as "translatable." It has been the frequent experience of several Javanese-speaking Americans, for instance, particularly those who in my estimation spoke phonetically correct Javanese, to be told that they spoke "excellent Indonesian." The very lack of phonetic incongruity allowed auditors not to attend to the sound of the language and to attribute a non-Javanese language to speakers.

The Javanese who claimed Javanese-speaking Americans were speaking Indonesian understood what they were hearing. By stating it was Indonesian, they acknowledged that they did not need to translate, but at the same time they denied that the foreigner was speaking "their" language. They had it both ways. On the one hand, the foreigner was not capable of Javanese, meaning he could not engage with them on their terms. On the other, they understood what he said, therefore he must be speaking a language that the Javanese themselves knew but that was not really their own language, and instead was the language used when people of different languages converse together. The foreigner spoke Indonesian, in this view, not as a national language, but as a lingua franca, a code that belongs to no one in particular.

To overcome this gap seems to mean to engage in risk. Yet the risk is present anytime one speaks a sentence. It is, however, only a risk to oneself. For one's auditors, that one is incapable of saying anything that need be connected with one's thoughts, or perhaps disconnected from them, is not a problem. Utterances that are unable to cross the border between languages can, in Javanese, be thought to be nonlinguistic in the way that the Javanese who deny that Chinese can speak *Kromo* also think of Chinese as being unintelligible, not only to the Javanese but, by implication, to anyone. For some Javanese, in some contexts, Chinese is mere gibberish. To think this way preserves for Javanese its status as a language. What is not translatable into Javanese is not a language. If it were, it could appear in Javanese and Javanese in it, a topic we shall return to.

The question of translation is central to Javanese. Linguists, for instance, would not be satisfied with my characterization of Javanese as two languages. Even though they are mutually incomprehensible, knowledge of one not ensuring knowledge of the other, there is only one community of speakers; anyone who speaks High Javanese also speaks Low Javanese. The introduction of High Javanese was thus the introduction of translation as a necessary and emphasized process of speaking what from a linguistic point of view is a single language.

Drawing a line through Javanese with the establishment of High and Low Javanese, introducing the necessity to translate, established not only a social and political hierarchy with the Sunan or ruler at the apex, but a hierarchy of translation as well. Low Javanese demanded translation into High Javanese, but the converse was not true. Low Javanese we have seen is thought to be one's "first" language; one needs to be able to convert it into High Javanese to be "Javanese" by the definition that the Javanese give of themselves. (A child who does not yet speak *Kromo* is "not yet Javanese.") No Javanese, however, is thought to need to learn Low Javanese. The demand for translation works from the bottom of the hierarchy up. The special place of High Javanese was, at one time, to be the sole receiver of that demand. High Javanese was capable of registering the conversion of Low Javanese, the result being Javanese state and society. The social reality so constituted was that Low Javanese demanded translation by High Javanese but only by High Javanese. No other language would do. It is in this way that Dutch was set outside the boundaries of Javanese at the same moment that the Dutch became Java's political masters.

To defer in Javanese meant that one did not defer in

Dutch. The process of deference, reservation of Low Javanese in favor of High Javanese, as a political gesture, meant that Low Javanese could be translated into High Javanese, that it demanded to be so translated, but that the demand for translation was satisfied "internally," within one's "own" community, a community of speakers. Dutch was left outside, one sign of which is that the word for "white foreigner" is *landa*, which means also "Dutch." The ruler as the figure receiving the highest deference and who deferred to no one indicated the top of the hierarchy within which the demand for translation could be met.

The situation opened up with the national revolution. Anderson has shown how Indonesian was made a form of High Javanese already in the Sukarno period.[9] The strong nationalist tendencies of the Solonese were in no conflict with their Javanism. The assumption was that Low Javanese could find itself translated by Indonesian; Java and Indonesia could be coterminous. I state this as a linguistic proposition, one that the Javanization of Indonesia and Indonesian verifies. The point is that "Javanese" in that sense incorporated Indonesian, the boundaries of the language being wider than its "own" two linguistic codes. This is but another example of Javanese taking a second language as its boundary.

Javanism thus defines itself in two ways. First, there is the demand for translation that is the power of Low Javanese to transmit itself, and in so doing to form a hierarchy. Second, there is the power of Javanese to translate other languages. To the degree that it does so, these languages submit themselves to Javanism. Thus the examples of Chinese in the neighborhood when Chinese speakers act like Javanese, or English when I spoke on the stage and English appeared in *Kromo*. Whether a code is a language or not, whether it is translatable or not, does not depend, in Javanese views, on the codes but the situations. Chinese is not a language when Chinese are said not to be able to speak *Kromo*. But when they act like Javanese, it is. The question is the ability to suppress one's "natural" language, whatever it is, to follow Javanese practice. By treating other languages as though they were Low Javanese and allowing their speakers into the community of discourse defined by High Javanese, making them part of the same speech community, Javanese incorporates "foreign" languages into itself. "Javanism," then, is not one code or two; it is a system of translation embodying any number of languages in order to draw boundaries around itself. This is the interest that the Javanese have in translation.

Such an interest, however, does not mean that Javanese always want to translate. Translation functions to draw boundaries; it would do, not to translate, but merely to place a language outside these boundaries, to consider it untranslatable. This means that I would lose my bet, that I would utter something on stage with no consequent opening of communication.

There were three possibilities in my anecdotes. I could have been speaking Javanese, which means that in some way the audience would sense that I was holding something back in order to speak "their" language. Or, they could comprehend what I said and yet deny that it was in their language, attributing it instead to a lingua franca, a language belonging to no one. The third possibility is that they did not comprehend what I said and thought it was not really language that I was speaking.

"I don't speak Javanese" is comparable to the sentence that Javanese frequently utter to foreigners, "You speak better Javanese than I do," meaning that High Javanese is a language into which the Javanese as well as the foreigner have to translate. What Javanese grant by understanding a foreigner or another Javanese speak High Javanese is that they hear another language behind it, the unspoken language. In a way, then, they hear what is inaudible. The claim of the speaker when speaking a second language is that there is something more, something that can be heard without having been sounded. At the moment when there is thought to be something more than is audible, the listener is obliged to listen, and the first possibility has been achieved. Given this, it is not surprising that the opening of communication occurs across a gap of misunderstanding when, indeed, more has been intended than was said.

Before I appeared on stage, the actors had been discussing a foreigner. The audience, then, was prepared for my arrival in a certain sense. Moreover, since the point of Sri Mulat is the consolidation of the *anéh* through figures such as Draculla, one could say that they were doubly prepared. However, one could also argue the opposite. What they were prepared for was an actor who would impersonate an outsider. What they had before them was a figure who, by the color of his skin and his height—a foot or so taller than the actors—would seem actually to be a foreigner. The question of whether it was an actor who arrived onstage or a person who was not acting doubles the question of whether I was really speaking Javanese. To the degree that an actor acts, he suppresses something of his everyday self to take on the persona given him in the play, a process similar to that in speaking High Javanese. To that extent, the question of whether or not I was acting duplicated the question of whether or not I was "really" speaking Javanese.

When I first came on stage, Pak Pandé asked me my name. I replied, "Jim Siegel." He called me by the name by which he knew me offstage, "Pak Jim." *Pak* is a title, something like "Mister." In Javanese, *jim* has a meaning. It derives from Arabic and means "spirit" or "ghost" and is found in English as *jin*. Pak Pandé, then, called me "Mr. Ghost," which could have been taken as my name or as a term meaning that I was a ghost.*

---

*My name was occasionally the cause of embarrassment to Javanese. In the most extreme instance, a young servant, a woman, could not cease her laughter for 15 or 20 minutes after hearing my name.

A proper name, as Jacques Derrida points out, should "transfer" but cannot truly "translate."[10] A translated word is linked to other concepts of the language. A proper name might have a meaning in the language. Yet to the extent that it is so taken, it is no longer the name proper to the person but something else.

It happens frequently in Java that names have a meaning, and it happens somewhat less frequently that Javanese change their names. The name change usually occurs after some misfortune. The reason often given is that the spirit who caused the misfortune will be confused, centering its attention on the name while the bearer has taken refuge under a new appellation. In such cases, the meaning of the name is secondary. It is not necessarily that the bearer hopes his new name will bring him new qualities; it is rather that regardless of what the name means, it is now attached to him, whereas his old name, regardless of what it meant, is no longer his. There is a necessary difference between the name as meaning and the proper name.

The name, then, transfers without becoming attached to other concepts of the language, either the native language of the bearer or the language into which he is introduced. It has the capacity to cross the line between languages without becoming a part of them.

In Java, ghosts cross the line between living and dead, there being frequent communication between the two realms. However, this is not the case with Draculla, who is not only a new ghost but explicitly a foreign one, "Mrs. Draculla from abroad," whose popularity is a way to accommodate the heterogeneous, given the failure of Javanese mythology to do so during the New Order. Draculla differs from other spirits precisely by not being a source of communication. When she appears, a chase always ensues as Draculla tries to bite and everyone flees. The chase makes apparent that something outside discourse threatens to enter it, that success in doing so means death and before that fear (*horor*). When Draculla is evaded, one kind of fear, *horor*, is transformed into another, *wedi*, the sort upon which respect is based. The domestication of the heterogeneous depends on this spirit being always unassimilable but being, also, always just outside the boundaries of social discourse.

It is in this light that we can place Sri Mulat, which marks the failure of High Javanese. In the theater of Sri Mulat, *Kromo* (and its substitute, Indonesian) is spoken, but it does not function as though translation from one language to the next is impossible. The point of Sri Mulat, however, is that Low Javanese keeps being produced. Through the figure of Draculla, the *anéh* is figured and disposed of, and Javanese keeps its boundaries around itself, uncontaminated by the intrusion of foreign elements. So long as Javanese keeps being produced, there is no essential danger. If present structures are not adequate to contain it, others will appear. If not now, then later.

This reassurance is directed at an anxiety that we can see in the difference between *horor* and *wedi*. The fear that is *horor* exceeds the fear that is *wedi*. *Wedi* always results in structure. *Horor*, however, indicates a fear not contained by respect that can permeate Javanese, causing translation not to function. It does no good to defer to Draculla. This linguistic terror has a political concomitant; present structures, those of High Javanese and Indonesian, are weak. Translation might occur only later. There could be no hierarchy for the moment.

Names transfer but do not translate. Ghosts, if they are Draculla, transfer without assimilation. The suggestion that I was like Draculla, contained in the meaning of my name and in my foreignness, only makes apparent a possibility already present in any name qua proper name: the possibility of a heterogeneous element in the midst of social discourse.

Since the audience expected the *anéh*, however, this should have been no problem. The problem becomes apparent when one sees that I stood in the place of Draculla and then notes the differences. Draculla is always separated from discourse through the concluding chase. Were that not so, she would be like other Javanese ghosts. But Draculla is different precisely because she is foreign and because she says nothing significant. What few words she does say make no difference. The only reply is flight.*

If someone onstage holds a conversation with Draculla, her words do not matter. Nothing in them can offer reassurance regardless of the speech levels used. No amount of deference can stave her off. Language at that point is divorced from intent and from effect. The actors could as well recite a string of numbers. Nonetheless, the codes used are Javanese. It is Javanese pictured as originating from nowhere, however, from a site unknown to Javanese geography and therefore called "abroad." It is Javanese produced without all the required operations of speech, without, in particular, suppression of the initial language. It is therefore Javanese infiltrated with alien elements heard, not as absent, but as present.

This was the possibility raised when I appeared onstage claiming not to speak Javanese, yet holding a conversation in that language under the name "Mr. Ghost." It was the possibility of there being no boundaries around languages, of there being, in that case, no Javanese. It was the chance of there being only one language, a set of signs unassimilable anywhere.

In the theater of Sri Mulat, High Javanese and Indonesian are set within the context of Low Javanese. Draculla emerges from the production of Low Javanese as translation fails. Though Sri Mulat manages to show the *horor* that is incompatible with the true functioning of lan-

*In fact, she sometimes does say a few words of Javanese before anyone is aware of who she is. There is never a conveyed message, however, since the chase prohibits it.

guage, it is ultimately domesticating because Draculla herself is an outgrowth of the continued production of Low
Javanese. The language still works so long as it has its
speakers; if the *anéh* rather than hierarchy is the product,
still, as we have said, the boundaries of Javanese are preserved.

The greater threat to Javanese comes when translation,
not production, is in question, and when this involves
translation, not from Low Javanese, but into any sort of
Javanese (or Indonesian) from a place outside. Draculla,
being a product of Javanese, can only allude to the outside. Any designation of the outside from within language suffers the same limitation. There is no other mode
of designation except the linguistic. The closest approxi-
mation is a representation ambiguously inside and outside language at the same time.

This is a fourth possibility, one the other three rule out.
It would admit that Javanese does not work, that it does
not maintain its borders. To admit this possibility would
be to say that Javanese does not have the capacity to capture whatever messages enter its field. If this were so, the
originator of these messages would stand in no defined
relation to the Javanese who receive them. He would not
be accepted as capable of operating within Javanese, nor
would he be dismissable because he had uttered a code,
Indonesian, that placed him outside Javanese hierarchy or
because he was a complete outsider who spoke no language at all. If none of these possibilities were realities, it
would mean that messages would "transfer but not translate," as Derrida puts it, and therefore that Javanese could
not define the place of the originator of these messages.
It would be necessary to make one of the other three
choices to avoid the loss of place of Javanese in the world,
its place as the definer of whatever enters its arena or
stands outside of it.

It is against this chance that the audience, judging by
their applause, decided I was speaking Javanese. It is still

not clear to me why they chose this possibility and not one of the other two. (Perhaps some did so choose.) To have done so would still have instituted cultural boundaries across which I could have operated at another time. I could, for instance, have relied solely on documents and thus made myself invisible to them and independent of their categorizations. But an interest in translation means necessarily drawing a line between myself and them, between my thinking and theirs, and thus giving myself a place in regard to them. To want to do so, I would in the first place have to feel myself in the presence of what might escape translation, choosing to believe that comprehension is possible in order to avoid being beset by its incompleteness. This, it seems to me, is the reason for taking the chance. For if risk is the foundation of communication, it itself rests on the avoidance of the fourth possibility, of transfer without translation.[11]

Notes

Introduction

1. J. Brandes, "Een Jayapatta of Acte van Eene Rechterlijke Uitspraak van Caka 849," *Tijdschrift voor Indische Taal-, Land, en Volkenkunde*, vol. 32 (1889): 98–149.
2. J. Brandes, "Een Jayapatta," 98–149.
3. See particularly, Jacques Derrida, *Of Grammatology*, trans. Gayatri Spivak (Baltimore, Md.: Johns Hopkins University Press, 1974).
4. Samuel Weber, *The Legend of Freud*, (Minneapolis: University of Minnesota Press, 1982). See especially pages 17–32.
5. An English version of Derrida's essay as well as the French can be found in Joseph F. Graham, ed., *Difference in Translation*, (Ithaca, N.Y.: Cornell University Press, 1985). The translator is Joseph F. Graham. A translation of Benjamin's piece can be found in Walter Benjamin, *Illuminations*, trans. Harry Zohn (New York: Schocken Books, 1969).

Readers interested in pursuing the question of translation in Southeast Asia should turn also to the excellent thesis of Vincente L. Rafael, *Contracting Christianity: Conversions and Translations in Early Tagalog Colonial Society* (Ph.D. diss., Cornell University, 1984).

Chapter One

1. Javanese is two languages in the sense that High Javanese is unintelligible to the person who knows only Low Javanese and vice versa. As virtually the only speakers of High Javanese are those who already speak Low Javanese, however, some linguists speak of speech styles or language levels. See, for instance, John U. Wolff and Soepomo Poedjosoedarmo, "Communicative Codes in Central Java," Cornell University Southeast Asia Program Data paper no. 116 (Ithaca, N.Y.: 1982).

2. For a linguistic description of Javanese language levels see Soepomo Poedjosoedarmo, "Javanese Speech Levels," *Indonesia* 6:54-81 (October 1968). Descriptions of usage can be found in Clifford Geertz, *The Religion of Java* (Glencoe, Ill.: The Free Press, 1960), 248–60; Hildred Geertz, *The Javanese Family* (Glencoe, Ill.: The Free Press, 1961), 18–22; Robert Jay, *Javanese Villagers: Social Relations in Rural Modjokuto* (Cambridge, Mass.: MIT Press, 1969), 240–46; Ward Keeler, *Javanese: A Cultural Approach* (Athens, Ohio: Center for Southeast Asian Studies, 1984); Leslie Palmier, *Social Status and Power in Java*, London School of Economics Monographs on Social Anthropology (London, 1960), 90 f., 111 f., 137; E. M. Uhlenbeck, *Beknopte Javaansche Grammatica* (Batavia: Bale-Poestaka, 1941) and especially John U. Wolff and Soepomo Poedjosoedarmo, "Communicative Codes."

3. Middle Javanese has a few words of its own.

4. There is sometimes disagreement amongst Javanese about the meaning of *alus*, perhaps in part because it can be applied to so many contexts; not merely behavior but craftsmanship and artistic enterprise can also be characterized as having or lacking "alusness." There is general agreement, however, that in behavior, "alusness" centers on refinement. Cf. Clifford Geertz, *The Religion of Java*, 232.

5. Hildred Geertz describes this as beginning at about age ten or twelve in rural East Java. *The Javanese Family*, 22. In his thesis, Ward Keeler describes it as occurring much earlier in rural Central Java. Keeler, "Father Puppeteer" (Ph.D. diss., University of Chicago, June 1982), 104. My own observations in Solo are limited, but what I did see confirmed Keeler's observations. The discrepancy no doubt reflects the heavier usage of High Javanese in Solo, something that the Javanese frequently comment on.

6. One might find this switching of levels complete with switching of tones between, say, a teacher and his students. I have often seen, for instance, the students of a teacher of Javanese mysticism tease each other quite mercilessly in front of their teacher but instantly, in speaking to the teacher, speak not only in High Javanese, but in tones entirely different from the ones they had been using to each other, switching back and forth easily. For an example of a conversation in which switching of levels is shown with great subtlety, see Jay, *Javanese Villagers*, 243.

7. Deference is attached only to relative status; it is always a question of the relation of the two speakers. However the fact, soon to be explicated, that Solonese want to speak High Javanese and that Middle Javanese is considered part of High Javanese makes it nearly certain that all adults will receive some form of deference; even if it is a lesser form than the one they themselves give.

8. Various forms of Javanese are named. Soepomo describes nine such varieties, showing how language levels can be mixed to take account of complexities of relative status. Thus, one speaks to a close relative who, however, is of quite high status in *Bosoantyo*, which combines *Kromo Inggil* words with *Ngoko* affixes when referring to the listener and his or her attributes but uses *Ngoko* otherwise. *Madyantoro* is used to speak to a low-ranking person whom one does not know well but who is older. It uses the few words reserved only for *Madyo*, *Kromo* words where these do not exist, plus *Ngoko* affixes. And so on. These forms are indeed practiced in Solo. However, for the most part speakers are not aware of their labels. The system is complex when it is described but flexible in practice. Solonese feel that there are rules, that they know these rules and, though they worry about mistakes, that they follow the rules in general practice. The wide differences that one can find between speakers in the same situation reflects Solonese feelings about rules. They exist as part of the world, and they are needed. Discrepancies in practice often go unnoticed, as each thinks he has done it "correctly." This is possible when Solonese attend more to the fact that they did not do what would have come naturally—speak *Ngoko*—than to the precise form of their practice.

9. In addition, Indonesian itself has been transformed on the model of Javanese, as has been pointed out by B.R.O'G. Anderson in his seminal article, "The Languages of Indonesian Politics," *Indonesia* 1 (April 1966): 89–116.

10. In this respect it is interesting that urban Acehnese speech has lost one of its formal elements, the balancing of phrases within the sentence, as it has tended to become a language of privacy, being thus reduced to sounding something like *Ngoko*.

11. The originator of this proposition was apparently G. P. Rouffaer, who asserted that only in the Kartasura period (1688–1744), when the Javanese court had been cut off from outside influences and had turned in on itself, did "Javanese court lan-

guage get its perfection and its polish." G. P. Rouffaer and H. H. Juynboll, *De Batikkunst in Nederlandsch-Indië en Haar Geschiedenis,* vol. 1 (Utrecht: A. Oosthoek, 1914), 306. This proposition was developed by D. H. Burger in his "Structuurveranderingen in de Javaanse Samenleving," *Indonesië,* 3rd year (1949–50): 1–18, 101–123. (English translation by Leslie Palmier, *Structural Changes in Javanese Society: The Supra-Village Sphere,* Cornell Modern Indonesia Project, Translation Series [Ithaca, N.Y., 1956].) Before Rouffaer, J. Brandes had pointed out that *Kromo* used antique forms but, in his view, it was merely a case of finding synonyms for *Ngoko,* which preceded it. J. Brandes, "Een Jayapatta," 98–149. Uhlenbeck refuses Brandes's judgment on the grounds that *Kromo* expresses social constellations between speakers, but he does not refute his argument about the historical primacy of *Ngoko.* E. M. Uhlenbeck, *De Tegenstelling Krama: Ngoko* (Groningen: J. B. Wolters, 1950), 21 f. See also C. C. Berg for the statement that literary Javanese contains *Kromo* forms but gives no data on differentiation of language types, and for interesting speculation on the relation between literary usage and the formation of *Kromo.* C. C. Berg, "Het Kramaiserings verschijnsel," in *Inleiding tot de Studie van het Oud Javaansh* (Soerakarta: De Bliksem, 1928), 188–96.

   That a court language existed early is seen by Tome Pires's account: "And that it may be known that there is no greater pride than in Java, there are two languages, one for the nobles and the other for the people. They do not differ as the language at court does with us; but the nobles have one name for things and the people another; this must certainly be the same for everything." Armando Cortesao, ed. and trans., *The Suma Oriental of Tome Pires and the Book of Francisco Rodrigues* (London: The Hakluyt Society, 1944), 199. Such a situation should not be confused with the bilingualism that pertains presently in Java.

   12. Compare Jay, *Javanese Villagers,* 245: "Control of higher speech forms by itself raises a villager's personal rank." Note the puzzle. It is not merely that one is praised for giving deference and thus for knowing one's place. Rather, as Jay accurately notes, to speak High Javanese does indeed raise one in the esteem of others, making them think the speaker is of higher status. Jay goes on to point out that "ability to handle higher forms of Javanese gracefully signals high political and social rank, while

awkward or crude speech, heavily larded with low forms characterizes the villager as rude and untutored" (p. 245).

13. On *iklas* see Clifford Geertz, *The Religion of Java*, 73, 240–41.

14. An extremely useful survey of the literature on *latah* can be found in Robert Winzeler, "The Study of Malayan *Latah*," *Indonesia* 37 (April 1984): 77–104.

15. I am indebted for this and other examples of *latah* to Wahyono M. of the Museum Nasional, Jakarta, who has collected much information on the subject.

16. Hildred Geertz, "Latah in Java: A Theoretical Paradox," *Indonesia* 5 (April 1968): 93–104. Some Javanese have told me of scatological utterances by *latah* sufferers.

17. Geertz's description of how *latah* is spread is worth quoting at this point:

On discovering that I was interested in *latah*, [an informant] told me that her next-door neighbor was a *latah*, and invited me to her house to meet her. Accordingly, several days later, I paid a formal call on my informant, in the Javanese manner. Tea was brought out, and we engaged in the usual politely elegant and empty conversation expected in such a call. My hostess meanwhile sent her daughter next door for the *latah*, Mbok Ti. Mbok Ti, a woman in her forties, slipped in quietly and sat down next to the hostess. We continued our formal interchange of courtly phrases until suddenly the hostess jabbed her finger into Mbok Ti's ribs and Mbok Ti blurted an obscene word that I didn't catch. She was obviously extremely embarrassed, and got up immediately to leave. The hostess urged her to stay and talk with us, but Mbok Ti was still upset and replied something like, "Stay and talk vagina." This made her even more embarrassed and she left rapidly. After some time she came back again, but sat very quietly at some distance from the rest of us. . . .

About a month later, Mbok Ti held a small feast in honor of her son's circumcision, and I attended it. All of the neighbors were there, politely drinking tea and conversing with proper subdued tones. A women came in and Mbok Ti came up to me and said, "Here is a real *latah*, just watch. You should study her not me." (I had never mentioned my interest in *latah*; someone must have been talking to her.) With that she exclaimed in a loud voice to the new woman, *"Dag!"* the Dutch greeting, "Good-day!" The second *latah*, Mbok Min, immediately responded, "Dag!" several times, raising her hand automatically each time. When she paused, the first *latah*, Mbok Ti, started her up again. Then, tiring of this game, Mbok Ti cried out, *"Merdeka!"* the Indonesian slogan, "Freedom!" and Mbok Min imitated her, and again repeated it over and over. Mbok Ti then left us to take care of her guests, and Mbok Min quieted down. She was a very tense-looking woman, with large nervous eyes, of about sixty. She said nothing unless spoken to. It is the custom in Java at one of these feasts, for all the guests to urge each other politely to eat, saying over and over, *"Mangga!"* "Please eat!" Mbok Min had been sitting at the side for sometime without speaking, when suddenly she burst out— this time without being teased—with *"Mangga, mangga, mangga!"* compulsively repeating the polite word and its accompanying gesture, over and over. People then began to tease her and she grew more and more rattled, and in this upset condition offered a cup of tea to someone, with the words "Please have some vagina." The word for tea has something of the same sound as the word for vagina.

Hildred Geertz, "Latah" in Java, 96–97.
18. Ibid., 96–97.
19. Geertz does not give the Javanese. The word for "tea" in Javanese is *teh*; the word used for vagina was probably *tempik*.
20. Hildred Geertz, "Latah in Java," 94. Again Geertz does not give the Javanese. "Hand me that basket" was probably *"Kekna jarang iku,"* while "Go have intercourse with a horse" might have been *"Lakikna jaran iku,"* or possibly *"Lakikna jaran iku."*
21. It is, of course, not possible to prove a negative. This statement is based on frequent questioning of people of various social rank and from various Solo neighborhoods. I feel somewhat less sure about Jogjakarta. I spent a day in Jogjakarta trying to find *latah* sufferers and met the same responses as in Solo.
22. The other incidents involved the same phrase and similar circumstances.
23. Hildred Geertz, "Latah in Java," 99.

24. The possibility of doing away with such forms, proposed as early as the 1920s, depended on the Indonesian Revolution being more than a national revolution. As B.R.O'G. Anderson has definitively shown, however, the possibility for a social revolution was lost. (This is the theme of Anderson, *Java in a Time of Revolution* [Ithaca, N.Y.: Cornell University Press, 1972.]) Occasionally in Solo today one can still see adults speaking *Ngoko* and being answered in *Kromo*. The likelihood is that these are the high nobility who maintain close association with the palace. Indeed, inside the palace such speech is common. The insistence today that all adults should be given some respectful form of address is an insistence that everyone has a place in the hierarchy—that, unlike prerevolutionary days, no one can be merely disregarded. The critical point, however, is that Javanese find an advantage less in the form of address they receive than in the role of deference-giver they accept, capitalizing on the suppression of *Ngoko* to preserve something from the social encounter.

Chapter Two

1. B.R.O'G. Anderson, "The Idea of Power in Java" in *Culture and Politics in Indonesia* ed. Claire Holt, B.R.O'G. Anderson, and J. T. Siegel (Ithaca, N.Y.: Cornell University Press, 1972), 9. Anderson describes the "quest for power" through various forms of meditation and self-denial. He points out that "self deprivation is more or less equivalent to self-aggrandizement within the ascetic mode"; that going without sleep, without sexual intercourse, without food, and so on results in the acquisition of power. I would only add that the locus of power before it is achieved by the ascetic is the realm associated with death—the place inhabited by spirits and often found at graves.

2. The recent history of Solo can be found in Anderson, *Java in a Time of Revolution*, 350–70 for the revolutionary period and the end of the sunanate's political role; for the prewar period see the Ph.D. dissertation of George Larson, *Prelude to Revolution: Palaces and Politics in Surakarta, 1912–1942* (Ann Arbor, Mich.: University Microfilms, 1979).

3. Anderson, "The Idea of Power," 20–21.

4. The problem these curers have with authority is also sometimes due to their own failure to accommodate themselves to the wishes of authorities in making the best use of their attraction. One curer began practicing in the countryside near Solo when he was interrogated by the local prosecuting attorney and military and civilian administrators. He demonstrated to them that he did, indeed, have special "power" that enabled him to cure, that he was not bilking the public. Despite this he was obliged to move on when he refused to change his venue to a nearby location where parking fees could be controlled by the local authorities. On the other hand, where such arrangements can be made, as in the case of a boy curer in Delanggu, outside Solo, matters can proceed smoothly. The cure itself is free, but various committees have been set up by the lurah to keep order at the boy's house, where he practices after school. These committees sell admission tickets and collect parking fees. Everything went well until the boy stabbed himself with a magical kris, considerably decreasing his popularity after he had recovered from his wounds.

5. On this subject see Hildred Geertz, *The Javanese Family*, 111 ff.; and also Keeler, "Father Puppeteer," 103, 106.

6. Kemlayan is a residential area that is located behind streets lined with shops. Solo's main streets block off the district, even intersecting it at one point. Lanes or alleyways, some paved, some not, run into the residential areas, which are densely settled. I surveyed a portion of this area that is not quite coterminous with what I call a neighborhood. They comprised two Rukun Tetangga, or subdivisions of the administrative district called Rukun Keluarga. The house of the head of the Rukun Keluarga is located on this lane, though the Rukun Keluarga itself includes several more Rukan Tetangga. According to estimates I made by pacing off the area, it contains 7,626 square meters and a total of 294 persons; it is, in other words, densely populated, particularly when one considers that there are only two houses that have more than one story. Twenty-seven of the 69 household heads were born in Kemlayan, seven have been there less than 10 years; there is a tendency for some children to move out but for one to stay. There is a cluster of four households with kinship ties to each other; most family households do not have such ties. Seven families are Catholic, 10 are pious Muslims, not

including four non-Javanese Muslim households. There are five Chinese families. The widow of the palace official, who was also a revolutionary hero, holds title to a good deal of the land; she does not, however, exercise much influence in the neighborhood. The land has been pawned to her under an arrangement, the legal validity of which is now under dispute. Rents are low (sometimes less than a dollar a year); they have not been raised to meet inflation, and in any case they often are not paid at all. As the woman told me, "All my tenants are widows," meaning that they were poor, they had been there a long time, and she was letting them stay there out of pity; anyway, evicting them could take substantial effort. Economic information is contained in the Appendix at the end of Chapter Three.

7. In fact there are robberies in the neighborhood. That three occurred during my 11 months in residence, however, did not stop people from saying that thieves do not dare set foot in the area.

8. His version of events, which he told me on several occasions, always concluded with ghost stories, that lots of people saw ghosts with holes in their heads, no heads at all, etc. during that period.

9. My information about neighborhood organizations comes from asking about it whenever I could. I have detailed information not only on Kemlayan but also on the batik neighborhood mentioned above. It was, however, beyond my capacity to find out details of *ronḍa* organizations throughout Solo. That there is variation is clear from the damage done to Chinese residences during the November 1980 incidents. Where the *ronḍa* was not strong, damage occurred. The members of the *ronḍa* do not feel themselves responsible for those who live on the road edge, that is, those whose residences and lives both face outward. It is socially desirable to live on the main road; those who do are usually wealthier, and their ties are often exclusively to the outside world, except for paying their *ronḍa* dues.

10. The average contribution to the *ronḍa* was Rp 750 per month. The highest contribution by a Javanese was Rp 2000 in the case of one wealthy merchant. Four Chinese paid Rp 3000 per month, and none are listed on the *ronḍa* list as paying less than Rp 1000. The lowest Javanese contribution was Rp 150; several paid Rp 250. The *ronḍa* collected from seven Rukun Kel-

318 — Notes to Pages 43–58

uarga, thus encompassing more than the single neighborhood I have been describing so far. The outer limit is marked by the main road; no one living on or across a main street is a member if participation in local events is the measure. Some events, however, involved the whole of the *ronḍa* territory. The real boundary of the neighborhood as a social entity is marked not so much by inclusion in any particular activity as by the use of *Ngoko* between those who think of themselves as being neighbors. The territory would then depend on who was doing the talking; but the assumption prevails that anyone within the whole area protected by the *ronḍa* was at least a potential *Ngoko* speaking partner.

11. It might be useful to say something more about thieves themselves. There are gangs of thieves in Solo. They seem to operate, however, primarily on the main roads, cooperating to steal bicycles, snatch purses, and pick pockets. Such gangs do not figure in the stories about thieves; it is always the individual thief who was caught that is talked about.

In my thinking about the beating of thieves I am in fact following the line of interpretation laid out by B.R.O'G. Anderson in an as yet unpublished analysis of a short story of Pramoedya Ananta Toer, "Dendam." The title of Anderson's piece is "Reading Modern Indonesian Literature: The Case of Pramoedya's 'Revenge'."

12. The semantics of thief-beating are not the same all over Java. Maria Paschalis Laksono informs me that in the area around Jogjakarta, for instance, a thief who keeps his eyes open is considered not yet to have learned his lesson (*kapok*). There the thief must find the beating unbearable and yell out, "*kapok, kapok*" or be in danger of losing his life. (Personal communication, June 1985.)

13. Anderson, "Reading Modern."

14. I have changed the names of all persons in this chapter and the next to preserve their anonymity.

15. I have tried to show how a "community" is formed by giving *Ngoko* the place of *Kromo* within an urban neighborhood. One might ask if I have not contradicted myself; in Chapter One I pointed out that *Ngoko* furnishes no sense of social locatedness or self-awareness, in Chapter Two I pointed out the opposite. The point, however, is that ordinarily *Ngoko* would not operate

as it does in the neighborhood. It is the sensed weakness of the present national hierarchy, a religious rather than a political weakness, that results in reliance on neighborhoods. Such reliance, however, has limits. It does not include everyone.

Those who live on the edge of the major roads are excluded; these people are nearly always the more well-to-do. There are areas without strong neighborhoods as well. What is more, even within the neighborhood, the self-awareness generated by *Ngoko* is limited. It is not convertible into status that can be used outside the neighborhood. And even within the neighborhood, it is not pervasive. I do not believe, for instance, that it operates between husbands and wives or between those whose sentiment is strong, such as lovers. My evidence for this, aside from the sort of observations I made in Chapter One, is the inability of *Ngoko* to suppress the spectral gestures that accompany excited speech in such contexts.

Chapter Three

1. A translation of the report may be found in the Appendix at the end of Chapter Three.

2. The meeting, as it was an official meeting of a governmental organization, was in Indonesian. People chatted in *Ngoko* till the meeting began. Bulet expressed his anger in Indonesian.

3. The accusations and the denials were made to me, not to each other.

4. Though I never encountered it in Kemlayan, I have heard that Christians, though they pay respects to their neighbors on Lebaran, will sometimes point out that it is not their holiday. That Christians eagerly participated in Lebaran in Kemlayan indicates how much of a local occasion it had become.

5. I was not present at the celebration; my knowledge of it comes from reports of those who attended.

6. An example of the usual dialogue on these occasions is contained in the set of Javanese lessons by Ward Keeler. These are as yet unpublished.

7. On the issue of writing in general as well as the question of replicability, see such works of Jacques Derrida as *On Grammatology*, trans. G. Spivak (Baltimore, Md.: Johns Hopkins University Press, 1974). On the question of replicability in particu-

lar, see Jacques Derrida, "Signature, Event, Context," *Glyph* 1 (1977): 172–97.

8. Were the group to be composed of traders I would make the same assertion because of the degree to which Muslim business in Solo has failed to transcend family concerns, whereas the family itself is still saturated in hierarchy. We shall touch on this in Chapter Five.

9. Thus one can buy a T-shirt with a picture of President Sukarno and the inscription "Nostalgia Proklamator," the proclamator of national independence being the referent.

Appendix, Chapter Three

10. The Camat is the administrative official superior to the lurah.

11. *Kampung* means "village" or "neighborhood" and is here part of the title of the *ronḍa* organization.

12. The failure to capitalize *ronḍa* in this line whereas it is capitalized below is one of many small slips that testify to the hurry with which this report was assembled.

13. LSD are the initials of the Lembaga Sosial Desa, the organization that preceded the LKMD.

14. BUKK is the organization responsible for garbage collection. The chairman was Chinese.

15. *Permukiman* means district.

16. Close readers of such exotica will note that this figure belongs in the income column. This major flaw in the BUKK financial report went unnoticed, showing again that it is filling in the blanks, not the content of the report that is crucial.

17. "Drawers" here refers to the people who pull the garbage cart through the alleys.

18. Note the incorrect arithmetic by means of which the books are balanced. This went unchallenged.

19. I do not know what *skah* means.

20. One notes the immense generality of this rubric.

21. The report was stamped with the official stamp of the Rukun Keluarga below this spot.

22. Signatures were reproduced on this line, with names printed beneath.

23. One notes the absence of mention of the *ronḍa* chairman.

Chapter Four

1. On this subject see Anderson, "The Languages of Indonesian Politics," 89–116.

2. Quotations from Teguh are from an interview with him on November 7, 1981.

3. The Surakarta weekly *Dharma Nyata* for the third week of October, 1981, reported that Draculla had been sighted in Java and also in Bali. There was a racket from the room of a Japanese construction worker in a hotel. Hotel employees broke in and found him "sprawled out bathed in blood," with two teeth marks in his neck. They rushed him to the hospital. Before he died he gasped out his story. He had first noticed peculiar smells, particularly the odor of fish and then of perfume. Then, "it was as though someone outside was calling." Thinking he had a guest, he opened the door. He was shocked when, apparently, what entered was a head without a body. The hair fluttered, the tongue protruded and the teeth were horrifying. The head attacked him at once mercilessly. Though the Japanese knew self-defense it was still not possible to prevent the bodyless head from latching onto his neck, he could not free himself and finally he collapsed.

"According to information received, the hotel is indeed haunted. The Hotel security guard included magicians. They explained that no one is allowed to act in any unusual way or to curse or to defecate except in certain places. . . ." The report continues with the experiences of Dutch and Indonesian airline pilots who also encountered spirits at the hotel. It is only with reports such as these that the paper sold out in my time in Solo.

See *Dharma Nyata* for the first week of October, 1981, for reports of Draculla having been seen in Madura, an island off Java.

4. This performance, and the others I will mention, occurred between October 1981 and December 1982. In all I watched 53 performances, including two in Surabaya and one in Jakarta. I also saw one performance in Solo in August 1979.

5. He was, indeed, gravely ill and died in 1982.

6. See T. W. Adorno, "Applaus," in *Musikalische Schriften*, vol. 1 (Frankfurt: Suhrkamp Verlag, 1978), 309–320.

7. I had been recording the performance and later noticed that the recorder had picked up the woman's comments.

Chapter Five

1. Walter Benjamin, "Brecht's *Threepenny Novel*," in *Reflections* trans. Edmond Jephcott (New York: Harcourt Brace Jovanovich, 1978), 199–200.
2. Information on the development of European-style landscape painting can be found in Claire Holt, *Art in Indonesia: Continuities and Change* (Ithaca, N.Y.: Cornell University Press, 1967), 192 ff.
3. Roland Barthes, *Camera Lucida: Reflections on Photography*, trans. Richard Howard (New York: Hill and Wang, 1981), 6.

Chapter Six

1. Anderson, *Java in a Time of Revolution*, 9.
2. The government has banned all forms of gambling including video games except the national lottery. Lottery bets can only legally be placed with government agents. Everyone I knew in Kemlayan bet with illegal agents in order to bet only the last numbers, something not possible with government agents.
3. Walter Benjamin, "Paris, Capital of the Nineteenth Century," in *Reflections*, 159.

Chapter Seven

1. Rouffaer and Juynboll, *De Batikkunst in Nederlandsch-Indië*, 1:55 ff.
2. See J. T. Siegel, *The Rope of God* (Berkeley: University of California Press, 1969), and also Chandra Jayawardena, "Women and Kinship in Acheh Besar," *Ethnology* 16 (1977): 21–38.
3. Hildred Geertz, *The Javanese Family*, 38.
4. B.R.O'G. Anderson, "The Idea of Power," 27.
5. Personal communication, June 1983.
6. Jay, *Javanese Villagers*, 50.
7. Ibid.
8. Ibid.
9. Hildred Geertz, *The Javanese Family*, 110.
10. Ibid.
11. Jay, *Javanese Villagers*, 105.

12. Ward Keeler makes this point throughout Chapter Eleven of "Father Puppeteer."
13. Jay, *Javanese Villagers*, 105.
14. Hildred Geertz, *The Javanese Family*, 120.
15. Jay, *Javanese Villagers*, 92.
16. Hildred Geertz, *The Javanese Family*, 124.
17. Ibid.
18. Ibid., 123.
19. Jay, *Javanese Villagers*, 92.
20. Keeler, "Father Puppeteer," 86.
21. Jay, *Javanese Villagers*, 92. Keeler notes in "Father Puppeteer" that gambling is not necessarily discordant with status: "That [a Javanese man] gamble away his money, or that he spend it on good food for himself and his friends, and that he 'discard' his semen in the belly of a prostitute matter little to his authority. If anything, these gestures may enhance it, since that he need not conserve money or semen means he is certain of his ability to generate them. Money and semen will always be his as long as his spiritual potency is great" (p. 88). Keeler adds, however, that "should a man refuse to hand over all or at least most of his earnings to his wife, he already appears irresponsible, unless his wife has previously shown herself incompetent at handling money" (p. 95). He notes further that men who do not willingly give up their money to their wives "not only encounter disapproval, they run the risk of losing it all at gambling" (p. 98). Those who can recoup their losses easily by virtue of their power and who thus have no fear of squandering cannot be numerous.
22. Hildred Geertz, *The Javanese Family*, 133.
23. Jay, *Javanese Villagers*, 92.

Chapter Eight

1. Letter from Herrybertus Subagyo, *Topchords* 31 (May 1979): 43.
2. *Topchords* 39 (March 1980).
3. Letter from Monang cs, *Topchords* 40 (April 1980): 2.
4. Letter from Lelly Y., *Topchords* 40 (April 1980): 2.
5. Letter from Sunardi, BA, *Topchords* 40 (April 1980): 2.

6. Letter from Sri Bagiati, *Topchords* 38 (February 1980): 2.
7. Letter from P. Tarigan, *Topchords* 38 (February 1980): 2.
8. Reply to letter from Roy, *Topchords* 42 (July 1980): 2.
9. Anonymous, "Artikel Penyanyi: Toar Tangkau: Aku ingin Maju dan . . . . [*sic*] Develop" (Singers: Toar Tangkau: I want to progress and . . . . develop"), *Topchords* 42 (July 1980): 23 ff.
10. Anonymous, "Artikel Pemusik: Yani Veronica Danu Widjaja [sic]: Bakat Manusia . . . Luar Biasa" (Musicians: Yani Veronica Danu Widjaja: human talent . . . extraordinary), *Topchords* 41 (June 1980): 58–59.
11. Anonymous, "Artikel Penyanyi: Toar Tangkau," 23 ff.
12. Anonymous, "Artikel Penyanyi: Astri Ivo: Kecil-kecil bernama gede." (Singers: Astri Ivo: small, but a big name), *Topchords* 38 (July 1980): 87.
13. Anonymous, "Artikel Pemusik Indonesia: Reynold dan Camelia: Bercolak-colek Dengan Dangdut" (Indonesian musicians: Reynold and Camelia: decked-out with Dangdut), *Topchords* 39 (March 1980): 60–61.
14. Anonymous, "Artikel Penyanyi: Toar Tangkau," 25.
15. See B.R.O'G. Anderson, "A Time of Darkness and a Time of Light: Transposition in Early Indonesian Nationalist Thought," in *Perceptions of the Past in Southeast Asia*, ed. Anthony Reid and David Marr (Singapore: Heineman Educational Books [Asia] Ltd., 1979), 219–49.
16. Anonymous, "Artikel Pemusik: Yani Veronica," 58.
17. Letter from Arban-sma loyala Semarang, *Topchords* 42 (July 1980): 2.
18. Anonymous, "Artikel Pemusik Indonesia: Reynold," 60.
19. One can speak of "national" fans in two senses. First, they are located across the nation and, so far as *Topchords* is concerned, lack any regional features. Indeed, if someone moves to a distant corner of the country, *Topchords* advises them to subscribe and remain part of the national scene. Additionally, *remaja*, as most fans would seem to class themselves, is a term only in the national language. It is not translatable into the regional languages I know about.
20. For information on Rhoma Irama, see William H. Frederick, "Rhoma Irama and Dangdut Style: Aspects of Contemporary Indonesian Popular Culture," *Indonesia* 34 (October 1982), 103–130.

21. Anonymous, "Artikel Pemusik Indonesia: Rhoma Irama: Dangdut atau Melayu sama saja" (Indonesian musicians: Rhoma Irama: Dangdut or Melayu, it's the same), *Topchords* 38 (February 1980): 32–33.
22. Ibid., 32.
23. Ibid.
24. Anonymous, "Artikel Pemusik Indonesia: Reynold," 60.
25. Frederick, "Rhoma Irama," 106.
26. Here it would be interesting to know more about the cases of *tayuban* and *jaipongan*, folk forms that have been nationalized.
27. Letter from Arban-sma Ioyala Semarang, *Topchords* 42 (July 1980): 2.
28. See the letter from Yadi Amela, *Topchords* 38 (February 1980): 2.
29. Letter from Arban-sma Ioyala Semarang, *Topchords* 42 (July 1980): 2.
30. Anonymous, "Artikel Pemusik Indonesia: Reynold," 60.
31. Anonymous, *Topchords* 41 (June 1980): 1.
32. These descriptions and others quoted can be found in many *Topchords* issues for the years 1979–1980.
33. See the "Centerfold" in *Topchords* 38 (February 1980).
34. On the term *pemuda*, see Anderson, *Java in a Time of Revolution*, 1–16.
35. Usually, but not always. For instance this song, "Joget" or "Dance" by Rhoma Irama has these lyrics:

Let's dance, hey, let's dance
Come on, hey, dancing's great
Rock away, swing those hips
Rock away, swing those hips
With a happy heart
Enjoy yourself, enjoy. . . .

(Quoted in Frederick, "Rhoma Irama," 110.)
36. Letter from Lelly Y., *Topchords* 40 (April 1980): 2.
37. Pramoedya Ananta Toer, "Revenge," trans. B.R.O'G. Anderson, *Indonesia* 26 (October 1978), translator's note 24.
38. Letter from Halimi Muniran, *Topchords* 33 (July 1979): 2.
39. Letter from Eddy SA, *Topchords* 41 (June 1980): 2.
40. Personal communication, March 1983.

Chapter Nine

1. "Karena Luapan Emosi Sejumlah Toko Jl. Sumoharjo Solo Dirusak" (Number of stores on Sumoharjo Street damaged as a result of overflowing emotions), *Suara Merdeka*, 21 November 1980.

2. "Keadaan di Jateng dan DIY Sudah Bisa Dikendalikan" (The situation in Central Java and the special district of Jogjakarta can now be controlled), *Kompas*, 4 December 1980; "Harry Mulyadi Mengaku Sebagai Pencetus Ide 'Peristiwa Solo' " (Harry Mulyadi confesses to igniting the idea of 'the events of Solo'), *Sinar Harapan*, 4 December 1980. See also "Tidak ada Lagi Jam Malam" (No more curfew), *Tempo* (13 December 1980): 12–14.

3. Unless otherwise noted, the remainder of the account of the riot is based on my interviews and observations.

4. "Walikota Solo Menghimbau Masyarakat Dan Pelajar Agar Tak Terpancing Emosi" (Mayor of Solo appeals to the people, and to students not to become provoked by emotions), *Suara Merdeka*, 22 November 1980.

5. Notes by a resident of Solo who wishes to remain anonymous.

6. Departement Dalam Negeri, Direktorat Jenderal Sosial Politik, "Inventarisari: Kronologi Kasus Aksi Kekerasan (Pengrusakan/Pembakaran) Secara Massal di Wilayah Propinsi Jawa Tengah" (Department of the Interior, Directorate General of Social-Political Affairs, "Inventory: chronology of cases of violent mass action [damage/burning] in the region of the province of Central Java), mimeographed, unsigned, n.d.

7. Shiraishi Takashi, based on his extensive research on this period, personal communication, April 1983.

8. P. de Kat Angelino, *Rapport Betreffende Eene Gehouden Enquete Naar de Arbeids Toestanden in de Batikkerijen op Java en Madoera door de Inspecteur bij het Kantoor van Arbeid P. De Kat Angelino*, vol. 3 (Weltevreden: Landsdrukkerii, 1930), 130.

9. James R. Rush, *Opium Farms in Nineteenth Century Java: Institutional Continuity and Change in a Colonial Society, 1860–1910* (Ann Arbor, Mich.: University Microfilms, 1977), 113.

10. One must set this against the extravagant praise the Javanese give to Europeans, who sometimes speak in bizarre accents and tempos.

11. Anderson, "The Idea of Power," 41.

12. See the thesis of Dede Oetomo, "The Chinese of Pasuruan: A Study of Language and Identity in a Minority Community in Transition," (Ph.D. diss., Cornell University, 1984).

13. Anderson, "The Idea of Power," 39.

14. To return to the comparison of the stoning of Chinese windows and the beating of thieves: The latter too was done deliberately and slowly. Indeed, it would be possible to argue that the blows directed to thieves are also compelled in the sense that no one thinks whether or not they should beat thieves or will or will not do so when the occasion arises. But whether the source of this necessity is the firmness of their intent or an automatic reaction to the thieves' intrusion is difficult to say. The reason it is difficult is because the blows, as I have shown, are thought to deliver a message. Whether this is the message in the minds of the men who beat thieves at the moment they perceive a thief or only afterwards is impossible to say. By contrast, the stoning of Chinese windows conveyed no message. It gave rise to no comments like those aroused by the treatment of thieves.

Chapter Ten

1. I attended 22 funerals and saw expressions of grief only on the occasions I note later. I was present shortly after deaths had occurred in three of the families. In one case, I was there minutes after the death; in another, within a couple of hours. In several other cases, I had ample opportunity to see if family members grieved in the months after the death.

Javanese do not think grief is in itself shameful. It is disapproved of only if it disrupts others. On three occasions Javanese freely admitted their grief to me, which makes me feel that the many others who denied grieving, who said they were instantly "detached" or *iklas*, were accurate in their statements. Occasionally someone would report another state, *bingung*, or "confusion," as their first reaction to learning of a death.

2. Clifford Geertz, "Ritual and Social Change: A Javanese Example," in *The Interpretation of Cultures* (New York: Basic Books, 1973), 153.

3. There are two exceptions: young children, sometimes

328 — Notes to Pages 258–259

through their early teens, whose parents die, and mothers whose children die.

4. On this topic, see especially Clifford Geertz, *The Religion of Java*, 68 ff. There are differences in detail between Geertz's description of ceremonies in rural East Java and what takes place in Solo: for instance, some Solonese Muslims do not consider the modin, or Islamic religious functionary, absolutely necessary to carry out the ritual of the funeral. However these differences do not figure in Solonese thinking about death. One can find manuals describing funerary customs such as R. Tanojo, *Tatatjaranipon Karipahan* (Surakarta: De Bliksem, 1933). I am indebted to John Pemberton for bringing this item to my attention. The people who come to a funeral include most of the deceased's acquaintances. It would be a solecism for neighbors and kin not to attend. One could expect also those with whom the person worked, members of his or her organizations and, in the case of prominent figures, those who knew of the deceased. On this topic see Jay, *Javanese Villagers*, 220 ff. One can expect amongst the speakers at least one or two figures of authority: in the case of someone from the palace, a palace official; in the case of someone local, the lurah and the head of the neighborhood. On the comfort these figures seem to bring to the deceased see Keeler, "Father Puppeteer," 162.

5. The effect of funerals and the other celebrations that follow upon a death is to ensure that the *roh* is acceptable to God. But Javanese thought does not include any notion of a place where this acceptance is finally accomplished. Even the Christians of the conventional denominations—Catholic and Protestant—put little stress on this dimension of the afterlife, whereas the Islamic belief that the soul of the dead continues to exist until the last judgment coincides with traditional Javanese belief. The Javanese live in the continual presence of the "dead," who take various forms. The question, then, is whether fear of the decaying corpse is not fear of the spirit, which might be thought to be still in the vicinity. The most definitive answer I can give to the question is that, despite persistent questioning, no one attributed the death that comes with the odor of the corpse to spirits. As I have said, those who had their relatives moved often believed that the *roh* was in the vicinity. But this was as true for fully decayed corpses as for more recent ones. Furthermore, the

presence of a spirit is, in a way, almost reassuring; one can appease it simply enough.

What I have described is a fear that has no solution, and no reassuring effects. *Wedi*, the word for fear in Javanese, means also respect. The connection between the two concepts comes through speech. Someone who is fearful will speak High Javanese. In speaking High Javanese, the speaker alleviates his fear by making it into a sign removed from himself. For example, as stated in Chapter One, Javanese intensely dislike being startled. They have an exclamation that they use not when they are startled, but in the places where, had they not spoken that word, they would be startled. By registering their "fear" in what they consider a second language, Javanese avoid the stress of feeling it. The fear that was generated by thoughts of the odiferous corpse, however, escaped this possibility. It is, indeed, precisely this evasion of speech that is the topic of this chapter.

6. Clifford Geertz, "Ritual and Social Change," 157.

7. At this point it is necessary to add a note about differences in funerals according to the gender and status of the deceased. The purpose of the funeral in all cases is to have the spirit of the person depart. If titles are available for use, then they add to the impression that only the relatively permanent attributes of the person are left in the visible world. The *arwah* or *roh* is not, however, completely lost. It is still somewhere else in the invisible world of spirits. As we saw in our example, when a prominent woman died she was treated as a man would also have been: she was eulogized in terms of her titles. In addition, however, as in all cases, there were prayers that called for the *arwah* or *roh* to be quickly "received" by God, leaving the corpse as a sign that the soul was, really, elsewhere. This is the central point of all funerals I witnessed, regardless of the sex or status of the deceased.

8. A translation by Joan Rivière is published in Sigmund Freud, *General Psychological Theory* (New York: Collier Books, 1963), 164–80.

9. See, for example, Georg Simmel, "The Aesthetic Significance of the Face," in *Georg Simmel*, ed. Kurt Wolff (Columbus: Ohio State University Press, 1959), 276–81.

10. On the historical background to this, see F.D.K. Bosch, *The Golden Germ* (The Hague: Mouton & Co., 1960), who traces

330 — Notes to Pages 265–273

the "soft" features of even "ruthless slayers of enemies" in plastic representation to lotus-symbolism (pp. 220 ff.).

11. Such a photograph, taken however by the author at the request of the deceased neighbors, can be found in J. T. Siegel, "Images and Odors in Javanese Practices Surrounding Death," *Indonesia* 36 (October 1983), between pages 6 and 7.

12. Compare this statement made to Clifford Geertz by a Javanese man that "it is a good thing to be dead." Geertz says, "He spoke happily, not in any weltschmerz mood. I asked why he thought this, and he said, 'Well, when you are dead, you don't want anything: you don't want an auto, you don't want money, you don't want a wife, you don't have any wants at all. Like God—God doesn't need any money, or wife, or auto, does he? Well, that's wonderful, not to want anything; and after you're dead, that's the way it is.' " Clifford Geertz, *The Religion of Java*, 75.

13. For a description of these spirits, see ibid., 26–29. *Arwah* is sometimes used to mean "life spirit."

14. There is a certain confirmation of this in the common warning of those with magical powers that no one can take their photograph without their permission. Should anyone try, the film will be blank. Such powers are obtained from the realm of the dead; they are an intrusion of the powers associated with spirits into everyday life. But when they are operative they leave no trace. By the same logic, the corpse, being visible, is set apart from the active powers of the dead.

15. At this point, one might ask how it is that, if Javanese imitate the "dead" and find it desirable to do so, they also expect blessings from them. Does not the expectation of blessings imply a difference that it would be in their interest to exaggerate? It is not the speaker of *Kromo* who goes out of existence when he or she dies; it is the speaker of *Ngoko*. It is the speaker of *Ngoko* who "exists," and who can die, and who receives the blessings of the dead.

16. Javanese, indeed, have another kind of incense, *ratus*, which is sweet-smelling. It is *menyan*, however, that is used for offerings.

17. I am aware of how difficult it can be to elicit associations. I can only say that people who ordinarily spoke to me most unreservedly, who spoke to me in *Ngoko* and under circum-

stances that seemed propitious, deny having any associations evoked by the smell of *menyan*.

Chapter Eleven

1. A concise description of these events can be found in B.R.O'G. Anderson and Ruth McVey, "What Happened in Indonesia?" *New York Review of Books* (1 June 1978). See also Anderson and McVey, "A Preliminary Analysis of the October 1, 1965, Coup in Indonesia," Cornell Modern Indonesia Project (Ithaca, N.Y.: 1971). An official Indonesian view can be found in Nugroho Notosusanto and Ismael Saleh, *The Coup Attempt of the "September 30th Movement" in Indonesia* (Jakarta: Pembimbing Masa, 1968).

2. I have not myself visited Lubang Buaya. A detailed description of the monuments with color photographs can be found in the anonymous article, "Monumem Pancasila Sakti: Untuk membina perjuangan Nasional," *Dialog* 29 (September–October, 1980): 2 ff.

3. *Giri* means "mountain" in Old Javanese. One Mangkunegaran site is Giri Layu. *Bangun* means "erect" or "arise" in Indonesian; *Mangadeg*, the name of another Mangkunegaran site, means the same.

4. Anderson, "The Idea of Power," 1–71.

5. Hildred Geertz, "Latah in Java," 97.

6. Ibid.

7. Joseph Errington, "Speech in the Royal Presence: Javanese Palace Language," *Indonesia* 34 (October 1982): 89–102.

Chapter Twelve

1. Clifford Geertz, "Deep Play: Notes on the Balinese Cockfight," in *The Interpretation of Cultures*, 143.

2. Ibid., 416.

3. Ibid., 415.

4. Ibid., 416.

5. Ibid., 413.

6. Ibid., 416.

7. Ibid., 415.

8. Ibid., 415.

9. For the insistence of Javanese on defining the world in Javanese terms, see B.R.O'G. Anderson, *Mythology and the Tolerance of the Javanese*, Cornell Modern Indonesia Project Publications no. 37, (Ithaca, N.Y.: 1965). On Indonesian as a form of Javanese, see Anderson, "The Languages of Indonesian Politics," 89–116.

10. Derrida, "Des Tours de Babel," 165–248. This is the place for me to thank Sam Weber for his suggestion that I include a piece on communication across cultures in this book.

11. I want to add a note on technique and method. I used a tape recorder only in a few instances. I recorded all the theatrical performances I attended, and I recorded certain interviews, primarily on historical topics which do not figure in this book. On most occasions I used the technique perfected by Clifford Geertz in his work on Java. I listened, remembered specific phrases, and transcribed my interviews as soon as possible after they occurred. Nothing appears in quotation marks unless it is verbatim.

The weakness of paraphrase is that one puts down one's understanding of what was said. In leaving out the actual words, pauses, hesitations, and so on, one leaves out the possibility of recording what one does not recognize. A certain degree of interpretation is necessarily inherent in paraphrase. Anthropologists usually justify their method on the grounds that verbatim recording imposes constraints on interviews. People tend to say less and to speak more formally. The possibility of intimate discourse, speech that flows without constraint between two parties, is given up. For reasons that by now should be clear, this does not necessarily apply in Java, though it still would be worth considering the differences made by using a tape recorder or taking notes in the presence of the people with whom one speaks.

The reason for not transcribing verbatim is both practical and theoretical. In a situation where numerous messages are reaching the ethnographer who wishes to know what the interests of Javanese are, he or she cannot record them all. To try and transcribe without paraphrase is unmanageable unless one already knows what topics interest one; then one can record verbatim only on that topic. The only way to keep open the possibility of recognizing a range of interests is through paraphrase. Paraphrase reduces to sense some of the enormous quantity of information that comes to one. The process of fieldwork is inevitably one of making sense of some of the language to which one is exposed. It is thus a way to become aware of the possibility of failure, the possibility of not being able to make sense, and therefore the possibility of untranslatable language.

This method both limits the ethnographer and opens new possibilities. When he or she feels Javanese is translatable, he or she must find another point where it may not be. Not to move on to the next topic means establishing a place for oneself in Java. At that point messages are only ordinarily problematic; they do not generate much explanation. The opening of communication is also its limitation.

Each place where I see Javanese being interested is the site of paraphrase and thus, in a way, of translation as well. It marks me as the translator, and in so doing "I" am marked off from "them." It is thus the site of the establishment of differences. This demarking, as Samuel Weber has termed it, has two modes. The "I" can be merely demarked; it can merely be "not them," not yet the translator. The "I" can also be constituted positively, as the observer or translator. But the consolidation cannot be sustained. We translate because there is an origin beyond us. No particular translation exhausts the possibility of language to posit that origin again. We observe only what we already know, but we also find ourselves merely demarked, merely "not them" in the presence of what we have missed.

Index

Library of Congress Cataloging-in-Publication Data

Siegel, James T., 1937-
   Solo in the new order.

   Bibliography: p.
   Includes index.
   1. Speech and social status—Indonesia—Solo.
2. Javanese language—Social aspects.   3. Solo
(Indonesia)—Social conditions.   4. Intercultural
communication.   I. Title.
P40.5.S632I57   1986   401'.9'09598   86-9432
ISBN 0-691-09427-6 (alk. paper)